The Supreme

NINJA Air Fryer

Cookbook

For Beginners

1500+ Days of Easy, Energy-Saving & Tasty Recipes to Fry, Roast, Bake, and Grill Your Way to Healthier Eating Habits, Incl. Tips and Tricks

Reece Hobbs

Table of Contents

INTRODUCTION

Welcome to the amazing world of the NINJA Air Fryer Cookbook!

Prepare to embark on a culinary adventure like no other, where air-frying reaches new levels of ninja-style awesomeness. Get ready to flip, toss, and slice your way through a collection of finger-licking, crispy creations that will leave your taste buds screaming for more.

Now, let's paint the scene for you. Picture yourself in a kitchen that's not just any ordinary kitchen—it's a dojo of flavor, a battlefield of sizzle, and a dojo where only the boldest culinary warriors dare to enter. Armed with the mystical NINJA Air Fryer and this extraordinary cookbook, you're about to unleash your inner food ninja!

But hold on a second, what exactly is a NINJA Air Fryer? Well, my friend, it's not your average fryer. It's a sleek and powerful machine that combines the mystique of ancient ninja techniques with the modern wizardry of hot air circulation. This remarkable contraption allows you to achieve that golden crispy texture you crave, while magically reducing the fat content of your favorite indulgent treats. It's like having a culinary superhero on your countertop!

Now, let's delve into the pages of this cookbook and discover the epic recipes that await you. From the moment you open it, you'll be greeted by a gang of whimsical food warriors, each with their own unique flavor-packed specialties. Meet Coconut Chicken Tender Sensei, the undisputed master of juicy, perfectly chicken that practically flies off the

plate. Or perhaps you'll encounter Veggie Frittata Ninja, a nimble master who can turn the simplest ingredients into a symphony of flavors with a flick of the wrist.

But our warriors don't stop there! They've also mastered the art of snack-foo, transforming humble ingredients into mouthwatering party pleasers. Think of Bacon, Egg, and Cheese Roll Ups, a delectable combination of sugar-free bacon and gooey cheese that'll make your guests do backflips of delight. And let's not forget the Pumpkin Cookie with Cream Cheese Frosting, a dessert ninja who can conjure up the perfect blend of chocolate chips, pumpkin cake spice, and ground cinnamon—all without a campfire!

In this cookbook, you'll find recipes that cater to every taste bud and occasion. Whether you're

in the mood for a quick and easy weekday dinner, an exotic international feast, or a blow-your-mind dessert extravaganza, our ninja warriors have got you covered. They'll guide you through each step with their signature flair, providing helpful tips, tricks, and even a few ninja secrets along the way.

So, are you ready to join the ranks of the fearless food ninjas? Grab your NINJA Air Fryer, sharpen your knives, and let the cooking battles begin! With the NINJA Air Fryer Cookbook by your side, you'll be flipping, frying, and feasting like a true culinary ninja. Get ready to take your taste buds on a wild ride they'll never forget!

Remember, my friend, in the world of air-frying, there are no limits. Embrace your inner ninja and let the crispy adventures begin!

Chapter 1

Breakfasts

Smoky Sausage Patties

Prep time: 30 minutes | Cook time: 9 minutes | Serves 8

1 pound (454 g) ground pork 1 tablespoon coconut aminos 2 teaspoons liquid smoke 1 teaspoon dried sage 1 teaspoon sea salt	½ teaspoon fennel seeds ½ teaspoon dried thyme ½ teaspoon freshly ground black pepper ¼ teaspoon cayenne pepper

1. In a large bowl, combine the pork, coconut aminos, liquid smoke, sage, salt, fennel seeds, thyme, black pepper, and cayenne pepper. Work the meat with your hands until the seasonings are fully incorporated. 2. Shape the mixture into 8 equal-size patties. Using your thumb, make a dent in the center of each patty. Place the patties on a plate and cover with plastic wrap. Refrigerate the patties for at least 30 minutes. 3. Working in batches if necessary, place the patties in a single layer in the air fryer, being careful not to overcrowd them. 4. Set the air fryer to 400°F (204°C) and air fry for 5 minutes. Flip and cook for about 4 minutes more.

Super Easy Bacon Cups

Prep time: 5 minutes | Cook time: 20 minutes | Serves 2

3 slices bacon, cooked, sliced in half 2 slices ham 1 slice tomato 2 eggs	2 teaspoons grated Parmesan cheese Salt and ground black pepper, to taste

1. Preheat the air fryer to 375°F (191°C). Line 2 greased muffin tins with 3 half-strips of bacon 2. Put one slice of ham and half slice of tomato in each muffin tin on top of the bacon 3. Crack one egg on top of the tomato in each muffin tin and sprinkle each with half a teaspoon of grated Parmesan cheese. Sprinkle with salt and ground black pepper, if desired. 4. Bake in the preheated air fryer for 20 minutes. Remove from the air fryer and let cool. 5. Serve warm.

Whole Wheat Blueberry Muffins

Prep time: 10 minutes | Cook time: 15 minutes | Serves 6

Olive oil cooking spray ½ cup unsweetened applesauce ¼ cup raw honey ½ cup nonfat plain Greek yogurt 1 teaspoon vanilla extract 1 large egg	1½ cups plus 1 tablespoon whole wheat flour, divided ½ teaspoon baking soda ½ teaspoon baking powder ½ teaspoon salt ½ cup blueberries, fresh or frozen

1. Preheat the air fryer to 360°F(182°C). Lightly coat the inside of six silicone muffin cups or a six-cup muffin tin with olive oil cooking spray. 2. In a large bowl, combine the applesauce, honey, yogurt, vanilla, and egg and mix until smooth. 3. Sift in 1½ cups of the flour, the baking soda, baking powder, and salt into the wet mixture, then stir until just combined. 4. In a small bowl, toss the blueberries with the remaining 1 tablespoon flour, then fold the mixture into the muffin batter. 5. Divide the mixture evenly among the prepared muffin cups and place into the basket of the air fryer. Bake for 12 to 15 minutes, or until golden brown on top and a toothpick inserted into the middle of one of the muffins comes out clean. 6. Allow to cool for 5 minutes before serving.

Egg and Bacon Muffins

Prep time: 5 minutes | Cook time: 15 minutes | Serves 1

2 eggs Salt and ground black pepper, to taste 1 tablespoon green pesto 3 ounces (85 g) shredded	Cheddar cheese 5 ounces (142 g) cooked bacon 1 scallion, chopped

1. Preheat the air fryer to 350°F (177°C). Line a cupcake tin with parchment paper. 2. Beat the eggs with pepper, salt, and pesto in a bowl. Mix in the cheese. 3. Pour the eggs into the cupcake tin and top with the bacon and scallion. 4. Bake in the preheated air fryer for 15 minutes, or until the egg is set. 5. Serve immediately.

Baked Egg and Mushroom Cups

Prep time: 5 minutes | Cook time: 15 minutes | Serves 6

Olive oil cooking spray 6 large eggs 1 garlic clove, minced ½ teaspoon salt ½ teaspoon black pepper Pinch red pepper flakes	8 ounces (227 g) baby bella mushrooms, sliced 1 cup fresh baby spinach 2 scallions, white parts and green parts, diced

1. Preheat the air fryer to 320°F (160°C). Lightly coat the inside of six silicone muffin cups or a six-cup muffin tin with olive oil cooking spray. 2. In a large bowl, beat the eggs, garlic, salt, pepper, and red pepper flakes for 1 to 2 minutes, or until well combined. 3. Fold in the mushrooms, spinach, and scallions. 4. Divide the mixture evenly among the muffin cups. 5. Place into the air fryer and bake for 12 to 15 minutes, or until the eggs are set. 6. Remove and allow to cool for 5 minutes before serving.

Ham and Cheese Crescents

Prep time: 5 minutes | Cook time: 7 minutes | Makes 8 rolls

Oil, for spraying 1 (8-ounce / 227-g) can refrigerated crescent rolls 4 slices deli ham	8 slices American cheese 2 tablespoons unsalted butter, melted

1. Line the air fryer basket with parchment and spray lightly with oil. 2. Separate the dough into 8 pieces. 3. Tear the ham slices in half and place 1 piece on each piece of dough. Top each with 1 slice of cheese. 4. Roll up each piece of dough, starting on the wider side. 5. Place the rolls in the prepared basket. Brush with the melted butter. 6. Air fry at 320°F (160°C) for 6 to 7 minutes, or until puffed and golden brown and the cheese is melted.

Everything Bagels

Prep time: 15 minutes | Cook time: 14 minutes | Makes 6 bagels

1¾ cups shredded Mozzarella cheese or goat cheese Mozzarella 2 tablespoons unsalted butter or coconut oil 1 large egg, beaten 1 tablespoon apple cider	vinegar 1 cup blanched almond flour 1 tablespoon baking powder ⅛ teaspoon fine sea salt 1½ teaspoons everything bagel seasoning

1. Make the dough: Put the Mozzarella and butter in a large microwave-safe bowl and microwave for 1 to 2 minutes, until the cheese is entirely melted. Stir well. Add the egg and vinegar. Using a hand mixer on medium, combine well. Add the almond flour, baking powder, and salt and, using the mixer, combine well. 2. Lay a piece of parchment paper on the countertop and place the dough on it. Knead it for about 3 minutes. The dough should be a little sticky but pliable. (If the dough is too sticky, chill it in the refrigerator for an hour or overnight.) 3. Preheat the air fryer to 350ºF (177ºC). Spray a baking sheet or pie pan that will fit into your air fryer with avocado oil. 4. Divide the dough into 6 equal portions. Roll 1 portion into a log that is 6 inches long and about ½ inch thick. Form the log into a circle and seal the edges together, making a bagel shape. Repeat with the remaining portions of dough, making 6 bagels. 5. Place the bagels on the greased baking sheet. Spray the bagels with avocado oil and top with everything bagel seasoning, pressing the seasoning into the dough with your hands. 6. Place the bagels in the air fryer and bake for 14 minutes, or until cooked through and golden brown, flipping after 6 minutes. 7. Remove the bagels from the air fryer and allow them to cool slightly before slicing them in half and serving. Store leftovers in an airtight container in the fridge for up to 4 days or in the freezer for up to a month.

Mozzarella Bacon Calzones

Prep time: 15 minutes | Cook time: 12 minutes | Serves 4

2 large eggs 1 cup blanched finely ground almond flour 2 cups shredded Mozzarella cheese	2 ounces (57 g) cream cheese, softened and broken into small pieces 4 slices cooked sugar-free bacon, crumbled

1. Beat eggs in a small bowl. Pour into a medium nonstick skillet over medium heat and scramble. Set aside. 2. In a large microwave-safe bowl, mix flour and Mozzarella. Add cream cheese to the bowl. 3. Place bowl in microwave and cook 45 seconds on high to melt cheese, then stir with a fork until a soft dough ball forms. 4. Cut a piece of parchment to fit air fryer basket. Separate dough into two sections and press each out into an 8-inch round. 5. On half of each dough round, place half of the scrambled eggs and crumbled bacon. Fold the other side of the dough over and press to seal the edges. 6. Place calzones on ungreased parchment and into air fryer basket. Adjust the temperature to 350ºF (177ºC) and set the timer for 12 minutes, turning calzones halfway through cooking. Crust will be golden and firm when done. 7. Let calzones cool on a cooking rack 5 minutes before serving.

Lemon-Blueberry Muffins

Prep time: 5 minutes | Cook time: 20 to 25 minutes | Makes 6 muffins

1¼ cups almond flour 3 tablespoons Swerve 1 teaspoon baking powder 2 large eggs 3 tablespoons melted butter	1 tablespoon almond milk 1 tablespoon fresh lemon juice ½ cup fresh blueberries

1. Preheat the air fryer to 350ºF (177ºC). Lightly coat 6 silicone muffin cups with vegetable oil. Set aside. 2. In a large mixing bowl, combine the almond flour, Swerve, and baking soda. Set aside. 3. In a separate small bowl, whisk together the eggs, butter, milk, and lemon juice. Add the egg mixture to the flour mixture and stir until just combined. Fold in the blueberries and let the batter sit for 5 minutes. 4. Spoon the muffin batter into the muffin cups, about two-thirds full. Air fry for 20 to 25 minutes, or until a toothpick inserted into the center of a muffin comes out clean. 5. Remove the basket from the air fryer and let the muffins cool for about 5 minutes before transferring them to a wire rack to cool completely.

Spinach Omelet

Prep time: 5 minutes | Cook time: 12 minutes | Serves 2

4 large eggs 1½ cups chopped fresh spinach leaves 2 tablespoons peeled and chopped yellow onion	2 tablespoons salted butter, melted ½ cup shredded mild Cheddar cheese ¼ teaspoon salt

1. In an ungreased round nonstick baking dish, whisk eggs. Stir in spinach, onion, butter, Cheddar, and salt. 2. Place dish into air fryer basket. Adjust the temperature to 320ºF (160ºC) and bake for 12 minutes. Omelet will be done when browned on the top and firm in the middle. 3. Slice in half and serve warm on two medium plates.

Veggie Frittata

Prep time: 7 minutes | Cook time: 21 to 23 minutes | Serves 2

Avocado oil spray ¼ cup diced red onion ¼ cup diced red bell pepper ¼ cup finely chopped broccoli 4 large eggs	3 ounces (85 g) shredded sharp Cheddar cheese, divided ½ teaspoon dried thyme Sea salt and freshly ground black pepper, to taste

1. Spray a pan well with oil. Put the onion, pepper, and broccoli in the pan, place the pan in the air fryer, and set to 350ºF (177ºC). Bake for 5 minutes. 2. While the vegetables cook, beat the eggs in a medium bowl. Stir in half of the cheese, and season with the thyme, salt, and pepper. 3. Add the eggs to the pan and top with the remaining cheese. Set the air fryer to 350ºF (177ºC). Bake for 16 to 18 minutes, until cooked through.

Pancake Cake

Prep time: 10 minutes | Cook time: 7 minutes | Serves 4

½ cup blanched finely ground almond flour ¼ cup powdered erythritol ½ teaspoon baking powder 2 tablespoons unsalted butter, softened	1 large egg ½ teaspoon unflavored gelatin ½ teaspoon vanilla extract ½ teaspoon ground cinnamon

1. In a large bowl, mix almond flour, erythritol, and baking powder. Add butter, egg, gelatin, vanilla, and cinnamon. Pour into a round baking pan. 2. Place pan into the air fryer basket. 3. Adjust the temperature to 300ºF (149ºC) and set the timer for 7 minutes. 4. When the cake is completely cooked, a toothpick will come out clean. Cut cake into four and serve.

Pita and Pepperoni Pizza

Prep time: 10 minutes | Cook time: 6 minutes | Serves 1

1 teaspoon olive oil 1 tablespoon pizza sauce 1 pita bread 6 pepperoni slices	¼ cup grated Mozzarella cheese ¼ teaspoon garlic powder ¼ teaspoon dried oregano

1. Preheat the air fryer to 350ºF (177ºC). Grease the air fryer basket with olive oil. 2. Spread the pizza sauce on top of the pita bread. Put the pepperoni slices over the sauce, followed by the Mozzarella cheese. 3. Season with garlic powder and oregano. 4. Put the pita pizza inside the air fryer and place a trivet on top. 5. Bake in the preheated air fryer for 6 minutes and serve.

Breakfast Cobbler

Prep time: 20 minutes | Cook time: 30 minutes | Serves 4

Filling:

10 ounces (283 g) bulk pork sausage, crumbled ¼ cup minced onions 2 cloves garlic, minced ½ teaspoon fine sea salt ½ teaspoon ground black pepper 1 (8-ounce / 227-g) package cream cheese (or Kite Hill brand cream cheese style spread for dairy-free), softened	¾ cup beef or chicken broth Biscuits: 3 large egg whites ¾ cup blanched almond flour 1 teaspoon baking powder ¼ teaspoon fine sea salt 2½ tablespoons very cold unsalted butter, cut into ¼-inch pieces Fresh thyme leaves, for garnish

1. Preheat the air fryer to 400ºF (204ºC). 2. Place the sausage, onions, and garlic in a pie pan. Using your hands, break up the sausage into small pieces and spread it evenly throughout the pie pan. Season with the salt and pepper. Place the pan in the air fryer and bake for 5 minutes. 3. While the sausage cooks, place the cream cheese and broth in a food processor or blender and purée until smooth. 4. Remove the pork from the air fryer and use a fork or metal spatula to crumble it more. Pour the cream cheese mixture into the sausage and stir to combine. Set aside. 5. Make the biscuits: Place the egg whites in a medium-sized mixing bowl or the bowl of a stand mixer and whip with a hand mixer or stand mixer until stiff peaks form. 6. In a separate medium-sized bowl, whisk together the almond flour, baking powder, and salt, then cut in the butter. When you are done, the mixture should still have chunks of butter. Gently fold the flour mixture into the egg whites with a rubber spatula. 7. Use a large spoon or ice cream scoop to scoop the dough into 4 equal-sized biscuits, making sure the butter is evenly distributed. Place the biscuits on top of the sausage and cook in the air fryer for 5 minutes, then turn the heat down to 325ºF (163ºC) and bake for another 17 to 20 minutes, until the biscuits are golden brown. Serve garnished with fresh thyme leaves. 8. Store leftovers in an airtight container in the refrigerator for up to 3 days. Reheat in a preheated 350ºF (177ºC) air fryer for 5 minutes, or until warmed through.

Bacon, Egg, and Cheese Roll Ups

Prep time: 15 minutes | Cook time: 15 minutes | Serves 4

2 tablespoons unsalted butter ¼ cup chopped onion ½ medium green bell pepper, seeded and chopped 6 large eggs	12 slices sugar-free bacon 1 cup shredded sharp Cheddar cheese ½ cup mild salsa, for dipping

1. In a medium skillet over medium heat, melt butter. Add onion and pepper to the skillet and sauté until fragrant and onions are translucent, about 3 minutes. 2. Whisk eggs in a small bowl and pour into skillet. Scramble eggs with onions and peppers until fluffy and fully cooked, about 5 minutes. Remove from heat and set aside. 3. On work surface, place three slices of bacon side by side, overlapping about ¼ inch. Place ¼ cup scrambled eggs in a heap on the side closest to you and sprinkle ¼ cup cheese on top of the eggs. 4. Tightly roll the bacon around the eggs and secure the seam with a toothpick if necessary. Place each roll into the air fryer basket. 5. Adjust the temperature to 350ºF (177ºC) and air fry for 15 minutes. Rotate the rolls halfway through the cooking time. 6. Bacon will be brown and crispy when completely cooked. Serve immediately with salsa for dipping.

Spaghetti Squash Fritters

Prep time: 15 minutes | Cook time: 8 minutes | Serves 4

2 cups cooked spaghetti squash 2 tablespoons unsalted butter, softened 1 large egg	¼ cup blanched finely ground almond flour 2 stalks green onion, sliced ½ teaspoon garlic powder 1 teaspoon dried parsley

1. Remove excess moisture from the squash using a cheesecloth or kitchen towel. 2. Mix all ingredients in a large bowl. Form into four patties. 3. Cut a piece of parchment to fit your air fryer basket. Place each patty on the parchment and place into the air fryer basket. 4. Adjust the temperature to 400ºF (204ºC) and set the timer for 8 minutes. 5. Flip the patties halfway through the cooking time. Serve warm.

Gyro Breakfast Patties with Tzatziki

Prep time: 10 minutes | Cook time: 20 minutes per batch | Makes 16 patties

Patties:	1 small cucumber, chopped
2 pounds (907 g) ground lamb or beef	½ teaspoon fine sea salt
½ cup diced red onions	½ teaspoon garlic powder, or
¼ cup sliced black olives	1 clove garlic, minced
2 tablespoons tomato sauce	¼ teaspoon dried dill weed,
1 teaspoon dried oregano leaves	or 1 teaspoon finely chopped fresh dill
1 teaspoon Greek seasoning	For Garnish/Serving:
2 cloves garlic, minced	½ cup crumbled feta cheese
1 teaspoon fine sea salt	(about 2 ounces / 57 g)
Tzatziki:	Diced red onions
1 cup full-fat sour cream	Sliced black olives
	Sliced cucumbers

1. Preheat the air fryer to 350ºF (177ºC). 2. Place the ground lamb, onions, olives, tomato sauce, oregano, Greek seasoning, garlic, and salt in a large bowl. Mix well to combine the ingredients. 3. Using your hands, form the mixture into sixteen 3-inch patties. Place about 5 of the patties in the air fryer and air fry for 20 minutes, flipping halfway through. Remove the patties and place them on a serving platter. Repeat with the remaining patties. 4. While the patties cook, make the tzatziki: Place all the ingredients in a small bowl and stir well. Cover and store in the fridge until ready to serve. Garnish with ground black pepper before serving. 5. Serve the patties with a dollop of tzatziki, a sprinkle of crumbled feta cheese, diced red onions, sliced black olives, and sliced cucumbers. 6. Store leftovers in an airtight container in the refrigerator for up to 5 days or in the freezer for up to a month. Reheat the patties in a preheated 390ºF (199ºC) air fryer for a few minutes, until warmed through.

Tomato and Mozzarella Bruschetta

Prep time: 5 minutes | Cook time: 4 minutes | Serves 1

6 small loaf slices	cheese, grated
½ cup tomatoes, finely chopped	1 tablespoon fresh basil, chopped
3 ounces (85 g) Mozzarella	1 tablespoon olive oil

1. Preheat the air fryer to 350ºF (177ºC). 2. Put the loaf slices inside the air fryer and air fry for about 3 minutes. 3. Add the tomato, Mozzarella, basil, and olive oil on top. 4. Air fry for an additional minute before serving.

Breakfast Hash

Prep time: 10 minutes | Cook time: 30 minutes | Serves 6

Oil, for spraying	2 tablespoons olive oil
3 medium russet potatoes, diced	2 teaspoons granulated garlic
½ yellow onion, diced	1 teaspoon salt
1 green bell pepper, seeded and diced	½ teaspoon freshly ground black pepper

1. Line the air fryer basket with parchment and spray lightly with oil. 2. In a large bowl, mix together the potatoes, onion, bell pepper, and olive oil. 3. Add the garlic, salt, and black pepper and stir until evenly coated. 4. Transfer the mixture to the prepared basket. 5. Air fry at 400ºF (204ºC) for 20 to 30 minutes, shaking or stirring every 10 minutes, until browned and crispy. If you spray the potatoes with a little oil each time you stir, they will get even crispier.

Pizza Eggs

Prep time: 5 minutes | Cook time: 10 minutes | Serves 2

1 cup shredded Mozzarella cheese	¼ teaspoon dried oregano
7 slices pepperoni, chopped	¼ teaspoon dried parsley
1 large egg, whisked	¼ teaspoon garlic powder
	¼ teaspoon salt

1. Place Mozzarella in a single layer on the bottom of an ungreased round nonstick baking dish. Scatter pepperoni over cheese, then pour egg evenly around baking dish. 2. Sprinkle with remaining ingredients and place into air fryer basket. Adjust the temperature to 330ºF (166ºC) and bake for 10 minutes. When cheese is brown and egg is set, dish will be done. 3. Let cool in dish 5 minutes before serving.

Vanilla Granola

Prep time: 5 minutes | Cook time: 40 minutes | Serves 4

1 cup rolled oats	¼ teaspoon vanilla
3 tablespoons maple syrup	¼ teaspoon cinnamon
1 tablespoon sunflower oil	¼ teaspoon sea salt
1 tablespoon coconut sugar	

1. Preheat the air fryer to 248ºF (120ºC). 2. Mix together the oats, maple syrup, sunflower oil, coconut sugar, vanilla, cinnamon, and sea salt in a medium bowl and stir to combine. Transfer the mixture to a baking pan. 3. Place the pan in the air fryer basket and bake for 40 minutes, or until the granola is mostly dry and lightly browned. Stir the granola four times during cooking. 4. Let the granola stand for 5 to 10 minutes before serving.

Cheesy Scrambled Eggs

Prep time: 2 minutes | Cook time: 9 minutes | Serves 2

1 teaspoon unsalted butter	Cheddar cheese
2 large eggs	Salt and freshly ground black pepper, to taste
2 tablespoons milk	
2 tablespoons shredded	

1. Preheat the air fryer to 300ºF (149ºC). Place the butter in a baking pan and cook for 1 to 2 minutes, until melted. 2. In a small bowl, whisk together the eggs, milk, and cheese. Season with salt and black pepper. Transfer the mixture to the pan. 3. Cook for 3 minutes. Stir the eggs and push them toward the center of the pan. 4. Cook for another 2 minutes, then stir again. Cook for another 2 minutes, until the eggs are just cooked. Serve warm.

Breakfast Pita

Prep time: 5 minutes | Cook time: 6 minutes | Serves 2

1 whole wheat pita	¼ teaspoon dried oregano
2 teaspoons olive oil	¼ teaspoon dried thyme
½ shallot, diced	⅛ teaspoon salt
¼ teaspoon garlic, minced	2 tablespoons shredded
1 large egg	Parmesan cheese

1. Preheat the air fryer to 380°F(193°C). 2. Brush the top of the pita with olive oil, then spread the diced shallot and minced garlic over the pita. 3. Crack the egg into a small bowl or ramekin, and season it with oregano, thyme, and salt. 4. Place the pita into the air fryer basket, and gently pour the egg onto the top of the pita. Sprinkle with cheese over the top. 5. Bake for 6 minutes. 6. Allow to cool for 5 minutes before cutting into pieces for serving.

Bacon and Cheese Quiche

Prep time: 5 minutes | Cook time: 12 minutes | Serves 2

3 large eggs	4 slices cooked sugar-free
2 tablespoons heavy	bacon, crumbled
whipping cream	½ cup shredded mild
¼ teaspoon salt	Cheddar cheese

1. In a large bowl, whisk eggs, cream, and salt together until combined. Mix in bacon and Cheddar. 2. Pour mixture evenly into two ungreased ramekins. Place into air fryer basket. Adjust the temperature to 320°F (160°C) and bake for 12 minutes. Quiche will be fluffy and set in the middle when done. 3. Let quiche cool in ramekins 5 minutes. Serve warm.

Strawberry Tarts

Prep time: 15 minutes | Cook time: 10 minutes | Serves 6

2 refrigerated piecrusts	at room temperature
½ cup strawberry preserves	3 tablespoons confectioners'
1 teaspoon cornstarch	sugar
Cooking oil spray	Rainbow sprinkles, for
½ cup low-fat vanilla yogurt	decorating
1 ounce (28 g) cream cheese,	

1. Place the piecrusts on a flat surface. Using a knife or pizza cutter, cut each piecrust into 3 rectangles, for 6 total. Discard any unused dough from the piecrust edges. 2. In a small bowl, stir together the preserves and cornstarch. Mix well, ensuring there are no lumps of cornstarch remaining. 3. Scoop 1 tablespoon of the strawberry mixture onto the top half of each piece of piecrust. 4. Fold the bottom of each piece up to enclose the filling. Using the back of a fork, press along the edges of each tart to seal. 5. Insert the crisper plate into the basket and the basket into the unit. Preheat the unit by selecting BAKE, setting the temperature to 375°F (191°C), and setting the time to 3 minutes. Select START/ STOP to begin. 6. Once the unit is preheated, spray the crisper plate with cooking oil. Working in batches, spray the breakfast tarts with cooking oil and place them into the basket in a single layer. Do not stack the tarts. 7. Select BAKE, set the temperature to 375°F (191°C), and set the time to 10 minutes. Select START/ STOP to begin. 8. When the cooking is complete, the tarts should be light golden brown. Let the breakfast tarts cool fully before removing them from the basket. 9. Repeat steps 5, 6, 7, and 8 for the remaining breakfast tarts. 10. In a small bowl, stir together the yogurt, cream cheese, and confectioners' sugar. Spread the breakfast tarts with the frosting and top with sprinkles.

Classic British Breakfast

Prep time: 5 minutes | Cook time: 25 minutes | Serves 2

1 cup potatoes, sliced and	1 tablespoon olive oil
diced	1 sausage
2 cups beans in tomato sauce	Salt, to taste
2 eggs	

1. Preheat the air fryer to 390°F (199°C) and allow to warm. 2. Break the eggs onto a baking dish and sprinkle with salt. 3. Lay the beans on the dish, next to the eggs. 4. In a bowl, coat the potatoes with the olive oil. Sprinkle with salt. 5. Transfer the bowl of potato slices to the air fryer and bake for 10 minutes. 6. Swap out the bowl of potatoes for the dish containing the eggs and beans. Bake for another 10 minutes. Cover the potatoes with parchment paper. 7. Slice up the sausage and throw the slices on top of the beans and eggs. Bake for another 5 minutes. 8. Serve with the potatoes.

Breakfast Sausage and Cauliflower

Prep time: 5 minutes | Cook time: 45 minutes | Serves 4

1 pound (454 g) sausage,	1 cup grated Cheddar cheese,
cooked and crumbled	plus more for topping
2 cups heavy whipping	8 eggs, beaten
cream	Salt and ground black
1 head cauliflower, chopped	pepper, to taste

1. Preheat the air fryer to 350°F (177°C). 2. In a large bowl, mix the sausage, heavy whipping cream, chopped cauliflower, cheese and eggs. Sprinkle with salt and ground black pepper. 3. Pour the mixture into a greased casserole dish. Bake in the preheated air fryer for 45 minutes or until firm. 4. Top with more Cheddar cheese and serve.

Strawberry Toast

Prep time: 10 minutes | Cook time: 8 minutes | Makes 4 toasts

4 slices bread, ½-inch thick	1 cup sliced strawberries
Butter-flavored cooking	1 teaspoon sugar
spray	

1. Spray one side of each bread slice with butter-flavored cooking spray. Lay slices sprayed side down. 2. Divide the strawberries among the bread slices. 3. Sprinkle evenly with the sugar and place in the air fryer basket in a single layer. 4. Air fry at 390°F (199°C) for 8 minutes. The bottom should look brown and crisp and the top should look glazed.

Egg Muffins

Prep time: 10 minutes | Cook time: 11 to 13 minutes | Serves 4

4 eggs Salt and pepper, to taste Olive oil 4 English muffins, split	1 cup shredded Colby Jack cheese 4 slices ham or Canadian bacon

1. Preheat the air fryer to 390ºF (199ºC). 2. Beat together eggs and add salt and pepper to taste. Spray a baking pan lightly with oil and add eggs. Bake for 2 minutes, stir, and continue cooking for 3 or 4 minutes, stirring every minute, until eggs are scrambled to your preference. Remove pan from air fryer. 3. Place bottom halves of English muffins in air fryer basket. Take half of the shredded cheese and divide it among the muffins. Top each with a slice of ham and one-quarter of the eggs. Sprinkle remaining cheese on top of the eggs. Use a fork to press the cheese into the egg a little so it doesn't slip off before it melts. 4. Air fry at 360ºF (182ºC) for 1 minute. Add English muffin tops and cook for 2 to 4 minutes to heat through and toast the muffins.

Broccoli-Mushroom Frittata

Prep time: 10 minutes | Cook time: 20 minutes | Serves 2

1 tablespoon olive oil 1½ cups broccoli florets, finely chopped ½ cup sliced brown mushrooms ¼ cup finely chopped onion	½ teaspoon salt ¼ teaspoon freshly ground black pepper 6 eggs ¼ cup Parmesan cheese

1. In a nonstick cake pan, combine the olive oil, broccoli, mushrooms, onion, salt, and pepper. Stir until the vegetables are thoroughly coated with oil. Place the cake pan in the air fryer basket and set the air fryer to 400ºF (204ºC). Air fry for 5 minutes until the vegetables soften. 2. Meanwhile, in a medium bowl, whisk the eggs and Parmesan until thoroughly combined. Pour the egg mixture into the pan and shake gently to distribute the vegetables. Air fry for another 15 minutes until the eggs are set. 3. Remove from the air fryer and let sit for 5 minutes to cool slightly. Use a silicone spatula to gently lift the frittata onto a plate before serving.

Tomato and Cheddar Rolls

Prep time: 30 minutes | Cook time: 25 minutes | Makes 12 rolls

4 Roma tomatoes ½ clove garlic, minced 1 tablespoon olive oil ¼ teaspoon dried thyme Salt and freshly ground black pepper, to taste 4 cups all-purpose flour 1 teaspoon active dry yeast	2 teaspoons sugar 2 teaspoons salt 1 tablespoon olive oil 1 cup grated Cheddar cheese, plus more for sprinkling at the end 1½ cups water

1. Cut the Roma tomatoes in half, remove the seeds with your fingers and transfer to a bowl. Add the garlic, olive oil, dried thyme, salt and freshly ground black pepper and toss well. 2. Preheat the air fryer to 390ºF (199ºC). 3. Place the tomatoes, cut side up in the air fryer basket and air fry for 10 minutes. The tomatoes should just start to brown. Shake the basket to redistribute the tomatoes, and air fry for another 5 to 10 minutes at 330ºF (166ºC) until the tomatoes are no longer juicy. Let the tomatoes cool and then rough chop them. 4. Combine the flour, yeast, sugar and salt in the bowl of a stand mixer. Add the olive oil, chopped roasted tomatoes and Cheddar cheese to the flour mixture and start to mix using the dough hook attachment. As you're mixing, add 1¼ cups of the water, mixing until the dough comes together. Continue to knead the dough with the dough hook for another 10 minutes, adding enough water to the dough to get it to the right consistency. 5. Transfer the dough to an oiled bowl, cover with a clean kitchen towel and let it rest and rise until it has doubled in volume, about 1 to 2 hours. Then, divide the dough into 12 equal portions. Roll each portion of dough into a ball. Lightly coat each dough ball with oil and let the dough balls rest and rise a second time, covered lightly with plastic wrap for 45 minutes. (Alternately, you can place the rolls in the refrigerator overnight and take them out 2 hours before you bake them.) 6. Preheat the air fryer to 360ºF (182ºC). 7. Spray the dough balls and the air fryer basket with a little olive oil. Place three rolls at a time in the basket and bake for 10 minutes. Add a little grated Cheddar cheese on top of the rolls for the last 2 minutes of air frying for an attractive finish.

New York Strip Steaks with Eggs

Prep time: 8 minutes | Cook time: 14 minutes per batch | Serves 4

Cooking oil spray 4 (4-ounce / 113-g) New York strip steaks 1 teaspoon granulated garlic, divided	1 teaspoon salt, divided 1 teaspoon freshly ground black pepper, divided 4 eggs ½ teaspoon paprika

1. Insert the crisper plate into the basket and the basket into the unit. Preheat the unit by selecting AIR FRY, setting the temperature to 360ºF (182ºC), and setting the time to 3 minutes. Select START/STOP to begin. 2. Once the unit is preheated, spray the crisper plate with cooking oil. Place 2 steaks into the basket; do not oil or season them at this time. 3. Select AIR FRY, set the temperature to 360ºF (182ºC), and set the time to 9 minutes. Select START/STOP to begin. 4. After 5 minutes, open the unit and flip the steaks. Sprinkle each with ¼ teaspoon of granulated garlic, ¼ teaspoon of salt, and ¼ teaspoon of pepper. Resume cooking until the steaks register at least 145ºF (63ºC) on a food thermometer. 5. When the cooking is complete, transfer the steaks to a plate and tent with aluminum foil to keep warm. Repeat steps 2, 3, and 4 with the remaining steaks. 6. Spray 4 ramekins with olive oil. Crack 1 egg into each ramekin. Sprinkle the eggs with the paprika and remaining ½ teaspoon each of salt and pepper. Working in batches, place 2 ramekins into the basket. 7. Select BAKE, set the temperature to 330ºF (166ºC), and set the time to 5 minutes. Select START/STOP to begin. 8. When the cooking is complete and the eggs are cooked to 160ºF (71ºC), remove the ramekins and repeat step 7 with the remaining 2 ramekins. 9. Serve the eggs with the steaks.

Coconut Brown Rice Porridge with Dates

Prep time: 10 minutes | Cook time: 23 minutes | Serves 1 to 2

1 cup canned coconut milk	¼ teaspoon ground
½ cup cooked brown rice	cardamom
¼ cup unsweetened shredded	4 large Medjool dates, pitted
coconut	and roughly chopped
¼ cup packed dark brown	Heavy cream, for serving
sugar	(optional)
½ teaspoon kosher salt	

1. In a cake pan, stir together the coconut milk, rice, shredded coconut, brown sugar, salt, cardamom, and dates and place in the air fryer. Bake at 375ºF (191ºC) until reduced and thickened and browned on top, about 23 minutes, stirring halfway through. 2. Remove the pan from the air fryer and divide the porridge among bowls. Drizzle the porridge with cream, if you like, and serve hot.

Onion Omelet

Prep time: 10 minutes | Cook time: 12 minutes | Serves 2

3 eggs	1 large onion, chopped
Salt and ground black	2 tablespoons grated Cheddar
pepper, to taste	cheese
½ teaspoons soy sauce	Cooking spray

1. Preheat the air fryer to 355ºF (179ºC). 2. In a bowl, whisk together the eggs, salt, pepper, and soy sauce. 3. Spritz a small pan with cooking spray. Spread the chopped onion across the bottom of the pan, then transfer the pan to the air fryer. 4. Bake in the preheated air fryer for 6 minutes or until the onion is translucent. 5. Add the egg mixture on top of the onions to coat well. Add the cheese on top, then continue baking for another 6 minutes. 6. Allow to cool before serving.

Cinnamon Rolls

Prep time: 10 minutes | Cook time: 20 minutes | Makes 12 rolls

2½ cups shredded	½ teaspoon vanilla extract
Mozzarella cheese	½ cup confectioners'
2 ounces (57 g) cream	erythritol
cheese, softened	1 tablespoon ground
1 cup blanched finely ground	cinnamon
almond flour	

1. In a large microwave-safe bowl, combine Mozzarella cheese, cream cheese, and flour. Microwave the mixture on high 90 seconds until cheese is melted. 2. Add vanilla extract and erythritol, and mix 2 minutes until a dough forms. 3. Once the dough is cool enough to work with your hands, about 2 minutes, spread it out into a 12 × 4-inch rectangle on ungreased parchment paper. Evenly sprinkle dough with cinnamon. 4. Starting at the long side of the dough, roll lengthwise to form a log. Slice the log into twelve even pieces. 5. Divide rolls between two ungreased round nonstick baking dishes. Place one dish into air fryer basket. Adjust the temperature to 375ºF (191ºC) and bake for 10 minutes.

6. Cinnamon rolls will be done when golden around the edges and mostly firm. Repeat with second dish. Allow rolls to cool in dishes 10 minutes before serving.

Asparagus and Bell Pepper Strata

Prep time: 10 minutes | Cook time: 14 to 20 minutes | Serves 4

8 large asparagus spears,	wheat bread, cut into ½-inch
trimmed and cut into 2-inch	cubes
pieces	3 egg whites
⅓ cup shredded carrot	1 egg
½ cup chopped red bell	3 tablespoons 1% milk
pepper	½ teaspoon dried thyme
2 slices low-sodium whole-	

1. In a baking pan, combine the asparagus, carrot, red bell pepper, and 1 tablespoon of water. Bake in the air fryer at 330ºF (166ºC) for 3 to 5 minutes, or until crisp-tender. Drain well. 2. Add the bread cubes to the vegetables and gently toss. 3. In a medium bowl, whisk the egg whites, egg, milk, and thyme until frothy. 4. Pour the egg mixture into the pan. Bake for 11 to 15 minutes, or until the strata is slightly puffy and set and the top starts to brown. Serve.

Pancake for Two

Prep time: 5 minutes | Cook time: 30 minutes | Serves 2

1 cup blanched finely ground	melted
almond flour	1 large egg
2 tablespoons granular	⅓ cup unsweetened almond
erythritol	milk
1 tablespoon salted butter,	½ teaspoon vanilla extract

1. In a large bowl, mix all ingredients together, then pour half the batter into an ungreased round nonstick baking dish. 2. Place dish into air fryer basket. Adjust the temperature to 320ºF (160ºC) and bake for 15 minutes. The pancake will be golden brown on top and firm, and a toothpick inserted in the center will come out clean when done. Repeat with remaining batter. 3. Slice in half in dish and serve warm.

Egg White Cups

Prep time: 10 minutes | Cook time: 15 minutes | Serves 4

2 cups 100% liquid egg	¼ teaspoon onion powder
whites	½ medium Roma tomato,
3 tablespoons salted butter,	cored and diced
melted	½ cup chopped fresh spinach
¼ teaspoon salt	leaves

1. In a large bowl, whisk egg whites with butter, salt, and onion powder. Stir in tomato and spinach, then pour evenly into four ramekins greased with cooking spray. 2. Place ramekins into air fryer basket. Adjust the temperature to 300ºF (149ºC) and bake for 15 minutes. Eggs will be fully cooked and firm in the center when done. Serve warm.

Scotch Eggs

Prep time: 10 minutes | Cook time: 20 to 25 minutes | Serves 4

2 tablespoons flour, plus extra for coating 1 pound (454 g) ground breakfast sausage 4 hard-boiled eggs, peeled 1 raw egg	1 tablespoon water Oil for misting or cooking spray Crumb Coating: ¾ cup panko bread crumbs ¾ cup flour

1. Combine flour with ground sausage and mix thoroughly. 2. Divide into 4 equal portions and mold each around a hard-boiled egg so the sausage completely covers the egg. 3. In a small bowl, beat together the raw egg and water. 4. Dip sausage-covered eggs in the remaining flour, then the egg mixture, then roll in the crumb coating. 5. Air fry at 360ºF (182ºC) for 10 minutes. Spray eggs, turn, and spray other side. 6. Continue cooking for another 10 to 15 minutes or until sausage is well done.

Italian Egg Cups

Prep time: 5 minutes | Cook time: 10 minutes | Serves 4

Olive oil 1 cup marinara sauce 4 eggs 4 tablespoons shredded Mozzarella cheese 4 teaspoons grated Parmesan	cheese Salt and freshly ground black pepper, to taste Chopped fresh basil, for garnish

1. Lightly spray 4 individual ramekins with olive oil. 2. Pour ¼ cup of marinara sauce into each ramekin. 3. Crack one egg into each ramekin on top of the marinara sauce. 4. Sprinkle 1 tablespoon of Mozzarella and 1 tablespoon of Parmesan on top of each egg. Season with salt and pepper. 5. Cover each ramekin with aluminum foil. Place two of the ramekins in the air fryer basket. 6. Air fry at 350ºF (177ºC) for 5 minutes and remove the aluminum foil. Air fry until the top is lightly browned and the egg white is cooked, another 2 to 4 minutes. If you prefer the yolk to be firmer, cook for 3 to 5 more minutes. 7. Repeat with the remaining two ramekins. Garnish with basil and serve.

Hearty Blueberry Oatmeal

Prep time: 10 minutes | Cook time: 25 minutes | Serves 6

1½ cups quick oats 1¼ teaspoons ground cinnamon, divided ½ teaspoon baking powder Pinch salt 1 cup unsweetened vanilla almond milk ¼ cup honey	1 teaspoon vanilla extract 1 egg, beaten 2 cups blueberries Olive oil 1½ teaspoons sugar, divided 6 tablespoons low-fat whipped topping (optional)

1. In a large bowl, mix together the oats, 1 teaspoon of cinnamon, baking powder, and salt. 2. In a medium bowl, whisk together the almond milk, honey, vanilla and egg. 3. Pour the liquid ingredients into the oats mixture and stir to combine. Fold in the blueberries. 4. Lightly spray a baking pan with oil. 5. Add half the blueberry mixture to the pan. 6. Sprinkle ⅛ teaspoon of cinnamon and ½ teaspoon sugar over the top. 7. Cover the pan with aluminum foil and place gently in the air fryer basket. 8. Air fry at 360ºF (182ºC) for 20 minutes. Remove the foil and air fry for an additional 5 minutes. Transfer the mixture to a shallow bowl. 9. Repeat with the remaining blueberry mixture, ½ teaspoon of sugar, and ⅛ teaspoon of cinnamon. 10. To serve, spoon into bowls and top with whipped topping.

Greek Bagels

Prep time: 10 minutes | Cook time: 10 minutes | Makes 2 bagels

½ cup self-rising flour, plus more for dusting ½ cup plain Greek yogurt 1 egg 1 tablespoon water	4 teaspoons everything bagel spice mix Cooking oil spray 1 tablespoon butter, melted

1. In a large bowl, using a wooden spoon, stir together the flour and yogurt until a tacky dough forms. Transfer the dough to a lightly floured work surface and roll the dough into a ball. 2. Cut the dough into 2 pieces and roll each piece into a log. Form each log into a bagel shape, pinching the ends together. 3. In a small bowl, whisk the egg and water. Brush the egg wash on the bagels. 4. Sprinkle 2 teaspoons of the spice mix on each bagel and gently press it into the dough. 5. Insert the crisper plate into the basket and the basket into the unit. Preheat the unit by selecting BAKE, setting the temperature to 330ºF (166ºC), and setting the time to 3 minutes. Select START/STOP to begin. 6. Once the unit is preheated, spray the crisper plate with cooking spray. Drizzle the bagels with the butter and place them into the basket. 7. Select BAKE, set the temperature to 330ºF (166ºC), and set the time to 10 minutes. Select START/STOP to begin. 8. When the cooking is complete, the bagels should be lightly golden on the outside. Serve warm.

Bourbon Vanilla French Toast

Prep time: 15 minutes | Cook time: 6 minutes | Serves 4

2 large eggs 2 tablespoons water ⅔ cup whole or 2% milk 1 tablespoon butter, melted 2 tablespoons bourbon	1 teaspoon vanilla extract 8 (1-inch-thick) French bread slices Cooking spray

1. Preheat the air fryer to 320ºF (160ºC). Line the air fryer basket with parchment paper and spray it with cooking spray. 2. Beat the eggs with the water in a shallow bowl until combined. Add the milk, melted butter, bourbon, and vanilla and stir to mix well. 3. Dredge 4 slices of bread in the batter, turning to coat both sides evenly. Transfer the bread slices onto the parchment paper. 4. Bake for 6 minutes until nicely browned. Flip the slices halfway through the cooking time. 5. Remove from the basket to a plate and repeat with the remaining 4 slices of bread. 6. Serve warm.

Chimichanga Breakfast Burrito

Prep time: 10 minutes | Cook time: 10 minutes | Serves 2

2 large (10- to 12-inch) flour tortillas ½ cup canned refried beans (pinto or black work equally well) 4 large eggs, cooked scrambled	4 corn tortilla chips, crushed ½ cup grated Pepper Jack cheese 12 pickled jalapeño slices 1 tablespoon vegetable oil Guacamole, salsa, and sour cream, for serving (optional)

1. Place the tortillas on a work surface and divide the refried beans between them, spreading them in a rough rectangle in the center of the tortillas. Top the beans with the scrambled eggs, crushed chips, pepper jack, and jalapeños. Fold one side over the fillings, then fold in each short side and roll up the rest of the way like a burrito. 2. Brush the outside of the burritos with the oil, then transfer to the air fryer, seam-side down. Air fry at 350ºF (177ºC) until the tortillas are browned and crisp and the filling is warm throughout, about 10 minutes. 3. Transfer the chimichangas to plates and serve warm with guacamole, salsa, and sour cream, if you like.

Keto Quiche

Prep time: 10 minutes | Cook time: 1 hour | Makes 1 (6-inch) quiche

Crust: 1¼ cups blanched almond flour 1¼ cups grated Parmesan or Gouda cheese ¼ teaspoon fine sea salt 1 large egg, beaten Filling: ½ cup chicken or beef broth (or vegetable broth for vegetarian) 1 cup shredded Swiss cheese	(about 4 ounces / 113 g) 4 ounces (113 g) cream cheese (½ cup) 1 tablespoon unsalted butter, melted 4 large eggs, beaten ⅓ cup minced leeks or sliced green onions ¾ teaspoon fine sea salt ⅛ teaspoon cayenne pepper Chopped green onions, for garnish

1. Preheat the air fryer to 325ºF (163ºC). Grease a pie pan. Spray two large pieces of parchment paper with avocado oil and set them on the countertop. 2. Make the crust: In a medium-sized bowl, combine the flour, cheese, and salt and mix well. Add the egg and mix until the dough is well combined and stiff. 3. Place the dough in the center of one of the greased pieces of parchment. Top with the other piece of parchment. Using a rolling pin, roll out the dough into a circle about 1/16 inch thick. 4. Press the pie crust into the prepared pie pan. Place it in the air fryer and bake for 12 minutes, or until it starts to lightly brown. 5. While the crust bakes, make the filling: In a large bowl, combine the broth, Swiss cheese, cream cheese, and butter. Stir in the eggs, leeks, salt, and cayenne pepper. When the crust is ready, pour the mixture into the crust. 6. Place the quiche in the air fryer and bake for 15 minutes. Turn the heat down to 300ºF (149ºC) and bake for an additional 30 minutes, or until a knife inserted 1 inch from the edge comes out clean. You may have to cover the edges of the crust with foil to prevent burning. 7. Allow the quiche to cool for 10 minutes before garnishing it with chopped green onions and

cutting it into wedges. 8. Store leftovers in an airtight container in the refrigerator for up to 4 days or in the freezer for up to a month. Reheat in a preheated 350ºF (177ºC) air fryer for a few minutes, until warmed through.

Breakfast Calzone

Prep time: 15 minutes | Cook time: 15 minutes | Serves 4

1½ cups shredded Mozzarella cheese ½ cup blanched finely ground almond flour 1 ounce (28 g) full-fat cream cheese	1 large whole egg 4 large eggs, scrambled ½ pound (227 g) cooked breakfast sausage, crumbled 8 tablespoons shredded mild Cheddar cheese

1. In a large microwave-safe bowl, add Mozzarella, almond flour, and cream cheese. Microwave for 1 minute. Stir until the mixture is smooth and forms a ball. Add the egg and stir until dough forms. 2. Place dough between two sheets of parchment and roll out to ¼-inch thickness. Cut the dough into four rectangles. 3. Mix scrambled eggs and cooked sausage together in a large bowl. Divide the mixture evenly among each piece of dough, placing it on the lower half of the rectangle. Sprinkle each with 2 tablespoons Cheddar. 4. Fold over the rectangle to cover the egg and meat mixture. Pinch, roll, or use a wet fork to close the edges completely. 5. Cut a piece of parchment to fit your air fryer basket and place the calzones onto the parchment. Place parchment into the air fryer basket. 6. Adjust the temperature to 380ºF (193ºC) and air fry for 15 minutes. 7. Flip the calzones halfway through the cooking time. When done, calzones should be golden in color. Serve immediately.

Turkey Breakfast Sausage Patties

Prep time: 5 minutes | Cook time: 10 minutes | Serves 4

1 tablespoon chopped fresh thyme 1 tablespoon chopped fresh sage 1¼ teaspoons kosher salt 1 teaspoon chopped fennel seeds ¾ teaspoon smoked paprika ½ teaspoon onion powder	½ teaspoon garlic powder ⅛ teaspoon crushed red pepper flakes ⅛ teaspoon freshly ground black pepper 1 pound (454 g) 93% lean ground turkey ½ cup finely minced sweet apple (peeled)

1. Thoroughly combine the thyme, sage, salt, fennel seeds, paprika, onion powder, garlic powder, red pepper flakes, and black pepper in a medium bowl. 2. Add the ground turkey and apple and stir until well incorporated. Divide the mixture into 8 equal portions and shape into patties with your hands, each about ¼ inch thick and 3 inches in diameter. 3. Preheat the air fryer to 400ºF (204ºC). 4. Place the patties in the air fryer basket in a single layer. You may need to work in batches to avoid overcrowding. 5. Air fry for 5 minutes. Flip the patties and air fry for 5 minutes, or until the patties are nicely browned and cooked through. 6. Remove from the basket to a plate and repeat with the remaining patties. 7. Serve warm.

Red Pepper and Feta Frittata

Prep time: 10 minutes | Cook time: 20 minutes | Serves 4

Olive oil cooking spray
8 large eggs
1 medium red bell pepper, diced
½ teaspoon salt

½ teaspoon black pepper
1 garlic clove, minced
½ cup feta, divided

1. Preheat the air fryer to 360°F(182°C). Lightly coat the inside of a 6-inch round cake pan with olive oil cooking spray. 2. In a large bowl, beat the eggs for 1 to 2 minutes, or until well combined. 3. Add the bell pepper, salt, black pepper, and garlic to the eggs, and mix together until the bell pepper is distributed throughout. 4. Fold in ¼ cup of the feta cheese. 5. Pour the egg mixture into the prepared cake pan, and sprinkle the remaining ¼ cup of feta over the top. 6. Place into the air fryer and bake for 18 to 20 minutes, or until the eggs are set in the center. 7. Remove from the air fryer and allow to cool for 5 minutes before serving.

Breakfast Pizza

Prep time: 5 minutes | Cook time: 8 minutes | Serves 1

2 large eggs
¼ cup unsweetened, unflavored almond milk (or unflavored hemp milk for nut-free)
¼ teaspoon fine sea salt
⅛ teaspoon ground black pepper

¼ cup diced onions
¼ cup shredded Parmesan cheese (omit for dairy-free)
6 pepperoni slices (omit for vegetarian)
¼ teaspoon dried oregano leaves
¼ cup pizza sauce, warmed, for serving

1. Preheat the air fryer to 350°F (177°C). Grease a cake pan. 2. In a small bowl, use a fork to whisk together the eggs, almond milk, salt, and pepper. Add the onions and stir to mix. Pour the mixture into the greased pan. Top with the cheese (if using), pepperoni slices (if using), and oregano. 3. Place the pan in the air fryer and bake for 8 minutes, or until the eggs are cooked to your liking. 4. Loosen the eggs from the sides of the pan with a spatula and place them on a serving plate. Drizzle the pizza sauce on top. Best served fresh.

Turkey Sausage Breakfast Pizza

Prep time: 15 minutes | Cook time: 24 minutes | Serves 2

4 large eggs, divided
1 tablespoon water
½ teaspoon garlic powder
½ teaspoon onion powder
½ teaspoon dried oregano
2 tablespoons coconut flour

3 tablespoons grated Parmesan cheese
½ cup shredded provolone cheese
1 link cooked turkey sausage, chopped (about 2 ounces / 57 g)
2 sun-dried tomatoes, finely chopped
2 scallions, thinly sliced

1. Preheat the air fryer to 400°F (204°C). Line a cake pan with parchment paper and lightly coat the paper with olive oil. 2. In a large bowl, whisk 2 of the eggs with the water, garlic powder, onion powder, and dried oregano. Add the coconut flour, breaking up any lumps with your hands as you add it to the bowl. Stir the coconut flour into the egg mixture, mixing until smooth. Stir in the Parmesan cheese. Allow the mixture to rest for a few minutes until thick and dough-like. 3. Transfer the mixture to the prepared pan. Use a spatula to spread it evenly and slightly up the sides of the pan. Air fry until the crust is set but still light in color, about 10 minutes. Top with the cheeses, sausage, and sun-dried tomatoes. 4. Break the remaining 2 eggs into a small bowl, then slide them onto the pizza. Return the pizza to the air fryer. Air fry 10 to 14 minutes until the egg whites are set and the yolks are the desired doneness. Top with the scallions and allow to rest for 5 minutes before serving.

2
Family Favorites

Cheesy Roasted Sweet Potatoes

Prep time: 7 minutes | Cook time: 18 to 23 minutes | Serves 4

2 large sweet potatoes, peeled and sliced 1 teaspoon olive oil 1 tablespoon white balsamic	vinegar 1 teaspoon dried thyme ¼ cup grated Parmesan cheese

1. In a large bowl, drizzle the sweet potato slices with the olive oil and toss. 2. Sprinkle with the balsamic vinegar and thyme and toss again. 3. Sprinkle the potatoes with the Parmesan cheese and toss to coat. 4. Roast the slices, in batches, in the air fryer basket at 400°F (204°C) for 18 to 23 minutes, tossing the sweet potato slices in the basket once during cooking, until tender. 5. Repeat with the remaining sweet potato slices. Serve immediately.

Meringue Cookies

Prep time: 15 minutes | Cook time: 1 hour 30 minutes | Makes 20 cookies

Oil, for spraying 4 large egg whites	1 cup sugar Pinch cream of tartar

1. Preheat the air fryer to 140°F (60°C). Line the air fryer basket with parchment and spray lightly with oil. 2. In a small heatproof bowl, whisk together the egg whites and sugar. Fill a small saucepan halfway with water, place it over medium heat, and bring to a light simmer. Place the bowl with the egg whites on the saucepan, making sure the bottom of the bowl does not touch the water. Whisk the mixture until the sugar is dissolved. 3. Transfer the mixture to a large bowl and add the cream of tartar. Using an electric mixer, beat the mixture on high until it is glossy and stiff peaks form. Transfer the mixture to a piping bag or a zip-top plastic bag with a corner cut off. 4. Pipe rounds into the prepared basket. You may need to work in batches, depending on the size of your air fryer. 5. Cook for 1 hour 30 minutes. 6. Turn off the air fryer and let the meringues cool completely inside. The residual heat will continue to dry them out.

Steak and Vegetable Kebabs

Prep time: 15 minutes | Cook time: 5 to 7 minutes | Serves 4

2 tablespoons balsamic vinegar 2 teaspoons olive oil ½ teaspoon dried marjoram ⅛ teaspoon freshly ground black pepper	¾ pound (340 g) round steak, cut into 1-inch pieces 1 red bell pepper, sliced 16 button mushrooms 1 cup cherry tomatoes

1. In a medium bowl, stir together the balsamic vinegar, olive oil, marjoram, and black pepper. 2. Add the steak and stir to coat. Let stand for 10 minutes at room temperature. 3. Alternating items, thread the beef, red bell pepper, mushrooms, and tomatoes onto 8 bamboo or metal skewers that fit in the air fryer. 4. Air fry at 390°F (199°C) for 5 to 7 minutes, or until the beef is browned and reaches at least 145°F (63°C) on a meat thermometer. Serve immediately.

Scallops with Green Vegetables

Prep time: 15 minutes | Cook time: 8 to 11 minutes | Serves 4

1 cup green beans 1 cup frozen peas 1 cup frozen chopped broccoli 2 teaspoons olive oil	½ teaspoon dried basil ½ teaspoon dried oregano 12 ounces (340 g) sea scallops

1. In a large bowl, toss the green beans, peas, and broccoli with the olive oil. Place in the air fryer basket. Air fry at 400°F (204°C) for 4 to 6 minutes, or until the vegetables are crisp-tender. 2. Remove the vegetables from the air fryer basket and sprinkle with the herbs. Set aside. 3. In the air fryer basket, put the scallops and air fry for 4 to 5 minutes, or until the scallops are firm and reach an internal temperature of just 145°F (63°C) on a meat thermometer. 4. Toss scallops with the vegetables and serve immediately.

Avocado and Egg Burrito

Prep time: 10 minutes | Cook time: 3 to 5 minutes | Serves 4

2 hard-boiled egg whites, chopped 1 hard-boiled egg, chopped 1 avocado, peeled, pitted, and chopped 1 red bell pepper, chopped 3 tablespoons low-sodium salsa, plus additional for	serving (optional) 1 (1.2-ounce / 34-g) slice low-sodium, low-fat American cheese, torn into pieces 4 low-sodium whole-wheat flour tortillas

1. In a medium bowl, thoroughly mix the egg whites, egg, avocado, red bell pepper, salsa, and cheese. 2. Place the tortillas on a work surface and evenly divide the filling among them. Fold in the edges and roll up. Secure the burritos with toothpicks if necessary. 3. Put the burritos in the air fryer basket. Air fry at 390°F (199°C) for 3 to 5 minutes, or until the burritos are light golden brown and crisp. Serve with more salsa (if using).

Fish and Vegetable Tacos

Prep time: 15 minutes | Cook time: 9 to 12 minutes | Serves 4

1 pound (454 g) white fish fillets, such as sole or cod 2 teaspoons olive oil 3 tablespoons freshly squeezed lemon juice, divided 1½ cups chopped red	cabbage 1 large carrot, grated ½ cup low-sodium salsa ⅓ cup low-fat Greek yogurt 4 soft low-sodium whole-wheat tortillas

1. Brush the fish with the olive oil and sprinkle with 1 tablespoon of lemon juice. Air fry in the air fryer basket at 390°F (199°C) for 9 to 12 minutes, or until the fish just flakes when tested with a fork. 2. Meanwhile, in a medium bowl, stir together the remaining 2 tablespoons of lemon juice, the red cabbage, carrot, salsa, and yogurt. 3. When the fish is cooked, remove it from the air fryer basket and break it up into large pieces. 4. Offer the fish, tortillas, and the cabbage mixture, and let each person assemble a taco.

Berry Cheesecake

Prep time: 5 minutes | Cook time: 10 minutes | Serves 4

Oil, for spraying	1 large egg
8 ounces (227 g) cream cheese	½ teaspoon vanilla extract
6 tablespoons sugar	¼ teaspoon lemon juice
1 tablespoon sour cream	½ cup fresh mixed berries

1. Preheat the air fryer to 350ºF (177ºC). Line the air fryer basket with parchment and spray lightly with oil. 2. In a blender, combine the cream cheese, sugar, sour cream, egg, vanilla, and lemon juice and blend until smooth. Pour the mixture into a 4-inch springform pan. 3. Place the pan in the prepared basket. 4. Cook for 8 to 10 minutes, or until only the very center jiggles slightly when the pan is moved. 5. Refrigerate the cheesecake in the pan for at least 2 hours. 6. Release the sides from the springform pan, top the cheesecake with the mixed berries, and serve.

Puffed Egg Tarts

Prep time: 10 minutes | Cook time: 42 minutes | Makes 4 tarts

Oil, for spraying	4 large eggs
All-purpose flour, for dusting	2 teaspoons chopped fresh parsley
1 (12-ounce / 340-g) sheet frozen puff pastry, thawed	Salt and freshly ground black pepper, to taste
¾ cup shredded Cheddar cheese, divided	

1. Preheat the air fryer to 390ºF (199ºC). Line the air fryer basket with parchment and spray lightly with oil. 2. Lightly dust your work surface with flour. Unfold the puff pastry and cut it into 4 equal squares. Place 2 squares in the prepared basket. 3. Cook for 10 minutes. 4. Remove the basket. Press the center of each tart shell with a spoon to make an indentation. 5. Sprinkle 3 tablespoons of cheese into each indentation and crack 1 egg into the center of each tart shell. 6. Cook for another 7 to 11 minutes, or until the eggs are cooked to your desired doneness. 7. Repeat with the remaining puff pastry squares, cheese, and eggs. 8. Sprinkle evenly with the parsley, and season with salt and black pepper. Serve immediately.

Steak Tips and Potatoes

Prep time: 10 minutes | Cook time: 20 minutes | Serves 4

Oil, for spraying	1 teaspoon Worcestershire sauce
8 ounces (227 g) baby gold potatoes, cut in half	1 teaspoon granulated garlic
½ teaspoon salt	½ teaspoon salt
1 pound (454 g) steak, cut into ½-inch pieces	½ teaspoon freshly ground black pepper

1. Line the air fryer basket with parchment and spray lightly with oil. 2. In a microwave-safe bowl, combine the potatoes and salt, then pour in about ½ inch of water. Microwave for 7 minutes, or until the potatoes are nearly tender. Drain. 3. In a large bowl, gently mix together the steak, potatoes, Worcestershire sauce, garlic, salt, and black pepper. Spread the mixture in an even layer in the prepared basket. 4. Air fry at 400ºF (204ºC) for 12 to 17 minutes, stirring after 5 to 6 minutes. The cooking time will depend on the thickness of the meat and preferred doneness.

Pecan Rolls

Prep time: 20 minutes | Cook time: 20 to 24 minutes | Makes 12 rolls

2 cups all-purpose flour, plus more for dusting	¼ cup packed light brown sugar
2 tablespoons granulated sugar, plus ¼ cup, divided	½ cup chopped pecans, toasted
1 teaspoon salt	1 to 2 tablespoons oil
3 tablespoons butter, at room temperature	¼ cup confectioners' sugar (optional)
¾ cup milk, whole or 2%	

1. In a large bowl, whisk the flour, 2 tablespoons granulated sugar, and salt until blended. Stir in the butter and milk briefly until a sticky dough forms. 2. In a small bowl, stir together the brown sugar and remaining ¼ cup of granulated sugar. 3. Place a piece of parchment paper on a work surface and dust it with flour. Roll the dough on the prepared surface to ¼ inch thickness. 4. Spread the sugar mixture over the dough. Sprinkle the pecans on top. Roll up the dough jelly roll-style, pinching the ends to seal. Cut the dough into 12 rolls. 5. Preheat the air fryer to 320ºF (160ºC). 6. Line the air fryer basket with parchment paper and spritz the parchment with oil. Place 6 rolls on the prepared parchment. 7. Bake for 5 minutes. Flip the rolls and bake for 5 to 7 minutes more until lightly browned. Repeat with the remaining rolls. 8. Sprinkle with confectioners' sugar (if using).

Apple Pie Egg Rolls

Prep time: 10 minutes | Cook time: 8 minutes | Makes 6 rolls

Oil, for spraying	½ teaspoon lemon juice
1 (21-ounce / 595-g) can apple pie filling	¼ teaspoon ground nutmeg
1 tablespoon all-purpose flour	¼ teaspoon ground cinnamon
	6 egg roll wrappers

1. Preheat the air fryer to 400ºF (204ºC). Line the air fryer basket with parchment and spray lightly with oil. 2. In a medium bowl, mix together the pie filling, flour, lemon juice, nutmeg, and cinnamon. 3. Lay out the egg roll wrappers on a work surface and spoon a dollop of pie filling in the center of each. 4. Fill a small bowl with water. Dip your finger in the water and, working one at a time, moisten the edges of the wrappers. Fold the wrapper like an envelope: First fold one corner into the center. Fold each side corner in, and then fold over the remaining corner, making sure each corner overlaps a bit and the moistened edges stay closed. Use additional water and your fingers to seal any open edges. 5. Place the rolls in the prepared basket and spray liberally with oil. You may need to work in batches, depending on the size of your air fryer. 6. Cook for 4 minutes, flip, spray with oil, and cook for another 4 minutes, or until crispy and golden brown. Serve immediately.

Old Bay Tilapia

Prep time: 15 minutes | Cook time: 6 minutes | Serves 4

Oil, for spraying	½ teaspoon salt
1 cup panko bread crumbs	¼ teaspoon freshly ground
2 tablespoons Old Bay	black pepper
seasoning	1 large egg
2 teaspoons granulated garlic	4 tilapia fillets
1 teaspoon onion powder	

1. Preheat the air fryer to 400°F (204°C). Line the air fryer basket with parchment and spray lightly with oil. 2. In a shallow bowl, mix together the bread crumbs, Old Bay, garlic, onion powder, salt, and black pepper. 3. In a small bowl, whisk the egg. 4. Coat the tilapia in the egg, then dredge in the bread crumb mixture until completely coated. 5. Place the tilapia in the prepared basket. You may need to work in batches, depending on the size of your air fryer. Spray lightly with oil. 6. Cook for 4 to 6 minutes, depending on the thickness of the fillets, until the internal temperature reaches 145°F (63°C). Serve immediately.

Fried Green Tomatoes

Prep time: 15 minutes | Cook time: 6 to 8 minutes | Serves 4

4 medium green tomatoes	½ cup panko bread crumbs
⅓ cup all-purpose flour	2 teaspoons olive oil
2 egg whites	1 teaspoon paprika
¼ cup almond milk	1 clove garlic, minced
1 cup ground almonds	

1. Rinse the tomatoes and pat dry. Cut the tomatoes into ½-inch slices, discarding the thinner ends. 2. Put the flour on a plate. In a shallow bowl, beat the egg whites with the almond milk until frothy. And on another plate, combine the almonds, bread crumbs, olive oil, paprika, and garlic and mix well. 3. Dip the tomato slices into the flour, then into the egg white mixture, then into the almond mixture to coat. 4. Place four of the coated tomato slices in the air fryer basket. Air fry at 400°F (204°C) for 6 to 8 minutes or until the tomato coating is crisp and golden brown. Repeat with remaining tomato slices and serve immediately.

Beef Jerky

Prep time: 30 minutes | Cook time: 2 hours | Serves 8

Oil, for spraying	brown sugar
1 pound (454 g) round steak,	1 tablespoon minced garlic
cut into thin, short slices	1 teaspoon ground ginger
¼ cup soy sauce	1 tablespoon water
3 tablespoons packed light	

1. Line the air fryer basket with parchment and spray lightly with oil. 2. Place the steak, soy sauce, brown sugar, garlic, ginger, and water in a zip-top plastic bag, seal, and shake well until evenly coated. Refrigerate for 30 minutes. 3. Place the steak in the prepared basket in a single layer. You may need to work in batches, depending on the size of your air fryer. 4. Air fry at 180°F (82°C) for at least 2 hours. Add more time if you like your jerky a bit tougher.

Coconut Chicken Tenders

Prep time: 10 minutes | Cook time: 12 minutes | Serves 4

Oil, for spraying	¾ cup panko bread crumbs
2 large eggs	1 teaspoon salt
¼ cup milk	½ teaspoon freshly ground
1 tablespoon hot sauce	black pepper
1½ cups sweetened flaked	1 pound (454 g) chicken
coconut	tenders

1. Line the air fryer basket with parchment and spray lightly with oil. 2. In a small bowl, whisk together the eggs, milk, and hot sauce. 3. In a shallow dish, mix together the coconut, bread crumbs, salt, and black pepper. 4. Coat the chicken in the egg mix, then dredge in the coconut mixture until evenly coated. 5. Place the chicken in the prepared basket and spray liberally with oil. 6. Air fry at 400°F (204°C) for 6 minutes, flip, spray with more oil, and cook for another 6 minutes, or until the internal temperature reaches 165°F (74°C).

Chinese-Inspired Spareribs

Prep time: 30 minutes | Cook time: 8 minutes | Serves 4

Oil, for spraying	½ cup beef or chicken stock
12 ounces (340 g) boneless	¼ cup honey
pork spareribs, cut into	2 tablespoons minced garlic
3-inch-long pieces	1 teaspoon ground ginger
1 cup soy sauce	2 drops red food coloring
¾ cup sugar	(optional)

1. Line the air fryer basket with parchment and spray lightly with oil. 2. Combine the ribs, soy sauce, sugar, beef stock, honey, garlic, ginger, and food coloring (if using) in a large zip-top plastic bag, seal, and shake well until completely coated. Refrigerate for at least 30 minutes. 3. Place the ribs in the prepared basket. 4. Air fry at 375°F (191°C) for 8 minutes, or until the internal temperature reaches 165°F (74°C).

Bacon-Wrapped Hot Dogs

Prep time: 5 minutes | Cook time: 10 minutes | Serves 4

Oil, for spraying	4 hot dog buns
4 bacon slices	Toppings of choice
4 all-beef hot dogs	

1. Line the air fryer basket with parchment and spray lightly with oil. 2. Wrap a strip of bacon tightly around each hot dog, taking care to cover the tips so they don't get too crispy. Secure with a toothpick at each end to keep the bacon from shrinking. 3. Place the hot dogs in the prepared basket. 4. Air fry at 380°F (193°C) for 8 to 9 minutes, depending on how crispy you like the bacon. For extra-crispy, cook the hot dogs at 400°F (204°C) for 6 to 8 minutes. 5. Place the hot dogs in the buns, return them to the air fryer, and cook for another 1 to 2 minutes, or until the buns are warm. Add your desired toppings and serve.

Meatball Subs

Prep time: 15 minutes | Cook time: 19 minutes | Serves 6

Oil, for spraying	1 teaspoon salt
1 pound (454 g) 85% lean ground beef	1 teaspoon freshly ground black pepper
½ cup Italian bread crumbs	6 hoagie rolls
1 tablespoon dried minced onion	1 (18-ounce / 510-g) jar marinara sauce
1 tablespoon minced garlic	1½ cups shredded Mozzarella cheese
1 large egg	

1. Line the air fryer basket with parchment and spray lightly with oil. 2. In a large bowl, mix together the ground beef, bread crumbs, onion, garlic, egg, salt, and black pepper. Roll the mixture into 18 meatballs. 3. Place the meatballs in the prepared basket. 4. Air fry at 390°F (199°C) for 15 minutes. 5. Place 3 meatballs in each hoagie roll. Top with marinara and Mozzarella cheese. 6. Place the loaded rolls in the air fryer and cook for 3 to 4 minutes, or until the cheese is melted. You may need to work in batches, depending on the size of your air fryer. Serve immediately.

Buffalo Cauliflower

Prep time: 15 minutes | Cook time: 5 minutes | Serves 6

1 large head cauliflower, separated into small florets	⅔ cup nonfat Greek yogurt
1 tablespoon olive oil	½ teaspoons Tabasco sauce
½ teaspoon garlic powder	1 celery stalk, chopped
⅓ cup low-sodium hot wing sauce	1 tablespoon crumbled blue cheese

1. In a large bowl, toss the cauliflower florets with the olive oil. Sprinkle with the garlic powder and toss again to coat. Put half of the cauliflower in the air fryer basket. Air fry at 380°F (193°C) for 5 to 7 minutes, until the cauliflower is browned, shaking the basket once during cooking. 2. Transfer to a serving bowl and toss with half of the wing sauce. Repeat with the remaining cauliflower and wing sauce. 3. In a small bowl, stir together the yogurt, Tabasco sauce, celery, and blue cheese. Serve with the cauliflower for dipping.

Pork Stuffing Meatballs

Prep time: 10 minutes | Cook time: 12 minutes | Makes 35 meatballs

Oil, for spraying	1 tablespoon dried rosemary
1½ pounds (680 g) ground pork	1 tablespoon dried thyme
1 cup bread crumbs	1 teaspoon salt
½ cup milk	1 teaspoon freshly ground black pepper
¼ cup minced onion	1 teaspoon finely chopped fresh parsley
1 large egg	

1. Line the air fryer basket with parchment and spray lightly with oil. 2. In a large bowl, mix together the ground pork, bread crumbs, milk, onion, egg, rosemary, thyme, salt, black pepper, and parsley. 3. Roll about 2 tablespoons of the mixture into a ball. Repeat with the rest of the mixture. You should have 30 to 35 meatballs. 4. Place the meatballs in the prepared basket in a single layer, leaving space between each one. You may need to work in batches, depending on the size of your air fryer. 5. Air fry at 390°F (199°C) for 10 to 12 minutes, flipping after 5 minutes, or until golden brown and the internal temperature reaches 160°F (71°C).

Cajun Shrimp

Prep time: 15 minutes | Cook time: 9 minutes | Serves 4

Oil, for spraying	¼-inch-thick slices
1 pound (454 g) jumbo raw shrimp, peeled and deveined	½ medium yellow squash, cut into ¼-inch-thick slices
1 tablespoon Cajun seasoning	1 green bell pepper, seeded and cut into 1-inch pieces
6 ounces (170 g) cooked kielbasa, cut into thick slices	2 tablespoons olive oil
½ medium zucchini, cut into	½ teaspoon salt

1. Preheat the air fryer to 400°F (204°C). Line the air fryer basket with parchment and spray lightly with oil. 2. In a large bowl, toss together the shrimp and Cajun seasoning. Add the kielbasa, zucchini, squash, bell pepper, olive oil, and salt and mix well. 3. Transfer the mixture to the prepared basket, taking care not to overcrowd. You may need to work in batches, depending on the size of your air fryer. 4. Cook for 9 minutes, shaking and stirring every 3 minutes. Serve immediately.

Phyllo Vegetable Triangles

Prep time: 15 minutes | Cook time: 6 to 11 minutes | Serves 6

3 tablespoons minced onion	2 tablespoons nonfat cream cheese, at room temperature
2 garlic cloves, minced	6 sheets frozen phyllo dough, thawed
2 tablespoons grated carrot	
1 teaspoon olive oil	Olive oil spray, for coating the dough
3 tablespoons frozen baby peas, thawed	

1. In a baking pan, combine the onion, garlic, carrot, and olive oil. Air fry at 390°F (199°C) for 2 to 4 minutes, or until the vegetables are crisp-tender. Transfer to a bowl. 2. Stir in the peas and cream cheese to the vegetable mixture. Let cool while you prepare the dough. 3. Lay one sheet of phyllo on a work surface and lightly spray with olive oil spray. Top with another sheet of phyllo. Repeat with the remaining 4 phyllo sheets; you'll have 3 stacks with 2 layers each. Cut each stack lengthwise into 4 strips (12 strips total). 4. Place a scant 2 teaspoons of the filling near the bottom of each strip. Bring one corner up over the filling to make a triangle; continue folding the triangles over, as you would fold a flag. Seal the edge with a bit of water. Repeat with the remaining strips and filling. 5. Air fry the triangles, in 2 batches, for 4 to 7 minutes, or until golden brown. Serve.

Chapter 3

Fast and Easy Everyday Favorites

Simple Baked Green Beans

Prep time: 5 minutes | Cook time: 10 minutes | Makes 2 cups

½ teaspoon lemon pepper	1 tablespoon olive oil
2 teaspoons granulated garlic	2 cups fresh green beans, trimmed and snapped in half
½ teaspoon salt	

1. Preheat the air fryer to 370ºF (188ºC). 2. Combine the lemon pepper, garlic, salt, and olive oil in a bowl. Stir to mix well. 3. Add the green beans to the bowl of mixture and toss to coat well. 4. Arrange the green beans in the preheated air fryer. Bake for 10 minutes or until tender and crispy. Shake the basket halfway through to make sure the green beans are cooked evenly. 5. Serve immediately.

Garlicky Zoodles

Prep time: 10 minutes | Cook time: 10 minutes | Serves 4

2 large zucchini, peeled and spiralized	½ teaspoon kosher salt
2 large yellow summer squash, peeled and spiralized	1 garlic clove, whole
1 tablespoon olive oil, divided	2 tablespoons fresh basil, chopped
	Cooking spray

1. Preheat the air fryer to 360ºF (182ºC). Spritz the air fryer basket with cooking spray. 2. Combine the zucchini and summer squash with 1 teaspoon olive oil and salt in a large bowl. Toss to coat well. 3. Transfer the zucchini and summer squash in the preheated air fryer and add the garlic. 4. Air fry for 10 minutes or until tender and fragrant. Toss the spiralized zucchini and summer squash halfway through the cooking time. 5. Transfer the cooked zucchini and summer squash onto a plate and set aside. 6. Remove the garlic from the air fryer and allow to cool for a few minutes. Mince the garlic and combine with remaining olive oil in a small bowl. Stir to mix well. 7. Drizzle the spiralized zucchini and summer squash with garlic oil and sprinkle with basil. Toss to serve.

Traditional Queso Fundido

Prep time: 10 minutes | Cook time: 25 minutes | Serves 4

4 ounces (113 g) fresh Mexican chorizo, casings removed	diced
	2 teaspoons ground cumin
1 medium onion, chopped	2 cups shredded Oaxaca or Mozzarella cheese
3 cloves garlic, minced	½ cup half-and-half
1 cup chopped tomato	Celery sticks or tortilla chips, for serving
2 jalapeños, deseeded and	

1. Preheat the air fryer to 400ºF (204ºC). 2. In a baking pan, combine the chorizo, onion, garlic, tomato, jalapeños, and cumin. Stir to combine. 3. Place the pan in the air fryer basket. Air fry for 15 minutes, or until the sausage is cooked, stirring halfway through the cooking time to break up the sausage. 4. Add the cheese and half-and-half; stir to combine. Air fry for 10 minutes, or until the cheese has melted. 5. Serve with celery sticks or tortilla chips.

Baked Halloumi with Greek Salsa

Prep time: 15 minutes | Cook time: 6 minutes | Serves 4

Salsa:	finely diced
1 small shallot, finely diced	2 teaspoons chopped fresh parsley
3 garlic cloves, minced	1 teaspoon snipped fresh dill
2 tablespoons fresh lemon juice	1 teaspoon snipped fresh oregano
2 tablespoons extra-virgin olive oil	Cheese:
1 teaspoon freshly cracked black pepper	8 ounces (227 g) Halloumi cheese, sliced into ½-inch-thick pieces
Pinch of kosher salt	1 tablespoon extra-virgin olive oil
½ cup finely diced English cucumber	
1 plum tomato, deseeded and	

1. Preheat the air fryer to 375ºF (191ºC). 2. For the salsa: Combine the shallot, garlic, lemon juice, olive oil, pepper, and salt in a medium bowl. Add the cucumber, tomato, parsley, dill, and oregano. Toss gently to combine; set aside. 3. For the cheese: Place the cheese slices in a medium bowl. Drizzle with the olive oil. Toss gently to coat. Arrange the cheese in a single layer in the air fryer basket. Bake for 6 minutes. 4. Divide the cheese among four serving plates. Top with the salsa and serve immediately.

Simple and Easy Croutons

Prep time: 5 minutes | Cook time: 8 minutes | Serves 4

2 slices friendly bread	Hot soup, for serving
1 tablespoon olive oil	

1. Preheat the air fryer to 390ºF (199ºC). 2. Cut the slices of bread into medium-size chunks. 3. Brush the air fryer basket with the oil. 4. Place the chunks inside and air fry for at least 8 minutes. 5. Serve with hot soup.

Beet Salad with Lemon Vinaigrette

Prep time: 10 minutes | Cook time: 12 to 15 minutes | Serves 4

6 medium red and golden beets, peeled and sliced	Cooking spray
	Vinaigrette:
1 teaspoon olive oil	2 teaspoons olive oil
¼ teaspoon kosher salt	2 tablespoons chopped fresh chives
½ cup crumbled feta cheese	Juice of 1 lemon
8 cups mixed greens	

1. Preheat the air fryer to 360ºF (182ºC). 2. In a large bowl, toss the beets, olive oil, and kosher salt. 3. Spray the air fryer basket with cooking spray, then place the beets in the basket and air fry for 12 to 15 minutes or until tender. 4. While the beets cook, make the vinaigrette in a large bowl by whisking together the olive oil, lemon juice, and chives. 5. Remove the beets from the air fryer, toss in the vinaigrette, and allow to cool for 5 minutes. Add the feta and serve on top of the mixed greens.

Corn Fritters

Prep time: 15 minutes | Cook time: 8 minutes | Serves 6

1 cup self-rising flour	¼ cup buttermilk
1 tablespoon sugar	¾ cup corn kernels
1 teaspoon salt	¼ cup minced onion
1 large egg, lightly beaten	Cooking spray

1. Preheat the air fryer to 350°F (177°C). Line the air fryer basket with parchment paper. 2. In a medium bowl, whisk the flour, sugar, and salt until blended. Stir in the egg and buttermilk. Add the corn and minced onion. Mix well. Shape the corn fritter batter into 12 balls. 3. Place the fritters on the parchment and spritz with oil. Bake for 4 minutes. Flip the fritters, spritz them with oil, and bake for 4 minutes more until firm and lightly browned. 4. Serve immediately.

Buttery Sweet Potatoes

Prep time: 5 minutes | Cook time: 10 minutes | Serves 4

2 tablespoons butter, melted	2 sweet potatoes, peeled and
1 tablespoon light brown sugar	cut into ½-inch cubes
	Cooking spray

1. Preheat the air fryer to 400°F (204°C). Line the air fryer basket with parchment paper. 2. In a medium bowl, stir together the melted butter and brown sugar until blended. Toss the sweet potatoes in the butter mixture until coated. 3. Place the sweet potatoes on the parchment and spritz with oil. 4. Air fry for 5 minutes. Shake the basket, spritz the sweet potatoes with oil, and air fry for 5 minutes more until they're soft enough to cut with a fork. 5. Serve immediately.

South Carolina Shrimp and Corn Bake

Prep time: 10 minutes | Cook time: 18 minutes | Serves 2

1 ear corn, husk and silk removed, cut into 2-inch rounds	pepper
	8 ounces (227 g) large shrimps (about 12 shrimps), deveined
8 ounces (227 g) red potatoes, unpeeled, cut into 1-inch pieces	6 ounces (170 g) andouille or chorizo sausage, cut into 1-inch pieces
2 teaspoons Old Bay Seasoning, divided	2 garlic cloves, minced
2 teaspoons vegetable oil, divided	1 tablespoon chopped fresh parsley
¼ teaspoon ground black	

1. Preheat the air fryer to 400°F (204°C). 2. Put the corn rounds and potatoes in a large bowl. Sprinkle with 1 teaspoon of Old Bay seasoning and drizzle with vegetable oil. Toss to coat well. 3. Transfer the corn rounds and potatoes on a baking sheet, then put in the preheated air fryer. 4. Bake for 12 minutes or until soft and browned. Shake the basket halfway through the cooking time. 5. Meanwhile, cut slits into the shrimps but be careful not to cut them through. Combine the shrimps, sausage, remaining Old Bay seasoning, and remaining vegetable oil in the large bowl. Toss to coat well. 6. When the baking of the potatoes and corn rounds is complete, add the shrimps and sausage and bake for 6 more minutes or until the shrimps are opaque. Shake the basket halfway through the cooking time. 7. When the baking is finished, serve them on a plate and spread with parsley before serving.

Cheesy Chile Toast

Prep time: 5 minutes | Cook time: 5 minutes | Serves 1

2 tablespoons grated Parmesan cheese	room temperature
	10 to 15 thin slices serrano
2 tablespoons grated Mozzarella cheese	chile or jalapeño
	2 slices sourdough bread
2 teaspoons salted butter, at	½ teaspoon black pepper

1. Preheat the air fryer to 325°F (163°C). 2. In a small bowl, stir together the Parmesan, Mozzarella, butter, and chiles. 3. Spread half the mixture onto one side of each slice of bread. Sprinkle with the pepper. Place the slices, cheese-side up, in the air fryer basket. Bake for 5 minutes, or until the cheese has melted and started to brown slightly. 4. Serve immediately.

Simple Air Fried Crispy Brussels Sprouts

Prep time: 5 minutes | Cook time: 20 minutes | Serves 4

¼ teaspoon salt	olive oil
⅛ teaspoon ground black pepper	1 pound (454 g) Brussels sprouts, trimmed and halved
1 tablespoon extra-virgin	Lemon wedges, for garnish

1. Preheat the air fryer to 350°F (177°C). 2. Combine the salt, black pepper, and olive oil in a large bowl. Stir to mix well. 3. Add the Brussels sprouts to the bowl of mixture and toss to coat well. 4. Arrange the Brussels sprouts in the preheated air fryer. Air fry for 20 minutes or until lightly browned and wilted. Shake the basket two times during the air frying. 5. Transfer the cooked Brussels sprouts to a large plate and squeeze the lemon wedges on top to serve.

Rosemary and Orange Roasted Chickpeas

Prep time: 5 minutes | Cook time: 10 to 12 minutes | Makes 4 cups

4 cups cooked chickpeas	1 teaspoon paprika
2 tablespoons vegetable oil	Zest of 1 orange
1 teaspoon kosher salt	1 tablespoon chopped fresh
1 teaspoon cumin	rosemary

1. Preheat the air fryer to 400°F (204°C). 2. Make sure the chickpeas are completely dry prior to roasting. In a medium bowl, toss the chickpeas with oil, salt, cumin, and paprika. 3. Working in batches, spread the chickpeas in a single layer in the air fryer basket. Air fry for 10 to 12 minutes until crisp, shaking once halfway through. 4. Return the warm chickpeas to the bowl and toss with the orange zest and rosemary. Allow to cool completely. 5. Serve.

Crispy Green Tomatoes Slices

Prep time: 10 minutes | Cook time: 8 minutes | Makes 12 slices

½ cup all-purpose flour	¼-inch-thick slices, patted
1 egg	dry
½ cup buttermilk	½ teaspoon salt
1 cup cornmeal	½ teaspoon ground black
1 cup panko	pepper
2 green tomatoes, cut into	Cooking spray

1. Preheat the air fryer to 400ºF (204ºC). Line the air fryer basket with parchment paper. 2. Pour the flour in a bowl. Whisk the egg and buttermilk in a second bowl. Combine the cornmeal and panko in a third bowl. 3. Dredge the tomato slices in the bowl of flour first, then into the egg mixture, and then dunk the slices into the cornmeal mixture. Shake the excess off. 4. Transfer the well-coated tomato slices in the preheated air fryer and sprinkle with salt and ground black pepper. 5. Spritz the tomato slices with cooking spray. Air fry for 8 minutes or until crispy and lightly browned. Flip the slices halfway through the cooking time. 6. Serve immediately.

Honey Bartlett Pears with Lemony Ricotta

Prep time: 10 minutes | Cook time: 8 minutes | Serves 4

2 large Bartlett pears, peeled, cut in half, cored	cheese
3 tablespoons melted butter	1 teaspoon pure lemon extract
½ teaspoon ground ginger	1 teaspoon pure almond
¼ teaspoon ground cardamom	extract
3 tablespoons brown sugar	1 tablespoon honey, plus additional for drizzling
½ cup whole-milk ricotta	

1. Preheat the air fryer to 375ºF (191ºC). 2. Toss the pears with butter, ginger, cardamom, and sugar in a large bowl. Toss to coat well. 3. Arrange the pears in the preheated air fryer, cut side down. Air fry for 5 minutes, then flip the pears and air fry for 3 more minutes or until the pears are soft and browned. 4. In the meantime, combine the remaining ingredients in a separate bowl. Whip for 1 minute with a hand mixer until the mixture is puffed. 5. Divide the mixture into four bowls, then put the pears over the mixture and drizzle with more honey to serve.

Easy Air Fried Edamame

Prep time: 5 minutes | Cook time: 7 minutes | Serves 6

1½ pounds (680 g) unshelled edamame	2 tablespoons olive oil
	1 teaspoon sea salt

1. Preheat the air fryer to 400ºF (204ºC). 2. Place the edamame in a large bowl, then drizzle with olive oil. Toss to coat well. 3. Transfer the edamame to the preheated air fryer. Cook for 7 minutes or until tender and warmed through. Shake the basket at least three times during the cooking. 4. Transfer the cooked edamame onto a plate and sprinkle with salt. Toss to combine well and set aside for 3 minutes to infuse before serving.

Bacon Pinwheels

Prep time: 10 minutes | Cook time: 10 minutes | Makes 8 pinwheels

1 sheet puff pastry	8 slices bacon
2 tablespoons maple syrup	Ground black pepper, to taste
¼ cup brown sugar	Cooking spray

1. Preheat the air fryer to 360ºF (182ºC). Spritz the air fryer basket with cooking spray. 2. Roll the puff pastry into a 10-inch square with a rolling pin on a clean work surface, then cut the pastry into 8 strips. 3. Brush the strips with maple syrup and sprinkle with sugar, leaving a 1-inch far end uncovered. 4. Arrange each slice of bacon on each strip, leaving a ⅛-inch length of bacon hang over the end close to you. Sprinkle with black pepper. 5. From the end close to you, roll the strips into pinwheels, then dab the uncovered end with water and seal the rolls. 6. Arrange the pinwheels in the preheated air fryer and spritz with cooking spray. 7. Air fry for 10 minutes or until golden brown. Flip the pinwheels halfway through. 8. Serve immediately.

Air Fried Tortilla Chips

Prep time: 5 minutes | Cook time: 10 minutes | Serves 4

4 six-inch corn tortillas, cut in half and slice into thirds	¼ teaspoon kosher salt
1 tablespoon canola oil	Cooking spray

1. Preheat the air fryer to 360ºF (182ºC). Spritz the air fryer basket with cooking spray. 2. On a clean work surface, brush the tortilla chips with canola oil, then transfer the chips in the preheated air fryer. 3. Air fry for 10 minutes or until crunchy and lightly browned. Shake the basket and sprinkle with salt halfway through the cooking time. 4. Transfer the chips onto a plate lined with paper towels. Serve immediately.

Air Fried Butternut Squash with Chopped Hazelnuts

Prep time: 10 minutes | Cook time: 20 minutes | Makes 3 cups

2 tablespoons whole hazelnuts	¼ teaspoon freshly ground black pepper
3 cups butternut squash, peeled, deseeded, and cubed	2 teaspoons olive oil
¼ teaspoon kosher salt	Cooking spray

1. Preheat the air fryer to 300ºF (149ºC). Spritz the air fryer basket with cooking spray. 2. Arrange the hazelnuts in the preheated air fryer. Air fry for 3 minutes or until soft. 3. Chopped the hazelnuts roughly and transfer to a small bowl. Set aside. 4. Set the air fryer temperature to 360ºF (182ºC). Spritz with cooking spray. 5. Put the butternut squash in a large bowl, then sprinkle with salt and pepper and drizzle with olive oil. Toss to coat well. 6. Transfer the squash in the air fryer. Air fry for 20 minutes or until the squash is soft. Shake the basket halfway through the frying time. 7. When the frying is complete, transfer the squash onto a plate and sprinkle with chopped hazelnuts before serving.

Beery and Crunchy Onion Rings

Prep time: 10 minutes | Cook time: 16 minutes | Serves 2 to 4

⅔ cup all-purpose flour	¾ cup beer
1 teaspoon paprika	1½ cups breadcrumbs
½ teaspoon baking soda	1 tablespoons olive oil
1 teaspoon salt	1 large Vidalia onion, peeled
½ teaspoon freshly ground	and sliced into ½-inch rings
black pepper	Cooking spray
1 egg, beaten	

1. Preheat the air fryer to 360°F (182°C). Spritz the air fryer basket with cooking spray. 2. Combine the flour, paprika, baking soda, salt, and ground black pepper in a bowl. Stir to mix well. 3. Combine the egg and beer in a separate bowl. Stir to mix well. 4. Make a well in the center of the flour mixture, then pour the egg mixture in the well. Stir to mix everything well. 5. Pour the breadcrumbs and olive oil in a shallow plate. Stir to mix well. 6. Dredge the onion rings gently into the flour and egg mixture, then shake the excess off and put into the plate of breadcrumbs. Flip to coat the both sides well. 7. Arrange the onion rings in the preheated air fryer. Air fry in batches for 16 minutes or until golden brown and crunchy. Flip the rings and put the bottom rings to the top halfway through. 8. Serve immediately.

Sweet Corn and Carrot Fritters

Prep time: 10 minutes | Cook time: 8 to 11 minutes | Serves 4

1 medium-sized carrot, grated	1 medium-sized egg, whisked
1 yellow onion, finely chopped	2 tablespoons plain milk
4 ounces (113 g) canned sweet corn kernels, drained	1 cup grated Parmesan cheese
1 teaspoon sea salt flakes	¼ cup flour
1 tablespoon chopped fresh cilantro	⅓ teaspoon baking powder
	⅓ teaspoon sugar
	Cooking spray

1. Preheat the air fryer to 350°F (177°C). 2. Place the grated carrot in a colander and press down to squeeze out any excess moisture. Dry it with a paper towel. 3. Combine the carrots with the remaining ingredients. 4. Mold 1 tablespoon of the mixture into a ball and press it down with your hand or a spoon to flatten it. Repeat until the rest of the mixture is used up. 5. Spritz the balls with cooking spray. 6. Arrange in the air fryer basket, taking care not to overlap any balls. Bake for 8 to 11 minutes, or until they're firm. 7. Serve warm.

Beef Bratwursts

Prep time: 5 minutes | Cook time: 15 minutes | Serves 4

4 (3-ounce / 85-g) beef bratwursts

1. Preheat the air fryer to 375°F (191°C). 2. Place the beef bratwursts in the air fryer basket and air fry for 15 minutes, turning once halfway through. 3. Serve hot.

Cheesy Jalapeño Cornbread

Prep time: 10 minutes | Cook time: 20 minutes | Serves 8

⅔ cup cornmeal	¾ cup whole milk
⅓ cup all-purpose flour	1 large egg, beaten
¾ teaspoon baking powder	1 jalapeño pepper, thinly
2 tablespoons buttery spread, melted	sliced
½ teaspoon kosher salt	⅓ cup shredded sharp Cheddar cheese
1 tablespoon granulated sugar	Cooking spray

1. Preheat the air fryer to 300°F (149°C). Spritz the air fryer basket with cooking spray. 2. Combine all the ingredients in a large bowl. Stir to mix well. Pour the mixture in a baking pan. 3. Arrange the pan in the preheated air fryer. Bake for 20 minutes or until a toothpick inserted in the center of the bread comes out clean. 4. When the cooking is complete, remove the baking pan from the air fryer and allow the bread to cool for a few minutes before slicing to serve.

Golden Salmon and Carrot Croquettes

Prep time: 15 minutes | Cook time: 10 minutes | Serves 6

2 egg whites	2 tablespoons minced garlic cloves
1 cup almond flour	
1 cup panko breadcrumbs	½ cup chopped onion
1 pound (454 g) chopped salmon fillet	2 tablespoons chopped chives
⅔ cup grated carrots	Cooking spray

1. Preheat the air fryer to 350°F (177°C). Spritz the air fryer basket with cooking spray. 2. Whisk the egg whites in a bowl. Put the flour in a second bowl. Pour the breadcrumbs in a third bowl. Set aside. 3. Combine the salmon, carrots, garlic, onion, and chives in a large bowl. Stir to mix well. 4. Form the mixture into balls with your hands. Dredge the balls into the flour, then egg, and then breadcrumbs to coat well. 5. Arrange the salmon balls in the preheated air fryer and spritz with cooking spray. 6. Air fry for 10 minutes or until crispy and browned. Shake the basket halfway through. 7. Serve immediately.

Easy Roasted Asparagus

Prep time: 5 minutes | Cook time: 6 minutes | Serves 4

1 pound (454 g) asparagus, trimmed and halved crosswise	oil
	Salt and pepper, to taste
	Lemon wedges, for serving
1 teaspoon extra-virgin olive	

1. Preheat the air fryer to 400°F (204°C). 2. Toss the asparagus with the oil, ⅛ teaspoon salt, and ⅛ teaspoon pepper in bowl. Transfer to air fryer basket. 3. Place the basket in air fryer and roast for 6 to 8 minutes, or until tender and bright green, tossing halfway through cooking. 4. Season with salt and pepper and serve with lemon wedges.

Cheesy Baked Grits

Prep time: 10 minutes | Cook time: 12 minutes | Serves 6

¾ cup hot water 2 (1-ounce / 28-g) packages instant grits 1 large egg, beaten 1 tablespoon butter, melted 2 cloves garlic, minced	½ to 1 teaspoon red pepper flakes 1 cup shredded Cheddar cheese or jalapeño Jack cheese

1. Preheat the air fryer to 400ºF (204ºC). 2. In a baking pan, combine the water, grits, egg, butter, garlic, and red pepper flakes. Stir until well combined. Stir in the shredded cheese. 3. Place the pan in the air fryer basket and air fry for 12 minutes, or until the grits have cooked through and a knife inserted near the center comes out clean. 4. Let stand for 5 minutes before serving.

Spinach and Carrot Balls

Prep time: 10 minutes | Cook time: 10 minutes | Serves 4

2 slices toasted bread 1 carrot, peeled and grated 1 package fresh spinach, blanched and chopped ½ onion, chopped 1 egg, beaten	½ teaspoon garlic powder 1 teaspoon minced garlic 1 teaspoon salt ½ teaspoon black pepper 1 tablespoon nutritional yeast 1 tablespoon flour

1. Preheat the air fryer to 390ºF (199ºC). 2. In a food processor, pulse the toasted bread to form bread crumbs. Transfer into a shallow dish or bowl. 3. In a bowl, mix together all the other ingredients. 4. Use your hands to shape the mixture into small-sized balls. Roll the balls in the bread crumbs, ensuring to cover them well. 5. Put in the air fryer basket and air fry for 10 minutes. 6. Serve immediately.

Southwest Corn and Bell Pepper Roast

Prep time: 10 minutes | Cook time: 10 minutes | Serves 4

For the Corn: 1½ cups thawed frozen corn kernels 1 cup mixed diced bell peppers 1 jalapeño, diced 1 cup diced yellow onion ½ teaspoon ancho chile powder 1 tablespoon fresh lemon	juice 1 teaspoon ground cumin ½ teaspoon kosher salt Cooking spray For Serving: ¼ cup feta cheese ¼ cup chopped fresh cilantro 1 tablespoon fresh lemon juice

1. Preheat the air fryer to 375ºF (191ºC). Spritz the air fryer with cooking spray. 2. Combine the ingredients for the corn in a large bowl. Stir to mix well. 3. Pout the mixture into the air fryer. Air fry for 10 minutes or until the corn and bell peppers are soft. Shake the basket halfway through the cooking time. 4. Transfer them onto a large plate, then spread with feta cheese and cilantro. Drizzle with lemon juice and serve.

Spicy Air Fried Old Bay Shrimp

Prep time: 7 minutes | Cook time: 10 minutes | Makes 2 cups

½ teaspoon Old Bay Seasoning 1 teaspoon ground cayenne pepper ½ teaspoon paprika	1 tablespoon olive oil ⅛ teaspoon salt ½ pound (227 g) shrimps, peeled and deveined Juice of half a lemon

1. Preheat the air fryer to 390ºF (199ºC). 2. Combine the Old Bay Seasoning, cayenne pepper, paprika, olive oil, and salt in a large bowl, then add the shrimps and toss to coat well. 3. Put the shrimps in the preheated air fryer. Air fry for 10 minutes or until opaque. Flip the shrimps halfway through. 4. Serve the shrimps with lemon juice on top.

Baked Chorizo Scotch Eggs

Prep time: 5 minutes | Cook time: 15 to 20 minutes | Makes 4 eggs

1 pound (454 g) Mexican chorizo or other seasoned sausage meat 4 soft-boiled eggs plus 1 raw egg	1 tablespoon water ½ cup all-purpose flour 1 cup panko bread crumbs Cooking spray

1. Divide the chorizo into 4 equal portions. Flatten each portion into a disc. Place a soft-boiled egg in the center of each disc. Wrap the chorizo around the egg, encasing it completely. Place the encased eggs on a plate and chill for at least 30 minutes. 2. Preheat the air fryer to 360ºF (182ºC). 3. Beat the raw egg with 1 tablespoon of water. Place the flour on a small plate and the panko on a second plate. Working with 1 egg at a time, roll the encased egg in the flour, then dip it in the egg mixture. Dredge the egg in the panko and place on a plate. Repeat with the remaining eggs. 4. Spray the eggs with oil and place in the air fryer basket. Bake for 10 minutes. Turn and bake for an additional 5 to 10 minutes, or until browned and crisp on all sides. 5. Serve immediately.

Purple Potato Chips with Rosemary

Prep time: 10 minutes | Cook time: 9 to 14 minutes | Serves 6

1 cup Greek yogurt 2 chipotle chiles, minced 2 tablespoons adobo sauce 1 teaspoon paprika 1 tablespoon lemon juice 10 purple fingerling potatoes	1 teaspoon olive oil 2 teaspoons minced fresh rosemary leaves ⅛ teaspoon cayenne pepper ¼ teaspoon coarse sea salt

1. Preheat the air fryer to 400ºF (204ºC). 2. In a medium bowl, combine the yogurt, minced chiles, adobo sauce, paprika, and lemon juice. Mix well and refrigerate. 3. Wash the potatoes and dry them with paper towels. Slice the potatoes lengthwise, as thinly as possible. You can use a mandoline, a vegetable peeler, or a very sharp knife. 4. Combine the potato slices in a medium bowl and drizzle with the olive oil; toss to coat. 5. Air fry the chips, in batches, in the air fryer basket, for 9 to 14 minutes. Use tongs to

gently rearrange the chips halfway during cooking time. 6. Sprinkle the chips with the rosemary, cayenne pepper, and sea salt. Serve with the chipotle sauce for dipping.

Chapter 4

Beef, Pork, and Lamb

Savory Sausage Cobbler

Prep time: 15 minutes | Cook time: 34 minutes | Serves 4

Filling: 1 pound (454 g) ground Italian sausage 1 cup sliced mushrooms 1 teaspoon fine sea salt 2 cups marinara sauce Biscuits: 3 large egg whites	¾ cup blanched almond flour 1 teaspoon baking powder ¼ teaspoon fine sea salt 2½ tablespoons very cold unsalted butter, cut into ¼-inch pieces Fresh basil leaves, for garnish

1. Preheat the air fryer to 400°F (204°C). 2. Place the sausage in a pie pan (or a pan that fits into your air fryer). Use your hands to break up the sausage and spread it evenly on the bottom of the pan. Place the pan in the air fryer and air fry for 5 minutes. 3. Remove the pan from the air fryer and use a fork or metal spatula to crumble the sausage more. Season the mushrooms with the salt and add them to the pie pan. Stir to combine the mushrooms and sausage, then return the pan to the air fryer and air fry for 4 minutes, or until the mushrooms are soft and the sausage is cooked through. 4. Remove the pan from the air fryer. Add the marinara sauce and stir well. Set aside. 5. Make the biscuits: Place the egg whites in a large mixing bowl or the bowl of a stand mixer. Using a hand mixer or stand mixer, whip the egg whites until stiff peaks form. 6. In a medium-sized bowl, whisk together the almond flour, baking powder, and salt, then cut in the butter. Gently fold the flour mixture into the egg whites with a rubber spatula. 7. Using a large spoon or ice cream scoop, spoon one-quarter of the dough on top of the sausage mixture, making sure the butter stays in separate clumps. Repeat with the remaining dough, spacing the biscuits about 1 inch apart. 8. Place the pan in the air fryer and cook for 5 minutes, then lower the heat to 325°F (163°C) and bake for another 15 to 20 minutes, until the biscuits are golden brown. Serve garnished with fresh basil leaves. 9. Store leftovers in an airtight container in the refrigerator for up to 3 days. Reheat in a preheated 350°F (177°C) air fryer for 5 minutes, or until warmed through.

Herbed Lamb Steaks

Prep time: 30 minutes | Cook time: 15 minutes | Serves 4

½ medium onion 2 tablespoons minced garlic 2 teaspoons ground ginger 1 teaspoon ground cinnamon 1 teaspoon onion powder	1 teaspoon cayenne pepper 1 teaspoon salt 4 (6-ounce / 170-g) boneless lamb sirloin steaks Oil, for spraying

1. In a blender, combine the onion, garlic, ginger, cinnamon, onion powder, cayenne pepper, and salt and pulse until the onion is minced. 2. Place the lamb steaks in a large bowl or zip-top plastic bag and sprinkle the onion mixture over the top. Turn the steaks until they are evenly coated. Cover with plastic wrap or seal the bag and refrigerate for 30 minutes. 3. Preheat the air fryer to 330°F (166°C). Line the air fryer basket with parchment and spray lightly with oil. 4. Place the lamb steaks in a single layer in the prepared basket, making sure they don't overlap. You may need to work in batches, depending on the size of your air fryer. 5. Cook for 8

minutes, flip, and cook for another 7 minutes, or until the internal temperature reaches 155°F (68°C).

Rack of Lamb with Pistachio Crust

Prep time: 10 minutes | Cook time: 19 minutes | Serves 2

½ cup finely chopped pistachios 3 tablespoons panko bread crumbs 1 teaspoon chopped fresh rosemary 2 teaspoons chopped fresh	oregano Salt and freshly ground black pepper, to taste 1 tablespoon olive oil 1 rack of lamb, bones trimmed of fat and frenched 1 tablespoon Dijon mustard

1. Preheat the air fryer to 380°F (193°C). 2. Combine the pistachios, bread crumbs, rosemary, oregano, salt and pepper in a small bowl. (This is a good job for your food processor if you have one.) Drizzle in the olive oil and stir to combine. 3. Season the rack of lamb with salt and pepper on all sides and transfer it to the air fryer basket with the fat side facing up. Air fry the lamb for 12 minutes. Remove the lamb from the air fryer and brush the fat side of the lamb rack with the Dijon mustard. Coat the rack with the pistachio mixture, pressing the bread crumbs onto the lamb with your hands and rolling the bottom of the rack in any of the crumbs that fall off. 4. Return the rack of lamb to the air fryer and air fry for another 3 to 7 minutes or until an instant read thermometer reads 140°F (60°C) for medium. Add or subtract a couple of minutes for lamb that is more or less well cooked. (Your time will vary depending on how big the rack of lamb is.) 5. Let the lamb rest for at least 5 minutes. Then, slice into chops and serve.

Greek Lamb Pita Pockets

Prep time: 15 minutes | Cook time: 6 minutes | Serves 4

Dressing: 1 cup plain yogurt 1 tablespoon lemon juice 1 teaspoon dried dill weed, crushed 1 teaspoon ground oregano ½ teaspoon salt Meatballs: ½ pound (227 g) ground lamb 1 tablespoon diced onion 1 teaspoon dried parsley 1 teaspoon dried dill weed,	crushed ¼ teaspoon oregano ¼ teaspoon coriander ¼ teaspoon ground cumin ¼ teaspoon salt 4 pita halves Suggested Toppings: 1 red onion, slivered 1 medium cucumber, deseeded, thinly sliced Crumbled feta cheese Sliced black olives Chopped fresh peppers

1. Preheat the air fryer to 390°F (199°C). 2. Stir the dressing ingredients together in a small bowl and refrigerate while preparing lamb. 3. Combine all meatball ingredients in a large bowl and stir to distribute seasonings. 4. Shape meat mixture into 12 small meatballs, rounded or slightly flattened if you prefer. 5. Transfer the meatballs in the preheated air fryer and air fry for 6 minutes, until well done. Remove and drain on paper towels. 6. To serve, pile meatballs and the choice of toppings in pita pockets and drizzle with dressing.

Beef Flank Steak with Sage

Prep time: 13 minutes | Cook time: 7 minutes | Serves 2

⅓ cup sour cream
½ cup green onion, chopped
1 tablespoon mayonnaise
3 cloves garlic, smashed
1 pound (454 g) beef flank steak, trimmed and cubed

2 tablespoons fresh sage, minced
½ teaspoon salt
⅓ teaspoon black pepper, or to taste

1. Season your meat with salt and pepper; arrange beef cubes on the bottom of a baking dish that fits in your air fryer. 2. Stir in green onions and garlic; air fry for about 7 minutes at 385ºF (196ºC). 3. Once your beef starts to tender, add the cream, mayonnaise, and sage; air fry an additional 8 minutes. Bon appétit!

Parmesan-Crusted Steak

Prep time: 30 minutes | Cook time: 12 minutes | Serves 6

½ cup (1 stick) unsalted butter, at room temperature
1 cup finely grated Parmesan cheese
¼ cup finely ground

blanched almond flour
1½ pounds (680 g) New York strip steak
Sea salt and freshly ground black pepper, to taste

1. Place the butter, Parmesan cheese, and almond flour in a food processor. Process until smooth. Transfer to a sheet of parchment paper and form into a log. Wrap tightly in plastic wrap. Freeze for 45 minutes or refrigerate for at least 4 hours. 2. While the butter is chilling, season the steak liberally with salt and pepper. Let the steak rest at room temperature for about 45 minutes. 3. Place the grill pan or basket in your air fryer, set it to 400ºF (204ºC), and let it preheat for 5 minutes. 4. Working in batches, if necessary, place the steak on the grill pan and air fry for 4 minutes. Flip and cook for 3 minutes more, until the steak is brown on both sides. 5. Remove the steak from the air fryer and arrange an equal amount of the Parmesan butter on top of each steak. Return the steak to the air fryer and continue cooking for another 5 minutes, until an instant-read thermometer reads 120ºF (49ºC) for medium-rare and the crust is golden brown (or to your desired doneness). 6. Transfer the cooked steak to a plate; let rest for 10 minutes before serving.

Greek Stuffed Tenderloin

Prep time: 10 minutes | Cook time: 10 minutes | Serves 4

1½ pounds (680 g) venison or beef tenderloin, pounded to ¼ inch thick
3 teaspoons fine sea salt
1 teaspoon ground black pepper
2 ounces (57 g) creamy goat cheese
½ cup crumbled feta cheese (about 2 ounces / 57 g)

¼ cup finely chopped onions
2 cloves garlic, minced
For Garnish/Serving (Optional):
Prepared yellow mustard
Halved cherry tomatoes
Extra-virgin olive oil
Sprigs of fresh rosemary
Lavender flowers

1. Spray the air fryer basket with avocado oil. Preheat the air fryer to 400ºF (204ºC). 2. Season the tenderloin on all sides with the salt and pepper. 3. In a medium-sized mixing bowl, combine the goat cheese, feta, onions, and garlic. Place the mixture in the center of the tenderloin. Starting at the end closest to you, tightly roll the tenderloin like a jelly roll. Tie the rolled tenderloin tightly with kitchen twine. 4. Place the meat in the air fryer basket and air fry for 5 minutes. Flip the meat over and cook for another 5 minutes, or until the internal temperature reaches 135ºF (57ºC) for medium-rare. 5. To serve, smear a line of prepared yellow mustard on a platter, then place the meat next to it and add halved cherry tomatoes on the side, if desired. Drizzle with olive oil and garnish with rosemary sprigs and lavender flowers, if desired. 6. Best served fresh. Store leftovers in an airtight container in the fridge for 3 days. Reheat in a preheated 350ºF (177ºC) air fryer for 4 minutes, or until heated through.

Ham with Sweet Potatoes

Prep time: 20 minutes | Cook time: 15 to 17 minutes | Serves 4

1 cup freshly squeezed orange juice
½ cup packed light brown sugar
1 tablespoon Dijon mustard
½ teaspoon salt
½ teaspoon freshly ground

black pepper
3 sweet potatoes, cut into small wedges
2 ham steaks (8 ounces / 227 g each), halved
1 to 2 tablespoons oil

1. In a large bowl, whisk the orange juice, brown sugar, Dijon, salt, and pepper until blended. Toss the sweet potato wedges with the brown sugar mixture. 2. Preheat the air fryer to 400ºF (204ºC). Line the air fryer basket with parchment paper and spritz with oil. 3. Place the sweet potato wedges on the parchment. 4. Cook for 10 minutes. 5. Place ham steaks on top of the sweet potatoes and brush everything with more of the orange juice mixture. 6. Cook for 3 minutes. Flip the ham and cook or 2 to 4 minutes more until the sweet potatoes are soft and the glaze has thickened. Cut the ham steaks in half to serve.

Mustard Lamb Chops

Prep time: 5 minutes | Cook time: 14 minutes | Serves 4

Oil, for spraying
1 tablespoon Dijon mustard
2 teaspoons lemon juice
½ teaspoon dried tarragon
¼ teaspoon salt

¼ teaspoon freshly ground black pepper
4 (1¼-inch-thick) loin lamb chops

1. Preheat the air fryer to 390ºF (199ºC). Line the air fryer basket with parchment and spray lightly with oil. 2. In a small bowl, mix together the mustard, lemon juice, tarragon, salt, and black pepper. 3. Pat dry the lamb chops with a paper towel. Brush the chops on both sides with the mustard mixture. 4. Place the chops in the prepared basket. You may need to work in batches, depending on the size of your air fryer. 5. Cook for 8 minutes, flip, and cook for another 6 minutes, or until the internal temperature reaches 125ºF (52ºC) for rare, 145ºF (63ºC) for medium-rare, or 155ºF (68ºC) for medium.

Mojito Lamb Chops

Prep time: 30 minutes | Cook time: 5 minutes | Serves 2

Marinade: 2 teaspoons grated lime zest ½ cup lime juice ¼ cup avocado oil ¼ cup chopped fresh mint leaves 4 cloves garlic, roughly chopped	2 teaspoons fine sea salt ½ teaspoon ground black pepper 4 (1-inch-thick) lamb chops Sprigs of fresh mint, for garnish (optional) Lime slices, for serving (optional)

1. Make the marinade: Place all the ingredients for the marinade in a food processor or blender and purée until mostly smooth with a few small chunks. Transfer half of the marinade to a shallow dish and set the other half aside for serving. Add the lamb to the shallow dish, cover, and place in the refrigerator to marinate for at least 2 hours or overnight. 2. Spray the air fryer basket with avocado oil. Preheat the air fryer to 390°F (199°C). 3. Remove the chops from the marinade and place them in the air fryer basket. Air fry for 5 minutes, or until the internal temperature reaches 145°F (63°C) for medium doneness. 4. Allow the chops to rest for 10 minutes before serving with the rest of the marinade as a sauce. Garnish with fresh mint leaves and serve with lime slices, if desired. Best served fresh.

Spice-Coated Steaks with Cucumber and Snap Pea Salad

Prep time: 15 minutes | Cook time: 15 to 20 minutes | Serves 4

1 (1½-pound / 680-g) boneless top sirloin steak, trimmed and halved crosswise 1½ teaspoons chili powder 1½ teaspoons ground cumin ¾ teaspoon ground coriander ⅛ teaspoon cayenne pepper ⅛ teaspoon ground cinnamon 1¼ teaspoons plus ⅛ teaspoon salt, divided ½ teaspoon plus ⅛ teaspoon ground black pepper, divided 1 teaspoon plus 1½ tablespoons extra-virgin	olive oil, divided 3 tablespoons mayonnaise 1½ tablespoons white wine vinegar 1 tablespoon minced fresh dill 1 small garlic clove, minced 8 ounces (227 g) sugar snap peas, strings removed and cut in half on bias ½ English cucumber, halved lengthwise and sliced thin 2 radishes, trimmed, halved and sliced thin 2 cups baby arugula

1. Preheat the air fryer to 400°F (204°C). 2. In a bowl, mix chili powder, cumin, coriander, cayenne pepper, cinnamon, 1¼ teaspoons salt and ½ teaspoon pepper until well combined. 3. Add the steaks to another bowl and pat dry with paper towels. Brush with 1 teaspoon oil and transfer to the bowl of spice mixture. Roll over to coat thoroughly. 4. Arrange the coated steaks in the air fryer basket, spaced evenly apart. Air fry for 15 to 20 minutes, or until an instant-read thermometer inserted in the thickest part of the meat registers at least 145°F (63°C). Flip halfway through to ensure even cooking. 5. Transfer the steaks to a clean work surface and wrap with aluminum foil. Let stand while preparing salad. 6. Make the salad: In a large bowl, stir together 1½ tablespoons

olive oil, mayonnaise, vinegar, dill, garlic, ⅛ teaspoon salt, and ⅛ teaspoon pepper. Add snap peas, cucumber, radishes and arugula. Toss to blend well. 7. Slice the steaks and serve with the salad.

Crescent Dogs

Prep time: 15 minutes | Cook time: 8 minutes | Makes 24 crescent dogs

Oil, for spraying 1 (8-ounce / 227-g) can refrigerated crescent rolls 8 slices Cheddar cheese, cut into thirds	24 cocktail sausages or 8 (6-inch) hot dogs, cut into thirds 2 tablespoons unsalted butter, melted 1 tablespoon sea salt flakes

1. Line the air fryer basket with parchment and spray lightly with oil. 2. Separate the dough into 8 triangles. Cut each triangle into 3 narrow triangles so you have 24 total triangles. 3. Top each triangle with 1 piece of cheese and 1 cocktail sausage. 4. Roll up each piece of dough, starting at the wide end and rolling toward the point. 5. Place the rolls in the prepared basket in a single layer. You may need to cook in batches, depending on the size of your air fryer. 6. Air fry at 325°F (163°C) for 3 to 4 minutes, flip, and cook for another 3 to 4 minutes, or until golden brown. 7. Brush with the melted butter and sprinkle with the sea salt flakes before serving.

Herb-Crusted Lamb Chops

Prep time: 10 minutes | Cook time: 5 minutes | Serves 2

1 large egg 2 cloves garlic, minced ¼ cup pork dust ¼ cup powdered Parmesan cheese 1 tablespoon chopped fresh oregano leaves 1 tablespoon chopped fresh rosemary leaves 1 teaspoon chopped fresh thyme leaves	½ teaspoon ground black pepper 4 (1-inch-thick) lamb chops For Garnish/Serving (Optional): Sprigs of fresh oregano Sprigs of fresh rosemary Sprigs of fresh thyme Lavender flowers Lemon slices

1. Spray the air fryer basket with avocado oil. Preheat the air fryer to 400°F (204°C). 2. Beat the egg in a shallow bowl, add the garlic, and stir well to combine. In another shallow bowl, mix together the pork dust, Parmesan, herbs, and pepper. 3. One at a time, dip the lamb chops into the egg mixture, shake off the excess egg, and then dredge them in the Parmesan mixture. Use your hands to coat the chops well in the Parmesan mixture and form a nice crust on all sides; if necessary, dip the chops again in both the egg and the Parmesan mixture. 4. Place the lamb chops in the air fryer basket, leaving space between them, and air fry for 5 minutes, or until the internal temperature reaches 145°F (63°C) for medium doneness. Allow to rest for 10 minutes before serving. 5. Garnish with sprigs of oregano, rosemary, and thyme, and lavender flowers, if desired. Serve with lemon slices, if desired. 6. Best served fresh. Store leftovers in an airtight container in the fridge for up to 4 days. Serve chilled over a salad, or reheat in a 350°F (177°C) air fryer for 3 minutes, or until heated through.

Hoisin BBQ Pork Chops

Prep time: 5 minutes | Cook time: 22 minutes | Serves 2 to 3

3 tablespoons hoisin sauce	1 to 2 teaspoons Sriracha
¼ cup honey	sauce, to taste
1 tablespoon soy sauce	2 to 3 bone-in center cut pork
3 tablespoons rice vinegar	chops, 1-inch thick (about
2 tablespoons brown sugar	1¼ pounds / 567 g)
1½ teaspoons grated fresh	Chopped scallions, for
ginger	garnish

1. Combine the hoisin sauce, honey, soy sauce, rice vinegar, brown sugar, ginger, and Sriracha sauce in a small saucepan. Whisk the ingredients together and bring the mixture to a boil over medium-high heat on the stovetop. Reduce the heat and simmer the sauce until it has reduced in volume and thickened slightly, about 10 minutes. 2. Preheat the air fryer to 400°F (204°C). 3. Place the pork chops into the air fryer basket and pour half the hoisin BBQ sauce over the top. Air fry for 6 minutes. Then, flip the chops over, pour the remaining hoisin BBQ sauce on top and air fry for 5 to 6 more minutes, depending on the thickness of the pork chops. The internal temperature of the pork chops should be 155°F (68°C) when tested with an instant read thermometer. 4. Let the pork chops rest for 5 minutes before serving. You can spoon a little of the sauce from the bottom drawer of the air fryer over the top if desired. Sprinkle with chopped scallions and serve.

Ritzy Skirt Steak Fajitas

Prep time: 15 minutes | Cook time: 30 minutes | Serves 4

2 tablespoons olive oil	1 green pepper, sliced
¼ cup lime juice	Salt and freshly ground black
1 clove garlic, minced	pepper, to taste
½ teaspoon ground cumin	8 flour tortillas
½ teaspoon hot sauce	Toppings:
½ teaspoon salt	Shredded lettuce
2 tablespoons chopped fresh	Crumbled Queso Fresco (or
cilantro	grated Cheddar cheese)
1 pound (454 g) skirt steak	Sliced black olives
1 onion, sliced	Diced tomatoes
1 teaspoon chili powder	Sour cream
1 red pepper, sliced	Guacamole

1. Combine the olive oil, lime juice, garlic, cumin, hot sauce, salt and cilantro in a shallow dish. Add the skirt steak and turn it over several times to coat all sides. Pierce the steak with a needle-style meat tenderizer or paring knife. Marinate the steak in the refrigerator for at least 3 hours, or overnight. When you are ready to cook, remove the steak from the refrigerator and let it sit at room temperature for 30 minutes. 2. Preheat the air fryer to 400°F (204°C). 3. Toss the onion slices with the chili powder and a little olive oil and transfer them to the air fryer basket. Air fry for 5 minutes. Add the red and green peppers to the air fryer basket with the onions, season with salt and pepper and air fry for 8 more minutes, until the onions and peppers are soft. Transfer the vegetables to a dish and cover with aluminum foil to keep warm. 4. Put the skirt steak in the air fryer basket and pour the marinade over the top. Air fry at 400°F (204°C) for 12 minutes.

Flip the steak over and air fry for an additional 5 minutes. Transfer the cooked steak to a cutting board and let the steak rest for a few minutes. If the peppers and onions need to be heated, return them to the air fryer for just 1 to 2 minutes. 5. Thinly slice the steak at an angle, cutting against the grain of the steak. Serve the steak with the onions and peppers, the warm tortillas and the fajita toppings on the side.

Pigs in a Blanket

Prep time: 10 minutes | Cook time: 7 minutes | Serves 2

½ cup shredded Mozzarella	cheese
cheese	2 (2-ounce / 57-g) beef
2 tablespoons blanched	smoked sausages
finely ground almond flour	½ teaspoon sesame seeds
1 ounce (28 g) full-fat cream	

1. Place Mozzarella, almond flour, and cream cheese in a large microwave-safe bowl. Microwave for 45 seconds and stir until smooth. Roll dough into a ball and cut in half. 2. Press each half out into a 4 × 5-inch rectangle. Roll one sausage up in each dough half and press seams closed. Sprinkle the top with sesame seeds. 3. Place each wrapped sausage into the air fryer basket. 4. Adjust the temperature to 400°F (204°C) and air fry for 7 minutes. 5. The outside will be golden when completely cooked. Serve immediately.

Steak, Broccoli, and Mushroom Rice Bowls

Prep time: 10 minutes | Cook time: 15 to 18 minutes | Serves 4

2 tablespoons cornstarch	1 onion, chopped
½ cup low-sodium beef broth	1 cup sliced cremini
1 teaspoon low-sodium soy	mushrooms
sauce	1 tablespoon grated peeled
12 ounces (340 g) sirloin	fresh ginger
strip steak, cut into 1-inch	Cooked brown rice
cubes	(optional), for serving
2½ cups broccoli florets	

1. In a medium bowl, stir together the cornstarch, beef broth, and soy sauce until the cornstarch is completely dissolved. 2. Add the beef cubes and toss to coat. Let stand for 5 minutes at room temperature. 3. Insert the crisper plate into the basket and the basket into the unit. Preheat the unit by selecting AIR FRY, setting the temperature to 400°F (204°C), and setting the time to 3 minutes. Select START/STOP to begin. 4. Once the unit is preheated, use a slotted spoon to transfer the beef from the broth mixture into a medium metal bowl that fits into the basket. Reserve the broth. Add the broccoli, onion, mushrooms, and ginger to the beef. Place the bowl into the basket. 5. Select AIR FRY, set the temperature to 400°F (204°C), and set the time to 18 minutes. Select START/STOP to begin. 6. After about 12 minutes, check the beef and broccoli. If a food thermometer inserted into the beef registers at least 145°F (63°C) and the vegetables are tender, add the reserved broth and resume cooking for about 3 minutes until the sauce boils. If not, resume cooking for about 3 minutes before adding the reserved broth. 7. When the cooking is complete, serve immediately over hot cooked brown rice, if desired.

Fajita Meatball Lettuce Wraps

Prep time: 10 minutes | Cook time: 10 minutes | Serves 4

1 pound (454 g) ground beef (85% lean)	1 teaspoon fine sea salt
½ cup salsa, plus more for serving if desired	½ teaspoon chili powder
¼ cup chopped onions	½ teaspoon ground cumin
¼ cup diced green or red bell peppers	1 clove garlic, minced
1 large egg, beaten	For Serving (Optional):
	8 leaves Boston lettuce
	Pico de gallo or salsa
	Lime slices

1. Spray the air fryer basket with avocado oil. Preheat the air fryer to 350°F (177°C). 2. In a large bowl, mix together all the ingredients until well combined. 3. Shape the meat mixture into eight 1-inch balls. Place the meatballs in the air fryer basket, leaving a little space between them. Air fry for 10 minutes, or until cooked through and no longer pink inside and the internal temperature reaches 145°F (63°C). 4. Serve each meatball on a lettuce leaf, topped with pico de gallo or salsa, if desired. Serve with lime slices if desired. 5. Store leftovers in an airtight container in the fridge for 3 days or in the freezer for up to a month. Reheat in a preheated 350°F (177°C) air fryer for 4 minutes, or until heated through.

Avocado Buttered Flank Steak

Prep time: 5 minutes | Cook time: 12 minutes | Serves 1

1 flank steak	2 avocados
Salt and ground black pepper, to taste	2 tablespoons butter, melted
	½ cup chimichurri sauce

1. Rub the flank steak with salt and pepper to taste and leave to sit for 20 minutes. 2. Preheat the air fryer to 400°F (204°C). 3. Halve the avocados and take out the pits. Spoon the flesh into a bowl and mash with a fork. Mix in the melted butter and chimichurri sauce, making sure everything is well combined. 4. Put the steak in the air fryer basket and air fry for 6 minutes. Flip over and allow to air fry for another 6 minutes. 5. Serve the steak with the avocado butter.

Easy Beef Satay

Prep time: 30 minutes | Cook time: 8 minutes | Serves 4

1 pound (454 g) beef flank steak, thinly sliced into long strips	1 tablespoon minced garlic
2 tablespoons vegetable oil	1 tablespoon sugar
1 tablespoon fish sauce	1 teaspoon Sriracha or other hot sauce
1 tablespoon soy sauce	1 teaspoon ground coriander
1 tablespoon minced fresh ginger	½ cup chopped fresh cilantro
	¼ cup chopped roasted peanuts

1. Place the beef strips in a large bowl or resealable plastic bag. Add the vegetable oil, fish sauce, soy sauce, ginger, garlic, sugar, Sriracha, coriander, and ¼ cup of the cilantro to the bag. Seal and massage the bag to thoroughly coat and combine. Marinate at room temperature for 30 minutes, or cover and refrigerate for up to 24 hours. 2. Using tongs, remove the beef strips from the bag and lay them flat in the air fryer basket, minimizing overlap as much as possible; discard the marinade. Set the air fryer to 400°F (204°C) for 8 minutes, turning the beef strips halfway through the cooking time. 3. Transfer the meat to a serving platter. Sprinkle with the remaining ¼ cup cilantro and the peanuts. Serve.

Cheddar Bacon Burst with Spinach

Prep time: 5 minutes | Cook time: 60 minutes | Serves 8

30 slices bacon	2 teaspoons Italian seasoning
1 tablespoon Chipotle seasoning	2½ cups Cheddar cheese
	4 cups raw spinach

1. Preheat the air fryer to 375°F (191°C). 2. Weave the bacon into 15 vertical pieces and 12 horizontal pieces. Cut the extra 3 in half to fill in the rest, horizontally. 3. Season the bacon with Chipotle seasoning and Italian seasoning. 4. Add the cheese to the bacon. 5. Add the spinach and press down to compress. 6. Tightly roll up the woven bacon. 7. Line a baking sheet with kitchen foil and add plenty of salt to it. 8. Put the bacon on top of a cooling rack and put that on top of the baking sheet. 9. Bake for 60 minutes. 10. Let cool for 15 minutes before slicing and serving.

Five-Spice Pork Belly

Prep time: 10 minutes | Cook time: 17 minutes | Serves 4

1 pound (454 g) unsalted pork belly	¼ to ½ cup Swerve confectioners'-style sweetener or equivalent amount of liquid or powdered sweetener
2 teaspoons Chinese five-spice powder	
Sauce:	3 tablespoons wheat-free tamari, or ½ cup coconut aminos
1 tablespoon coconut oil	
1 (1-inch) piece fresh ginger, peeled and grated	
2 cloves garlic, minced	1 green onion, sliced, plus more for garnish
½ cup beef or chicken broth	

1. Spray the air fryer basket with avocado oil. Preheat the air fryer to 400°F (204°C). 2. Cut the pork belly into ½-inch-thick slices and season well on all sides with the five-spice powder. Place the slices in a single layer in the air fryer basket (if you're using a smaller air fryer, work in batches if necessary) and cook for 8 minutes, or until cooked to your liking, flipping halfway through. 3. While the pork belly cooks, make the sauce: Heat the coconut oil in a small saucepan over medium heat. Add the ginger and garlic and sauté for 1 minute, or until fragrant. Add the broth, sweetener, and tamari and simmer for 10 to 15 minutes, until thickened. Add the green onion and cook for another minute, until the green onion is softened. Taste and adjust the seasoning to your liking. 4. Transfer the pork belly to a large bowl. Pour the sauce over the pork belly and coat well. Place the pork belly slices on a serving platter and garnish with sliced green onions. 5. Best served fresh. Store leftovers in an airtight container in the fridge for up to 4 days. Reheat in a preheated 400°F (204°C) air fryer for 3 minutes, or until heated through.

New York Strip with Honey-Mustard Butter

Prep time: 5 minutes | Cook time: 14 minutes | Serves 4

2 pounds (907 g) New York Strip 1 teaspoon cayenne pepper 1 tablespoon honey 1 tablespoon Dijon mustard	½ stick butter, softened Sea salt and freshly ground black pepper, to taste Cooking spray

1. Preheat the air fryer to 400ºF (204ºC) and spritz with cooking spray. 2. Sprinkle the New York Strip with cayenne pepper, salt, and black pepper on a clean work surface. 3. Arrange the New York Strip in the preheated air fryer and spritz with cooking spray. 4. Air fry for 14 minutes or until browned and reach your desired doneness. Flip the New York Strip halfway through. 5. Meanwhile, combine the honey, mustard, and butter in a small bowl. Stir to mix well. 6. Transfer the air fried New York Strip onto a plate and baste with the honey-mustard butter before serving.

Marinated Steak Tips with Mushrooms

Prep time: 30 minutes | Cook time: 10 minutes | Serves 4

1½ pounds (680 g) sirloin, trimmed and cut into 1-inch pieces 8 ounces (227 g) brown mushrooms, halved ¼ cup Worcestershire sauce 1 tablespoon Dijon mustard	1 tablespoon olive oil 1 teaspoon paprika 1 teaspoon crushed red pepper flakes 2 tablespoons chopped fresh parsley (optional)

1. Place the beef and mushrooms in a gallon-size resealable bag. In a small bowl, whisk together the Worcestershire, mustard, olive oil, paprika, and red pepper flakes. Pour the marinade into the bag and massage gently to ensure the beef and mushrooms are evenly coated. Seal the bag and refrigerate for at least 4 hours, preferably overnight. Remove from the refrigerator 30 minutes before cooking. 2. Preheat the air fryer to 400ºF (204ºC). 3. Drain and discard the marinade. Arrange the steak and mushrooms in the air fryer basket. Air fry for 10 minutes, pausing halfway through the baking time to shake the basket. Transfer to a serving plate and top with the parsley, if desired.

Poblano Pepper Cheeseburgers

Prep time: 5 minutes | Cook time: 30 minutes | Serves 4

2 poblano chile peppers 1½ pounds (680 g) 85% lean ground beef 1 clove garlic, minced 1 teaspoon salt	½ teaspoon freshly ground black pepper 4 slices Cheddar cheese (about 3 ounces / 85 g) 4 large lettuce leaves

1. Preheat the air fryer to 400ºF (204ºC). 2. Arrange the poblano peppers in the basket of the air fryer. Pausing halfway through the cooking time to turn the peppers, air fry for 20 minutes, or until they are softened and beginning to char. Transfer the peppers to a large bowl and cover with a plate. When cool enough to handle, peel off the skin, remove the seeds and stems, and slice into strips. Set aside. 3. Meanwhile, in a large bowl, combine the ground beef with the garlic, salt, and pepper. Shape the beef into 4 patties. 4. Lower the heat on the air fryer to 360ºF (182ºC). Arrange the burgers in a single layer in the basket of the air fryer. Pausing halfway through the cooking time to turn the burgers, air fry for 10 minutes, or until a thermometer inserted into the thickest part registers 160ºF (71ºC). 5. Top the burgers with the cheese slices and continue baking for a minute or two, just until the cheese has melted. Serve the burgers on a lettuce leaf topped with the roasted poblano peppers.

Pork and Beef Egg Rolls

Prep time: 30 minutes | Cook time: 7 to 8 minutes per batch | Makes 8 egg rolls

¼ pound (113 g) very lean ground beef ¼ pound (113 g) lean ground pork 1 tablespoon soy sauce 1 teaspoon olive oil ½ cup grated carrots 2 green onions, chopped 2 cups grated Napa cabbage ¼ cup chopped water	chestnuts ¼ teaspoon salt ¼ teaspoon garlic powder ¼ teaspoon black pepper 1 egg 1 tablespoon water 8 egg roll wraps Oil for misting or cooking spray

1. In a large skillet, brown beef and pork with soy sauce. Remove cooked meat from skillet, drain, and set aside. 2. Pour off any excess grease from skillet. Add olive oil, carrots, and onions. Sauté until barely tender, about 1 minute. 3. Stir in cabbage, cover, and cook for 1 minute or just until cabbage slightly wilts. Remove from heat. 4. In a large bowl, combine the cooked meats and vegetables, water chestnuts, salt, garlic powder, and pepper. Stir well. If needed, add more salt to taste. 5. Beat together egg and water in a small bowl. 6. Fill egg roll wrappers, using about ¼ cup of filling for each wrap. Roll up and brush all over with egg wash to seal. Spray very lightly with olive oil or cooking spray. 7. Place 4 egg rolls in air fryer basket and air fry at 390ºF (199ºC) for 4 minutes. Turn over and cook 3 to 4 more minutes, until golden brown and crispy. 8. Repeat to cook remaining egg rolls.

Mexican Pork Chops

Prep time: 5 minutes | Cook time: 15 minutes | Serves 2

¼ teaspoon dried oregano 1½ teaspoons taco seasoning mix 2 (4-ounce / 113-g) boneless	pork chops 2 tablespoons unsalted butter, divided

1. Preheat the air fryer to 400ºF (204ºC). 2. Combine the dried oregano and taco seasoning in a small bowl and rub the mixture into the pork chops. Brush the chops with 1 tablespoon butter. 3. In the air fryer, air fry the chops for 15 minutes, turning them over halfway through to air fry on the other side. 4. When the chops are a brown color, check the internal temperature has reached 145ºF (63ºC) and remove from the air fryer. Serve with a garnish of remaining butter.

Vietnamese "Shaking" Beef

Prep time: 30 minutes | Cook time: 4 minutes per batch | Serves 4

Meat:
4 garlic cloves, minced
2 teaspoons soy sauce
2 teaspoons sugar
1 teaspoon toasted sesame oil
1 teaspoon kosher salt
¼ teaspoon black pepper
1½ pounds (680 g) flat iron or top sirloin steak, cut into 1-inch cubes
Salad:
2 tablespoons rice vinegar or apple cider vinegar
2 tablespoons vegetable oil

1 garlic clove, minced
2 teaspoons sugar
¼ teaspoon kosher salt
¼ teaspoon black pepper
½ red onion, halved and very thinly sliced
1 head Bibb lettuce, leaves separated and torn into large pieces
½ cup halved grape tomatoes
¼ cup fresh mint leaves
For Serving:
Lime wedges

Coarse salt and freshly cracked black pepper, to taste

1. For the meat: In a small bowl, combine the garlic, soy sauce, sugar, sesame oil, salt, and pepper. Place the meat in a gallon-size resealable plastic bag. Pour the marinade over the meat. Seal and place the bag in a large bowl. Marinate for 30 minutes, or cover and refrigerate for up to 24 hours. 2. Place half the meat in the air fryer basket. Set the air fryer to 450ºF (232ºC) for 4 minutes, shaking the basket to redistribute the meat halfway through the cooking time. Transfer the meat to a plate (it should be medium-rare, still pink in the middle). Cover lightly with aluminum foil. Repeat to cook the remaining meat. 3. Meanwhile, for the salad: In a large bowl, whisk together the vinegar, vegetable oil, garlic, sugar, salt, and pepper. Add the onion. Stir to combine. Add the lettuce, tomatoes, and mint and toss to combine. Arrange the salad on a serving platter. 4. Arrange the cooked meat over the salad. Drizzle any accumulated juices from the plate over the meat. Serve with lime wedges, coarse salt, and cracked black pepper.

Bean and Beef Meatball Taco Pizza

Prep time: 10 minutes | Cook time: 7 to 9 minutes per batch | Serves 4

¾ cup refried beans (from a 16-ounce / 454-g can)
½ cup salsa
10 frozen precooked beef meatballs, thawed and sliced
1 jalapeño pepper, sliced
4 whole-wheat pita breads

1 cup shredded pepper Jack cheese
½ cup shredded Colby cheese
Cooking oil spray
⅓ cup sour cream

1. In a medium bowl, stir together the refried beans, salsa, meatballs, and jalapeño. 2. Insert the crisper plate into the basket and the basket into the unit. Preheat the unit by selecting BAKE, setting the temperature to 375ºF (191ºC), and setting the time to 3 minutes. Select START/STOP to begin. 3. Top the pitas with the refried bean mixture and sprinkle with the cheeses. 4. Once the unit is preheated, spray the crisper plate with cooking oil. Working in batches, place the pizzas into the basket. Select BAKE, set the temperature to 375ºF (191ºC), and set the time to 9 minutes. Select START/STOP to begin. 5. After about 7 minutes, check the pizzas. They are done when the cheese is melted and starts to brown. If not ready, resume cooking. 6. When the cooking is complete, top each pizza with a dollop of sour cream and serve warm.

Greek Pork with Tzatziki Sauce

Prep time: 30 minutes | Cook time: 50 minutes | Serves 4

Greek Pork:
2 pounds (907 g) pork sirloin roast
Salt and black pepper, to taste
1 teaspoon smoked paprika
½ teaspoon mustard seeds
½ teaspoon celery seeds
1 teaspoon fennel seeds
1 teaspoon Ancho chili powder
1 teaspoon turmeric powder
½ teaspoon ground ginger

2 tablespoons olive oil
2 cloves garlic, finely chopped
Tzatziki:
½ cucumber, finely chopped and squeezed
1 cup full-fat Greek yogurt
1 garlic clove, minced
1 tablespoon extra-virgin olive oil
1 teaspoon balsamic vinegar
1 teaspoon minced fresh dill
A pinch of salt

1. Toss all ingredients for Greek pork in a large mixing bowl. Toss until the meat is well coated. 2. Cook in the preheated air fryer at 360ºF (182ºC) for 30 minutes; turn over and cook another 20 minutes. 3. Meanwhile, prepare the tzatziki by mixing all the tzatziki ingredients. Place in your refrigerator until ready to use. 4. Serve the pork sirloin roast with the chilled tzatziki on the side. Enjoy!

Broccoli and Pork Teriyaki

Prep time: 10 minutes | Cook time: 13 minutes | Serves 4

1 head broccoli, trimmed into florets
1 tablespoon extra-virgin olive oil
¼ teaspoon sea salt
¼ teaspoon freshly ground black pepper

1 pound (454 g) pork tenderloin, trimmed and cut into 1-inch pieces
½ cup teriyaki sauce, divided
Olive oil spray
2 cups cooked brown rice
Sesame seeds, for garnish

1. Insert the crisper plate into the basket and the basket into the unit. Preheat the unit by selecting AIR ROAST, setting the temperature to 400ºF (204ºC), and setting the time to 3 minutes. Select START/STOP to begin. 2. In a large bowl, toss together the broccoli, olive oil, salt, and pepper. 3. In a medium bowl, toss together the pork and 3 tablespoons of teriyaki sauce to coat the meat. 4. Once the unit is preheated, spray the crisper plate with olive oil. Put the broccoli and pork into the basket. Spray them with olive oil and drizzle with 1 tablespoon of teriyaki sauce. 5. Select AIR ROAST, set the temperature to 400ºF (204ºC), and set the time to 13 minutes. Select START/STOP to begin. 6. After 10 to 12 minutes, the broccoli is tender and light golden brown and a food thermometer inserted into the pork should register 145ºF (63ºC). Remove the basket and drizzle the broccoli and pork with the remaining ¼ cup of teriyaki sauce and toss to coat. Reinsert the basket to resume cooking for 1 minute. 7. When the cooking is complete, serve immediately over the hot cooked rice, if desired, garnished with the sesame seeds.

Spicy Sirloin Tip Steak

Prep time: 25 minutes | Cook time: 12 to 18 minutes | Serves 4

2 tablespoons salsa	black pepper
1 tablespoon minced chipotle pepper	⅛ teaspoon red pepper flakes
1 tablespoon apple cider vinegar	12 ounces (340 g) sirloin tip steak, cut into 4 pieces and gently pounded to about ⅓ inch thick
1 teaspoon ground cumin	
⅛ teaspoon freshly ground	Cooking oil spray

1. In a small bowl, thoroughly mix the salsa, chipotle pepper, vinegar, cumin, black pepper, and red pepper flakes. Rub this mixture into both sides of each steak piece. Let stand for 15 minutes at room temperature. 2. Insert the crisper plate into the basket and place the basket into the unit. Preheat the unit by selecting AIR FRY, setting the temperature to 390ºF (199ºC), and setting the time to 3 minutes. Select START/STOP to begin. 3. Once the unit is preheated, spray the crisper plate with cooking oil. Working in batches, place 2 steaks into the basket. 4. Select AIR FRY, set the temperature to 390ºF (199ºC), and set the time to 9 minutes. Select START/STOP to begin. 5. After about 6 minutes, check the steaks. If a food thermometer inserted into the meat registers at least 145ºF (63ºC), they are done. If not, resume cooking. 6. When the cooking is done, transfer the steaks to a clean plate and cover with aluminum foil to keep warm. Repeat steps 3, 4, and 5 with the remaining steaks. 7. Thinly slice the steaks against the grain and serve.

Pork and Pinto Bean Gorditas

Prep time: 20 minutes | Cook time: 21 minutes | Serves 4

1 pound (454 g) lean ground pork	Salt and freshly ground black pepper, to taste
2 tablespoons chili powder	2 cups grated Cheddar cheese
2 tablespoons ground cumin	5 (12-inch) flour tortillas
1 teaspoon dried oregano	4 (8-inch) crispy corn tortilla shells
2 teaspoons paprika	
1 teaspoon garlic powder	4 cups shredded lettuce
½ cup water	1 tomato, diced
1 (15-ounce / 425-g) can pinto beans, drained and rinsed	⅓ cup sliced black olives
	Sour cream, for serving
	Tomato salsa, for serving
½ cup taco sauce	Cooking spray

1. Preheat the air fryer to 400ºF (204ºC). Spritz the air fryer basket with cooking spray. 2. Put the ground pork in the air fryer basket and air fry at 400ºF (204ºC) for 10 minutes, stirring a few times to gently break up the meat. Combine the chili powder, cumin, oregano, paprika, garlic powder and water in a small bowl. Stir the spice mixture into the browned pork. Stir in the beans and taco sauce and air fry for an additional minute. Transfer the pork mixture to a bowl. Season with salt and freshly ground black pepper. 3. Sprinkle ½ cup of the grated cheese in the center of the flour tortillas, leaving a 2-inch border around the edge free of cheese and filling. Divide the pork mixture among the four tortillas, placing it on top of the cheese. Put a crunchy corn tortilla on top of the pork and top with shredded lettuce, diced tomatoes,

and black olives. Cut the remaining flour tortilla into 4 quarters. These quarters of tortilla will serve as the bottom of the gordita. Put one quarter tortilla on top of each gordita and fold the edges of the bottom flour tortilla up over the sides, enclosing the filling. While holding the seams down, brush the bottom of the gordita with olive oil and place the seam side down on the countertop while you finish the remaining three gorditas. 4. Adjust the temperature to 380ºF (193ºC). 5. Air fry one gordita at a time. Transfer the gordita carefully to the air fryer basket, seam side down. Brush or spray the top tortilla with oil and air fry for 5 minutes. Carefully turn the gordita over and air fry for an additional 4 to 5 minutes until both sides are browned. When finished air frying all four gorditas, layer them back into the air fryer for an additional minute to make sure they are all warm before serving with sour cream and salsa.

Goat Cheese-Stuffed Flank Steak

Prep time: 10 minutes | Cook time: 14 minutes | Serves 6

1 pound (454 g) flank steak	black pepper
1 tablespoon avocado oil	2 ounces (57 g) goat cheese, crumbled
½ teaspoon sea salt	
½ teaspoon garlic powder	1 cup baby spinach, chopped
¼ teaspoon freshly ground	

1. Place the steak in a large zip-top bag or between two pieces of plastic wrap. Using a meat mallet or heavy-bottomed skillet, pound the steak to an even ¼-inch thickness. 2. Brush both sides of the steak with the avocado oil. 3. Mix the salt, garlic powder, and pepper in a small dish. Sprinkle this mixture over both sides of the steak. 4. Sprinkle the goat cheese over top, and top that with the spinach. 5. Starting at one of the long sides, roll the steak up tightly. Tie the rolled steak with kitchen string at 3-inch intervals. 6. Set the air fryer to 400ºF (204ºC). Place the steak roll-up in the air fryer basket. Air fry for 7 minutes. Flip the steak and cook for an additional 7 minutes, until an instant-read thermometer reads 120ºF (49ºC) for medium-rare (adjust the cooking time for your desired doneness).

Easy Lamb Chops with Asparagus

Prep time: 10 minutes | Cook time: 15 minutes | Serves 4

4 asparagus spears, trimmed	2 teaspoons chopped fresh thyme, for serving
2 tablespoons olive oil, divided	
	Salt and ground black pepper, to taste
1 pound (454 g) lamb chops	
1 garlic clove, minced	

1. Preheat the air fryer to 400ºF (204ºC). Spritz the air fryer basket with cooking spray. 2. On a large plate, brush the asparagus with 1 tablespoon olive oil, then sprinkle with salt. Set aside. 3. On a separate plate, brush the lamb chops with remaining olive oil and sprinkle with salt and ground black pepper. 4. Arrange the lamb chops in the preheated air fryer. Air fry for 10 minutes. 5. Flip the lamb chops and add the asparagus and garlic. Air fry for 5 more minutes or until the lamb is well browned and the asparagus is tender. 6. Serve them on a plate with thyme on top.

Pork Kebab with Yogurt Sauce

Prep time: 25 minutes | Cook time: 12 minutes | Serves 4

2 teaspoons olive oil	½ teaspoon celery seeds
½ pound (227 g) ground pork	Yogurt Sauce:
½ pound (227 g) ground beef	2 tablespoons olive oil
1 egg, whisked	2 tablespoons fresh lemon
Sea salt and ground black	juice
pepper, to taste	Sea salt, to taste
1 teaspoon paprika	¼ teaspoon red pepper
2 garlic cloves, minced	flakes, crushed
1 teaspoon dried marjoram	½ cup full-fat yogurt
1 teaspoon mustard seeds	1 teaspoon dried dill weed

1. Spritz the sides and bottom of the air fryer basket with 2 teaspoons of olive oil. 2. In a mixing dish, thoroughly combine the ground pork, beef, egg, salt, black pepper, paprika, garlic, marjoram, mustard seeds, and celery seeds. 3. Form the mixture into kebabs and transfer them to the greased basket. Cook at 365°F (185°C) for 11 to 12 minutes, turning them over once or twice. In the meantime, mix all the sauce ingredients and place in the refrigerator until ready to serve. Serve the pork kebabs with the yogurt sauce on the side. Enjoy!

Apple Cornbread Stuffed Pork Loin

Prep time: 15 minutes | Cook time: 1 hour | Serves 4 to 6

4 strips of bacon, chopped	Apple Gravy:
1 Granny Smith apple,	2 tablespoons butter
peeled, cored and finely	1 shallot, minced
chopped	1 Granny Smith apple,
2 teaspoons fresh thyme	peeled, cored and finely
leaves	chopped
¼ cup chopped fresh parsley	3 sprigs fresh thyme
2 cups cubed cornbread	2 tablespoons flour
½ cup chicken stock	1 cup chicken stock
Salt and freshly ground black	½ cup apple cider
pepper, to taste	Salt and freshly ground black
1 (2-pound / 907-g) boneless	pepper, to taste
pork loin	

1. Preheat the air fryer to 400°F (204°C). 2. Add the bacon to the air fryer and air fry for 6 to 8 minutes until crispy. While the bacon is cooking, combine the apple, fresh thyme, parsley and cornbread in a bowl and toss well. Moisten the mixture with the chicken stock and season to taste with salt and freshly ground black pepper. Add the cooked bacon to the mixture. 3. Butterfly the pork loin by holding it flat on the cutting board with one hand, while slicing into the pork loin parallel to the cutting board with the other. Slice into the longest side of the pork loin, but stop before you cut all the way through. You should then be able to open the pork loin up like a book, making it twice as wide as it was when you started. Season the inside of the pork with salt and freshly ground black pepper. 4. Spread the cornbread mixture onto the butterflied pork loin, leaving a one-inch border around the edge of the pork. Roll the pork loin up around the stuffing to enclose the stuffing, and tie the rolled pork in several places with kitchen twine or secure with toothpicks. Try to replace any stuffing that falls out of the roast as

you roll it, by stuffing it into the ends of the rolled pork. Season the outside of the pork with salt and freshly ground black pepper. 5. Preheat the air fryer to 360°F (182°C). 6. Place the stuffed pork loin into the air fryer, seam side down. Air fry the pork loin for 15 minutes at 360°F (182°C). Turn the pork loin over and air fry for an additional 15 minutes. Turn the pork loin a quarter turn and air fry for an additional 15 minutes. Turn the pork loin over again to expose the fourth side, and air fry for an additional 10 minutes. The pork loin should register 155°F (68°C) on an instant read thermometer when it is finished. 7. While the pork is cooking, make the apple gravy. Preheat a saucepan over medium heat on the stovetop and melt the butter. Add the shallot, apple and thyme sprigs and sauté until the apple starts to soften and brown a little. Add the flour and stir for a minute or two. Whisk in the stock and apple cider vigorously to prevent the flour from forming lumps. Bring the mixture to a boil to thicken and season to taste with salt and pepper. 8. Transfer the pork loin to a resting plate and loosely tent with foil, letting the pork rest for at least 5 minutes before slicing and serving with the apple gravy poured over the top.

Bacon-Wrapped Vegetable Kebabs

Prep time: 10 minutes | Cook time: 10 to 12 minutes | Serves 4

4 ounces (113 g) mushrooms, sliced	bacon, halved
1 small zucchini, sliced	Avocado oil spray
12 grape tomatoes	Sea salt and freshly ground
4 ounces (113 g) sliced	black pepper, to taste

1. Stack 3 mushroom slices, 1 zucchini slice, and 1 grape tomato. Wrap a bacon strip around the vegetables and thread them onto a skewer. Repeat with the remaining vegetables and bacon. Spray with oil and sprinkle with salt and pepper. 2. Set the air fryer to 400°F (204°C). Place the skewers in the air fryer basket in a single layer, working in batches if necessary, and air fry for 5 minutes. Flip the skewers and cook for 5 to 7 minutes more, until the bacon is crispy and the vegetables are tender. 3. Serve warm.

Lemony Pork Loin Chop Schnitzel

Prep time: 15 minutes | Cook time: 15 minutes | Serves 4

4 thin boneless pork loin chops	1 teaspoon salt
2 tablespoons lemon juice	1 cup panko breadcrumbs
½ cup flour	2 eggs
¼ teaspoon marjoram	Lemon wedges, for serving
	Cooking spray

1. Preheat the air fryer to 390°F (199°C) and spritz with cooking spray. 2. On a clean work surface, drizzle the pork chops with lemon juice on both sides. 3. Combine the flour with marjoram and salt on a shallow plate. Pour the breadcrumbs on a separate shallow dish. Beat the eggs in a large bowl. 4. Dredge the pork chops in the flour, then dunk in the beaten eggs to coat well. Shake the excess off and roll over the breadcrumbs. 5. Arrange the chops in the preheated air fryer and spritz with cooking spray. Air fry for 15 minutes or until the chops are golden and crispy. Flip the chops halfway through. Squeeze the lemon wedges over the fried chops and serve immediately.

Mediterranean Beef Steaks

Prep time: 20 minutes | Cook time: 20 minutes | Serves 4

2 tablespoons coconut aminos	pepper
3 heaping tablespoons fresh chives	½ teaspoon dried basil
2 tablespoons olive oil	½ teaspoon dried rosemary
3 tablespoons dry white wine	1 teaspoon freshly ground black pepper
4 small-sized beef steaks	1 teaspoon sea salt, or more to taste
2 teaspoons smoked cayenne	

1. Firstly, coat the steaks with the cayenne pepper, black pepper, salt, basil, and rosemary. 2. Drizzle the steaks with olive oil, white wine, and coconut aminos. 3. Finally, roast in the air fryer for 20 minutes at 340ºF (171ºC). Serve garnished with fresh chives. Bon appétit!

Sumptuous Pizza Tortilla Rolls

Prep time: 10 minutes | Cook time: 6 minutes | Serves 4

1 teaspoon butter	8 flour tortillas
½ medium onion, slivered	8 thin slices deli ham
½ red or green bell pepper, julienned	24 pepperoni slices
4 ounces (113 g) fresh white mushrooms, chopped	1 cup shredded Mozzarella cheese
½ cup pizza sauce	Cooking spray

1. Preheat the air fryer to 390ºF (199ºC). 2. Put butter, onions, bell pepper, and mushrooms in a baking pan. Bake in the preheated air fryer for 3 minutes. Stir and cook 3 to 4 minutes longer until just crisp and tender. Remove pan and set aside. 3. To assemble rolls, spread about 2 teaspoons of pizza sauce on one half of each tortilla. Top with a slice of ham and 3 slices of pepperoni. Divide sautéed vegetables among tortillas and top with cheese. 4. Roll up tortillas, secure with toothpicks if needed, and spray with oil. 5. Put 4 rolls in air fryer basket and air fry for 4 minutes. Turn and air fry 4 minutes, until heated through and lightly browned. 6. Repeat step 4 to air fry remaining pizza rolls. 7. Serve immediately.

Bacon-Wrapped Pork Tenderloin

Prep time: 30 minutes | Cook time: 22 to 25 minutes | Serves 6

½ cup minced onion	¼ teaspoon freshly ground black pepper
½ cup hard apple cider, or apple juice	2 pounds (907 g) pork tenderloin
¼ cup honey	1 to 2 tablespoons oil
1 tablespoon minced garlic	8 uncooked bacon slices
¼ teaspoon salt	

1. In a medium bowl, stir together the onion, hard cider, honey, garlic, salt, and pepper. Transfer to a large resealable bag or airtight container and add the pork. Seal the bag. Refrigerate to marinate for at least 2 hours. 2. Preheat the air fryer to 400ºF (204ºC). Line the air fryer basket with parchment paper. 3. Remove the pork from the marinade and place it on the parchment. Spritz with oil. 4. Cook for 15 minutes. 5. Wrap the bacon slices around the pork and secure them with toothpicks. Turn the pork roast and spritz with oil. Cook for 7 to 10 minutes more until the internal temperature reaches 145ºF (63ºC), depending on how well-done you like pork loin. It will continue cooking after it's removed from the fryer, so let it sit for 5 minutes before serving.

Provolone Stuffed Beef and Pork Meatballs

Prep time: 15 minutes | Cook time: 12 minutes | Serves 4 to 6

1 tablespoon olive oil	parsley
1 small onion, finely chopped	½ teaspoon dried oregano
1 to 2 cloves garlic, minced	1½ teaspoons salt
¾ pound (340 g) ground beef	Freshly ground black pepper, to taste
¾ pound (340 g) ground pork	2 eggs, lightly beaten
¾ cup bread crumbs	5 ounces (142 g) sharp or aged provolone cheese, cut into 1-inch cubes
¼ cup grated Parmesan cheese	
¼ cup finely chopped fresh	

1. Preheat a skillet over medium-high heat. Add the oil and cook the onion and garlic until tender, but not browned. 2. Transfer the onion and garlic to a large bowl and add the beef, pork, bread crumbs, Parmesan cheese, parsley, oregano, salt, pepper and eggs. Mix well until all the ingredients are combined. Divide the mixture into 12 evenly sized balls. Make one meatball at a time, by pressing a hole in the meatball mixture with the finger and pushing a piece of provolone cheese into the hole. Mold the meat back into a ball, enclosing the cheese. 3. Preheat the air fryer to 380ºF (193ºC). 4. Working in two batches, transfer six of the meatballs to the air fryer basket and air fry for 12 minutes, shaking the basket and turning the meatballs twice during the cooking process. Repeat with the remaining 6 meatballs. Serve warm.

Fruited Ham

Prep time: 15 minutes | Cook time: 8 to 10 minutes | Serves 4

1 cup orange marmalade	1 pound (454 g) cooked ham, cut into 1-inch cubes
¼ cup packed light brown sugar	½ cup canned mandarin oranges, drained and chopped
¼ teaspoon ground cloves	
½ teaspoon dry mustard	
1 to 2 tablespoons oil	

1. In a small bowl, stir together the orange marmalade, brown sugar, cloves, and dry mustard until blended. Set aside. 2. Preheat the air fryer to 320ºF (160ºC). Spritz a baking pan with oil. 3. Place the ham cubes in the prepared pan. Pour the marmalade sauce over the ham to glaze it. 4. Cook for 4 minutes. Stir and cook for 2 minutes more. 5. Add the mandarin oranges and cook for 2 to 4 minutes more until the sauce begins to thicken and the ham is tender.

Pepper Steak

Prep time: 30 minutes | Cook time: 16 to 20 minutes | Serves 4

1 pound (454 g) cube steak, cut into 1-inch pieces	black pepper
1 cup Italian dressing	¼ cup cornstarch
1½ cups beef broth	1 cup thinly sliced bell pepper, any color
1 tablespoon soy sauce	1 cup chopped celery
½ teaspoon salt	1 tablespoon minced garlic
¼ teaspoon freshly ground	1 to 2 tablespoons oil

1. In a large resealable bag, combine the beef and Italian dressing. Seal the bag and refrigerate to marinate for 8 hours. 2. In a small bowl, whisk the beef broth, soy sauce, salt, and pepper until blended. 3. In another small bowl, whisk ¼ cup water and the cornstarch until dissolved. Stir the cornstarch mixture into the beef broth mixture until blended. 4. Preheat the air fryer to 375°F (191°C). 5. Pour the broth mixture into a baking pan. Cook for 4 minutes. Stir and cook for 4 to 5 minutes more. Remove and set aside. 6. Increase the air fryer temperature to 400°F (204°C). Line the air fryer basket with parchment paper. 7. Remove the steak from the marinade and place it in a medium bowl. Discard the marinade. Stir in the bell pepper, celery, and garlic. 8. Place the steak and pepper mixture on the parchment. Spritz with oil. 9. Cook for 4 minutes. Shake the basket and cook for 4 to 7 minutes more, until the vegetables are tender and the meat reaches an internal temperature of 145°F (63°C). Serve with the gravy.

Barbecue Ribs

Prep time: 5 minutes | Cook time: 30 minutes | Serves 4

1 (2-pound / 907-g) rack baby back ribs	1 teaspoon dried oregano
1 teaspoon onion powder	Salt and freshly ground black pepper, to taste
1 teaspoon garlic powder	Cooking oil spray
1 teaspoon light brown sugar	½ cup barbecue sauce

1. Use a sharp knife to remove the thin membrane from the back of the ribs. Cut the rack in half, or as needed, so the ribs fit in the air fryer basket. The best way to do this is to cut the ribs into 4- or 5-rib sections. 2. In a small bowl, stir together the onion powder, garlic powder, brown sugar, and oregano and season with salt and pepper. Rub the spice seasoning onto the front and back of the ribs. 3. Cover the ribs with plastic wrap or foil and let sit at room temperature for 30 minutes. 4. Insert the crisper plate into the basket and the basket into the unit. Preheat the unit by selecting AIR ROAST, setting the temperature to 360°F (182°C), and setting the time to 3 minutes. Select START/STOP to begin. 5. Once the unit is preheated, spray the crisper plate with cooking oil. Place the ribs into the basket. It is okay to stack them. 6. Select AIR ROAST, set the temperature to 360°F (182°C), and set the time to 30 minutes. Select START/STOP to begin. 7. After 15 minutes, flip the ribs. Resume cooking for 15 minutes, or until a

food thermometer registers 190°F (88°C). 8. When the cooking is complete, transfer the ribs to a serving dish. Drizzle the ribs with the barbecue sauce and serve.

Italian Sausages with Peppers and Onions

Prep time: 5 minutes | Cook time: 28 minutes | Serves 3

1 medium onion, thinly sliced	¼ cup avocado oil or melted coconut oil
1 yellow or orange bell pepper, thinly sliced	1 teaspoon fine sea salt
1 red bell pepper, thinly sliced	6 Italian sausages
	Dijon mustard, for serving (optional)

1. Preheat the air fryer to 400°F (204°C). 2. Place the onion and peppers in a large bowl. Drizzle with the oil and toss well to coat the veggies. Season with the salt. 3. Place the onion and peppers in a pie pan and cook in the air fryer for 8 minutes, stirring halfway through. Remove from the air fryer and set aside. 4. Spray the air fryer basket with avocado oil. Place the sausages in the air fryer basket and air fry for 20 minutes, or until crispy and golden brown. During the last minute or two of cooking, add the onion and peppers to the basket with the sausages to warm them through. 5. Place the onion and peppers on a serving platter and arrange the sausages on top. Serve Dijon mustard on the side, if desired. 6. Store leftovers in an airtight container in the fridge for up to 7 days or in the freezer for up to a month. Reheat in a preheated 390°F (199°C) air fryer for 3 minutes, or until heated through.

Spicy Lamb Sirloin Chops

Prep time: 30 minutes | Cook time: 15 minutes | Serves 4

½ yellow onion, coarsely chopped	1 teaspoon ground turmeric
4 coin-size slices peeled fresh ginger	½ to 1 teaspoon cayenne pepper
5 garlic cloves	½ teaspoon ground cardamom
1 teaspoon garam masala	1 teaspoon kosher salt
1 teaspoon ground fennel	1 pound (454 g) lamb sirloin chops
1 teaspoon ground cinnamon	

1. In a blender, combine the onion, ginger, garlic, garam masala, fennel, cinnamon, turmeric, cayenne, cardamom, and salt. Pulse until the onion is finely minced and the mixture forms a thick paste, 3 to 4 minutes. 2. Place the lamb chops in a large bowl. Slash the meat and fat with a sharp knife several times to allow the marinade to penetrate better. Add the spice paste to the bowl and toss the lamb to coat. Marinate at room temperature for 30 minutes or cover and refrigerate for up to 24 hours. 3. Place the lamb chops in a single layer in the air fryer basket. Set the air fryer to 325°F (163°C) for 15 minutes, turning the chops halfway through the cooking time. Use a meat thermometer to ensure the lamb has reached an internal temperature of 145°F (63°C) (medium-rare).

Cheese Wine Pork Cutlets

Prep time: 30 minutes | Cook time: 15 minutes | Serves 2

1 cup water
1 cup red wine
1 tablespoon sea salt
2 pork cutlets
¼ cup almond meal
¼ cup flaxseed meal
½ teaspoon baking powder

1 teaspoon shallot powder
½ teaspoon porcini powder
Sea salt and ground black pepper, to taste
1 egg
¼ cup yogurt
1 teaspoon brown mustard
⅓ cup Parmesan cheese, grated

1. In a large ceramic dish, combine the water, wine and salt. Add the pork cutlets and put for 1 hour in the refrigerator. 2. In a shallow bowl, mix the almond meal, flaxseed meal, baking powder, shallot powder, porcini powder, salt, and ground pepper. In another bowl, whisk the eggs with yogurt and mustard. 3. In a third bowl, place the grated Parmesan cheese. 4. Dip the pork cutlets in the seasoned flour mixture and toss evenly; then, in the egg mixture. Finally, roll them over the grated Parmesan cheese. 5. Spritz the bottom of the air fryer basket with cooking oil. Add the breaded pork cutlets and cook at 395ºF (202ºC) and for 10 minutes. 6. Flip and cook for 5 minutes more on the other side. Serve warm.

Teriyaki Rump Steak with Broccoli and Capsicum

Prep time: 5 minutes | Cook time: 13 minutes | Serves 4

½ pound (227 g) rump steak
⅓ cup teriyaki marinade
1½ teaspoons sesame oil
½ head broccoli, cut into florets

2 red capsicums, sliced
Fine sea salt and ground black pepper, to taste
Cooking spray

1. Toss the rump steak in a large bowl with teriyaki marinade. Wrap the bowl in plastic and refrigerate to marinate for at least an hour. 2. Preheat the air fryer to 400ºF (204ºC) and spritz with cooking spray. 3. Discard the marinade and transfer the steak in the preheated air fryer. Spritz with cooking spray. 4. Air fry for 13 minutes or until well browned. Flip the steak halfway through. 5. Meanwhile, heat the sesame oil in a nonstick skillet over medium heat. Add the broccoli and capsicum. Sprinkle with salt and ground black pepper. Sauté for 5 minutes or until the broccoli is tender. 6. Transfer the air fried rump steak on a plate and top with the sautéed broccoli and capsicum. Serve hot.

Chapter 5

Poultry

Chicken Paillard

Prep time: 10 minutes | Cook time: 10 minutes | Serves 2

2 large eggs, room temperature 1 tablespoon water ½ cup powdered Parmesan cheese (about 1½ ounces / 43 g) or pork dust 2 teaspoons dried thyme leaves 1 teaspoon ground black pepper 2 (5-ounce / 142-g) boneless,	skinless chicken breasts, pounded to ½ inch thick Lemon Butter Sauce: 2 tablespoons unsalted butter, melted 2 teaspoons lemon juice ¼ teaspoon finely chopped fresh thyme leaves, plus more for garnish ⅛ teaspoon fine sea salt Lemon slices, for serving

1. Spray the air fryer basket with avocado oil. Preheat the air fryer to 390ºF (199ºC). 2. Beat the eggs in a shallow dish, then add the water and stir well. 3. In a separate shallow dish, mix together the Parmesan, thyme, and pepper until well combined. 4. One at a time, dip the chicken breasts in the eggs and let any excess drip off, then dredge both sides of the chicken in the Parmesan mixture. As you finish, set the coated chicken in the air fryer basket. 5. Roast the chicken in the air fryer for 5 minutes, then flip the chicken and cook for another 5 minutes, or until cooked through and the internal temperature reaches 165ºF (74ºC). 6. While the chicken cooks, make the lemon butter sauce: In a small bowl, mix together all the sauce ingredients until well combined. 7. Plate the chicken and pour the sauce over it. Garnish with chopped fresh thyme and serve with lemon slices. 8. Store leftovers in an airtight container in the refrigerator for up to 4 days. Reheat in a preheated 390ºF (199ºC) air fryer for 5 minutes, or until heated through.

Chicken Croquettes with Creole Sauce

Prep time: 30 minutes | Cook time: 10 minutes | Serves 4

2 cups shredded cooked chicken ½ cup shredded Cheddar cheese 2 eggs ¼ cup finely chopped onion ¼ cup almond meal 1 tablespoon poultry seasoning	Olive oil Creole Sauce: ¼ cup mayonnaise ¼ cup sour cream 1½ teaspoons Dijon mustard 1½ teaspoons fresh lemon juice ½ teaspoon garlic powder ½ teaspoon Creole seasoning

1. In a large bowl, combine the chicken, Cheddar, eggs, onion, almond meal, and poultry seasoning. Stir gently until thoroughly combined. Cover and refrigerate for 30 minutes. 2. Meanwhile, to make the Creole sauce: In a small bowl, whisk together the mayonnaise, sour cream, Dijon mustard, lemon juice, garlic powder, and Creole seasoning until thoroughly combined. Cover and refrigerate until ready to serve. 3. Preheat the air fryer to 400ºF (204ºC). Divide the chicken mixture into 8 portions and shape into patties. 4. Working in batches if necessary, arrange the patties in a single layer in the air fryer basket and coat both sides lightly with olive oil. Pausing halfway through the cooking time to flip the patties, air fry for 10 minutes, or until lightly browned and the cheese is melted. Serve with the Creole sauce.

Tex-Mex Chicken Breasts

Prep time: 10 minutes | Cook time: 17 to 20 minutes | Serves 4

1 pound (454 g) low-sodium boneless, skinless chicken breasts, cut into 1-inch cubes 1 medium onion, chopped 1 red bell pepper, chopped 1 jalapeño pepper, minced	2 teaspoons olive oil ⅔ cup canned low-sodium black beans, rinsed and drained ½ cup low-sodium salsa 2 teaspoons chili powder

1. Preheat the air fryer to 400ºF (204ºC). 2. In a medium metal bowl, mix the chicken, onion, bell pepper, jalapeño, and olive oil. Roast for 10 minutes, stirring once during cooking. 3. Add the black beans, salsa, and chili powder. Roast for 7 to 10 minutes more, stirring once, until the chicken reaches an internal temperature of 165ºF (74ºC) on a meat thermometer. Serve immediately.

Cranberry Curry Chicken

Prep time: 12 minutes | Cook time: 18 minutes | Serves 4

3 (5-ounce / 142-g) low-sodium boneless, skinless chicken breasts, cut into 1½-inch cubes 2 teaspoons olive oil 2 tablespoons cornstarch 1 tablespoon curry powder 1 tart apple, chopped	½ cup low-sodium chicken broth ⅓ cup dried cranberries 2 tablespoons freshly squeezed orange juice Brown rice, cooked (optional)

1. Preheat the air fryer to 380ºF (193ºC). 2. In a medium bowl, mix the chicken and olive oil. Sprinkle with the cornstarch and curry powder. Toss to coat. Stir in the apple and transfer to a metal pan. Bake in the air fryer for 8 minutes, stirring once during cooking. 3. Add the chicken broth, cranberries, and orange juice. Bake for about 10 minutes more, or until the sauce is slightly thickened and the chicken reaches an internal temperature of 165ºF (74ºC) on a meat thermometer. Serve over hot cooked brown rice, if desired.

Butter and Bacon Chicken

Prep time: 10 minutes | Cook time: 65 minutes | Serves 6

1 (4-pound / 1.8-kg) whole chicken 2 tablespoons salted butter, softened 1 teaspoon dried thyme	½ teaspoon garlic powder 1 teaspoon salt ½ teaspoon ground black pepper 6 slices sugar-free bacon

1. Pat chicken dry with a paper towel, then rub with butter on all sides. Sprinkle thyme, garlic powder, salt, and pepper over chicken. 2. Place chicken into ungreased air fryer basket, breast side up. Lay strips of bacon over chicken and secure with toothpicks. 3. Adjust the temperature to 350ºF (177ºC) and air fry for 65 minutes. Halfway through cooking, remove and set aside bacon and flip chicken over. Chicken will be done when the skin is golden and crispy and the internal temperature is at least 165ºF (74ºC). Serve warm with bacon.

Chicken with Pineapple and Peach

Prep time: 10 minutes | Cook time: 14 to 15 minutes | Serves 4

1 pound (454 g) low-sodium boneless, skinless chicken breasts, cut into 1-inch pieces 1 medium red onion, chopped 1 (8-ounce / 227-g) can pineapple chunks, drained, ¼ cup juice reserved 1 tablespoon peanut oil or	safflower oil 1 peach, peeled, pitted, and cubed 1 tablespoon cornstarch ½ teaspoon ground ginger ¼ teaspoon ground allspice Brown rice, cooked (optional)

1. Preheat the air fryer to 380ºF (193ºC). 2. In a medium metal bowl, mix the chicken, red onion, pineapple, and peanut oil. Bake in the air fryer for 9 minutes. Remove and stir. 3. Add the peach and return the bowl to the air fryer. Bake for 3 minutes more. Remove and stir again. 4. In a small bowl, whisk the reserved pineapple juice, the cornstarch, ginger, and allspice well. Add to the chicken mixture and stir to combine. 5. Bake for 2 to 3 minutes more, or until the chicken reaches an internal temperature of 165ºF (74ºC) on a meat thermometer and the sauce is slightly thickened. 6. Serve immediately over hot cooked brown rice, if desired.

Chicken Thighs in Waffles

Prep time: 1 hour 20 minutes | Cook time: 40 minutes | Serves 4

For the chicken: 4 chicken thighs, skin on 1 cup low-fat buttermilk ½ cup all-purpose flour ½ teaspoon garlic powder ½ teaspoon mustard powder 1 teaspoon kosher salt ½ teaspoon freshly ground black pepper ¼ cup honey, for serving Cooking spray	For the waffles: ½ cup all-purpose flour ½ cup whole wheat pastry flour 1 large egg, beaten 1 cup low-fat buttermilk 1 teaspoon baking powder 2 tablespoons canola oil ½ teaspoon kosher salt 1 tablespoon granulated sugar

1. Combine the chicken thighs with buttermilk in a large bowl. Wrap the bowl in plastic and refrigerate to marinate for at least an hour. 2. Preheat the air fryer to 360ºF (182ºC). Spritz the air fryer basket with cooking spray. 3. Combine the flour, mustard powder, garlic powder, salt, and black pepper in a shallow dish. Stir to mix well. 4. Remove the thighs from the buttermilk and pat dry with paper towels. Sit the bowl of buttermilk aside. 5. Dip the thighs in the flour mixture first, then into the buttermilk, and then into the flour mixture. Shake the excess off. 6. Arrange 2 thighs in the preheated air fryer and spritz with cooking spray. Air fryer for 20 minutes or until an instant-read thermometer inserted in the thickest part of the chicken thighs registers at least 165ºF (74ºC). flip the thighs halfway through. Repeat with remaining thighs. 7. Meanwhile, make the waffles: combine the ingredients for the waffles in a large bowl. Stir to mix well, then arrange the mixture in a waffle iron and cook until a golden and fragrant waffle forms. 8. Remove the waffles from the waffle iron and slice into 4 pieces. Remove the chicken thighs from the air fryer and allow to cool for 5 minutes. 9. Arrange each chicken thigh on each waffle piece and

drizzle with 1 tablespoon of honey. Serve warm.

Bell Pepper Stuffed Chicken Roll-Ups

Prep time: 10 minutes | Cook time: 12 minutes | Serves 4

2 (4-ounce / 113-g) boneless, skinless chicken breasts, slice in half horizontally 1 tablespoon olive oil Juice of ½ lime 2 tablespoons taco seasoning	½ green bell pepper, cut into strips ½ red bell pepper, cut into strips ¼ onion, sliced

1. Preheat the air fryer to 400ºF (204ºC). 2. Unfold the chicken breast slices on a clean work surface. Rub with olive oil, then drizzle with lime juice and sprinkle with taco seasoning. 3. Top the chicken slices with equal amount of bell peppers and onion. Roll them up and secure with toothpicks. 4. Arrange the chicken roll-ups in the preheated air fryer. Air fry for 12 minutes or until the internal temperature of the chicken reaches at least 165ºF (74ºC). Flip the chicken roll-ups halfway through. 5. Remove the chicken from the air fryer. Discard the toothpicks and serve immediately.

Italian Crispy Chicken

Prep time: 10 minutes | Cook time: 20 minutes | Serves 4

2 (4-ounce / 113-g) boneless, skinless chicken breasts 2 egg whites, beaten 1 cup Italian bread crumbs ½ cup grated Parmesan cheese 2 teaspoons Italian seasoning	Salt and freshly ground black pepper, to taste Cooking oil spray ¾ cup marinara sauce ½ cup shredded Mozzarella cheese

1. With your knife blade parallel to the cutting board, cut the chicken breasts in half horizontally to create 4 thin cutlets. On a solid surface, pound the cutlets to flatten them. You can use your hands, a rolling pin, a kitchen mallet, or a meat hammer. 2. Pour the egg whites into a bowl large enough to dip the chicken. 3. In another bowl large enough to dip a chicken cutlet in, stir together the bread crumbs, Parmesan cheese, and Italian seasoning, and season with salt and pepper. 4. Dip each cutlet into the egg whites and into the breadcrumb mixture to coat. 5. Insert the crisper plate into the basket and the basket into the unit. Preheat the unit by selecting AIR FRY, setting the temperature to 375ºF (191ºC), and setting the time to 3 minutes. Select START/STOP to begin. 6. Once the unit is preheated, spray the crisper plate with cooking oil. Working in batches, place 2 chicken cutlets into the basket. Spray the top of the chicken with cooking oil. 7. Select AIR FRY, set the temperature to 375ºF (191ºC), and set the time to 7 minutes. Select START/STOP to begin. 8. When the cooking is complete, repeat steps 6 and 7 with the remaining cutlets. 9. Top the chicken cutlets with the marinara sauce and shredded Mozzarella cheese. If the chicken will fit into the basket without stacking, you can prepare all 4 at once. Otherwise, do this 2 cutlets at a time. 10. Select AIR FRY, set the temperature to 375ºF (191ºC), and set the time to 3 minutes. Select START/STOP to begin. 11. The cooking is complete when the cheese is melted and the chicken reaches an internal temperature of 165ºF (74ºC). Cool for 5 minutes before serving.

Bacon-Wrapped Stuffed Chicken Breasts

Prep time: 15 minutes | Cook time: 30 minutes | Serves 4

½ cup chopped frozen spinach, thawed and squeezed dry	½ teaspoon kosher salt
	1 teaspoon black pepper
¼ cup cream cheese, softened	2 large boneless, skinless chicken breasts, butterflied and pounded to ½-inch thickness
¼ cup grated Parmesan cheese	
1 jalapeño, seeded and chopped	4 teaspoons salt-free Cajun seasoning
	6 slices bacon

1. In a small bowl, combine the spinach, cream cheese, Parmesan cheese, jalapeño, salt, and pepper. Stir until well combined. 2. Place the butterflied chicken breasts on a flat surface. Spread the cream cheese mixture evenly across each piece of chicken. Starting with the narrow end, roll up each chicken breast, ensuring the filling stays inside. Season chicken with the Cajun seasoning, patting it in to ensure it sticks to the meat. 3. Wrap each breast in 3 slices of bacon. Place in the air fryer basket. Set the air fryer to 350ºF (177ºC) for 30 minutes. Use a meat thermometer to ensure the chicken has reached an internal temperature of 165ºF (74ºC). 4. Let the chicken stand 5 minutes before slicing each rolled-up breast in half to serve.

Thai Game Hens with Cucumber and Chile Salad

Prep time: 25 minutes | Cook time: 25 minutes | Serves 6

2 (1¼-pound / 567-g) Cornish game hens, giblets discarded	Salt and ground black pepper, to taste
	1 English cucumber, halved lengthwise and sliced thin
1 tablespoon fish sauce	
6 tablespoons chopped fresh cilantro	1 Thai chile, stemmed, deseeded, and minced
2 teaspoons lime zest	2 tablespoons chopped dry-roasted peanuts
1 teaspoon ground coriander	
2 garlic cloves, minced	1 small shallot, sliced thinly
2 tablespoons packed light brown sugar	1 tablespoon lime juice
	Lime wedges, for serving
2 teaspoons vegetable oil	Cooking spray

1. Arrange a game hen on a clean work surface, remove the backbone with kitchen shears, then pound the hen breast to flat. Cut the breast in half. Repeat with the remaining game hen. 2. Loose the breast and thigh skin with your fingers, then pat the game hens dry and pierce about 10 holes into the fat deposits of the hens. Tuck the wings under the hens. 3. Combine 2 teaspoons of fish sauce, ¼ cup of cilantro, lime zest, coriander, garlic, 4 teaspoons of sugar, 1 teaspoon of vegetable oil, ½ teaspoon of salt, and ⅛ teaspoon of ground black pepper in a small bowl. Stir to mix well. 4. Rub the fish sauce mixture under the breast and thigh skin of the game hens, then let sit for 10 minutes to marinate. 5. Preheat the air fryer to 400ºF (204ºC). Spritz the air fryer basket with cooking spray. 6. Arrange the marinated game hens in the preheated air fryer, skin side down. 7. Air fry for 15 minutes, then gently turn the game hens over and air fry for 10 more minutes

or until the skin is golden brown and the internal temperature of the hens reads at least 165ºF (74ºC). 8. Meanwhile, combine all the remaining ingredients, except for the lime wedges, in a large bowl and sprinkle with salt and black pepper. Toss to mix well. 9. Transfer the fried hens on a large plate, then sit the salad aside and squeeze the lime wedges over before serving.

Chicken Cordon Bleu

Prep time: 20 minutes | Cook time: 15 to 20 minutes | Serves 4

4 small boneless, skinless chicken breasts	(about 3 to 4 inches square)
	2 tablespoons olive oil
Salt and pepper, to taste	2 teaspoons marjoram
4 slices deli ham	¼ teaspoon paprika
4 slices deli Swiss cheese	

1. Split each chicken breast horizontally almost in two, leaving one edge intact. 2. Lay breasts open flat and sprinkle with salt and pepper to taste. 3. Place a ham slice on top of each chicken breast. 4. Cut cheese slices in half and place one half atop each breast. Set aside remaining halves of cheese slices. 5. Roll up chicken breasts to enclose cheese and ham and secure with toothpicks. 6. Mix together the olive oil, marjoram, and paprika. Rub all over outsides of chicken breasts. 7. Place chicken in air fryer basket and air fry at 360ºF (182ºC) for 15 to 20 minutes, until well done and juices run clear. 8. Remove all toothpicks. To avoid burns, place chicken breasts on a plate to remove toothpicks, then immediately return them to the air fryer basket. 9. Place a half cheese slice on top of each chicken breast and cook for a minute or so just to melt cheese.

Barbecued Chicken with Creamy Coleslaw

Prep time: 10 minutes | Cook time: 20 minutes | Serves 2

3 cups shredded coleslaw mix	sauce, plus extra for serving
	2 tablespoons mayonnaise
Salt and pepper	2 tablespoons sour cream
2 (12-ounce / 340-g) bone-in split chicken breasts, trimmed	1 teaspoon distilled white vinegar, plus extra for seasoning
1 teaspoon vegetable oil	¼ teaspoon sugar
2 tablespoons barbecue	

1. Preheat the air fryer to 350ºF (177ºC). 2. Toss coleslaw mix and ¼ teaspoon salt in a colander set over bowl. Let sit until wilted slightly, about 30 minutes. Rinse, drain, and dry well with a dish towel. 3. Meanwhile, pat chicken dry with paper towels, rub with oil, and season with salt and pepper. Arrange breasts skin-side down in air fryer basket, spaced evenly apart, alternating ends. Bake for 10 minutes. Flip breasts and brush skin side with barbecue sauce. Return basket to air fryer and bake until well browned and chicken registers 160ºF (71ºC), 10 to 15 minutes. 4. Transfer chicken to serving platter, tent loosely with aluminum foil, and let rest for 5 minutes. While chicken rests, whisk mayonnaise, sour cream, vinegar, sugar, and pinch pepper together in a large bowl. Stir in coleslaw mix and season with salt, pepper, and additional vinegar to taste. Serve chicken with coleslaw, passing extra barbecue sauce separately.

Chicken with Lettuce

Prep time: 15 minutes | Cook time: 14 minutes | Serves 4

1 pound (454 g) chicken breast tenders, chopped into bite-size pieces	and thinly sliced
	1 tablespoon olive oil
½ onion, thinly sliced	1 tablespoon fajita seasoning
½ red bell pepper, seeded and thinly sliced	1 teaspoon kosher salt
	Juice of ½ lime
½ green bell pepper, seeded	8 large lettuce leaves
	1 cup prepared guacamole

1. Preheat the air fryer to 400ºF (204ºC). 2. In a large bowl, combine the chicken, onion, and peppers. Drizzle with the olive oil and toss until thoroughly coated. Add the fajita seasoning and salt and toss again. 3. Working in batches if necessary, arrange the chicken and vegetables in a single layer in the air fryer basket. Pausing halfway through the cooking time to shake the basket, air fry for 14 minutes, or until the vegetables are tender and a thermometer inserted into the thickest piece of chicken registers 165ºF (74ºC). 4. Transfer the mixture to a serving platter and drizzle with the fresh lime juice. Serve with the lettuce leaves and top with the guacamole.

Chicken Rochambeau

Prep time: 15 minutes | Cook time: 20 minutes | Serves 4

1 tablespoon butter	Sauce:
4 chicken tenders, cut in half crosswise	2 tablespoons butter
	½ cup chopped green onions
Salt and pepper, to taste	½ cup chopped mushrooms
¼ cup flour	2 tablespoons flour
Oil for misting	1 cup chicken broth
4 slices ham, ¼- to ⅜-inches thick and large enough to cover an English muffin	¼ teaspoon garlic powder
	1½ teaspoons Worcestershire sauce
2 English muffins, split	

1. Place 1 tablespoon of butter in a baking pan and air fry at 390ºF (199ºC) for 2 minutes to melt. 2. Sprinkle chicken tenders with salt and pepper to taste, then roll in the ¼ cup of flour. 3. Place chicken in baking pan, turning pieces to coat with melted butter. 4. Air fry at 390ºF (199ºC) for 5 minutes. Turn chicken pieces over, and spray tops lightly with olive oil. Cook 5 minutes longer or until juices run clear. The chicken will not brown. 5. While chicken is cooking, make the sauce: In a medium saucepan, melt the 2 tablespoons of butter. 6. Add onions and mushrooms and sauté until tender, about 3 minutes. 7. Stir in the flour. Gradually add broth, stirring constantly until you have a smooth gravy. 8. Add garlic powder and Worcestershire sauce and simmer on low heat until sauce thickens, about 5 minutes. 9. When chicken is cooked, remove baking pan from air fryer and set aside. 10. Place ham slices directly into air fryer basket and air fry at 390ºF (199ºC) for 5 minutes or until hot and beginning to sizzle a little. Remove and set aside on top of the chicken for now. 11. Place the English muffin halves in air fryer basket and air fry at 390ºF (199ºC) for 1 minute. 12. Open air fryer and place a ham slice on top of each English muffin half. Stack 2 pieces of chicken on top of each ham slice. Air fry for 1 to 2 minutes to heat through. 13.

Place each English muffin stack on a serving plate and top with plenty of sauce.

African Piri-Piri Chicken Drumsticks

Prep time: 30 minutes | Cook time: 20 minutes | Serves 2

Chicken:	1 teaspoon smoked paprika
1 tablespoon chopped fresh thyme leaves	½ teaspoon kosher salt
	½ teaspoon black pepper
1 tablespoon minced fresh ginger	4 chicken drumsticks
	Glaze:
1 small shallot, finely chopped	2 tablespoons butter or ghee
2 garlic cloves, minced	1 teaspoon chopped fresh thyme leaves
⅓ cup piri-piri sauce or hot sauce	1 garlic clove, minced
	1 tablespoon piri-piri sauce
3 tablespoons extra-virgin olive oil	1 tablespoon fresh lemon juice
Zest and juice of 1 lemon	

1. For the chicken: In a small bowl, stir together all the ingredients except the chicken. Place the chicken and the marinade in a gallon-size resealable plastic bag. Seal the bag and massage to coat. Refrigerate for at least 2 hours or up to 24 hours, turning the bag occasionally. 2. Place the chicken legs in the air fryer basket. Set the air fryer to 400ºF (204ºC) for 20 minutes, turning the chicken halfway through the cooking time. 3. Meanwhile, for the glaze: Melt the butter in a small saucepan over medium-high heat. Add the thyme and garlic. Cook, stirring, until the garlic just begins to brown, 1 to 2 minutes. Add the piri-piri sauce and lemon juice. Reduce the heat to medium-low and simmer for 1 to 2 minutes. 4. Transfer the chicken to a serving platter. Pour the glaze over the chicken. Serve immediately.

Thanksgiving Turkey Breast

Prep time: 5 minutes | Cook time: 30 minutes | Serves 4

1½ teaspoons fine sea salt	tarragon
1 teaspoon ground black pepper	1 teaspoon chopped fresh thyme leaves
1 teaspoon chopped fresh rosemary leaves	1 (2-pound / 907-g) turkey breast
1 teaspoon chopped fresh sage	3 tablespoons ghee or unsalted butter, melted
1 teaspoon chopped fresh	3 tablespoons Dijon mustard

1. Spray the air fryer with avocado oil. Preheat the air fryer to 390ºF (199ºC). 2. In a small bowl, stir together the salt, pepper, and herbs until well combined. Season the turkey breast generously on all sides with the seasoning. 3. In another small bowl, stir together the ghee and Dijon. Brush the ghee mixture on all sides of the turkey breast. 4. Place the turkey breast in the air fryer basket and air fry for 30 minutes, or until the internal temperature reaches 165ºF (74ºC). Transfer the breast to a cutting board and allow it to rest for 10 minutes before cutting it into ½-inch-thick slices. 5. Store leftovers in an airtight container in the refrigerator for up to 4 days or in the freezer for up to a month. Reheat in a preheated 350ºF (177ºC) air fryer for 4 minutes, or until warmed through.

Breaded Turkey Cutlets

Prep time: 5 minutes | Cook time: 8 minutes | Serves 4

½ cup whole wheat bread crumbs	⅛ teaspoon garlic powder
¼ teaspoon paprika	1 egg
¼ teaspoon salt	4 turkey breast cutlets
¼ teaspoon black pepper	Chopped fresh parsley, for serving
⅛ teaspoon dried sage	

1. Preheat the air fryer to 380°F(193ºC). 2. In a medium shallow bowl, whisk together the bread crumbs, paprika, salt, black pepper, sage, and garlic powder. 3. In a separate medium shallow bowl, whisk the egg until frothy. 4. Dip each turkey cutlet into the egg mixture, then into the bread crumb mixture, coating the outside with the crumbs. Place the breaded turkey cutlets in a single layer in the bottom of the air fryer basket, making sure that they don't touch each other. 5. Bake for 4 minutes. Turn the cutlets over, then bake for 4 minutes more, or until the internal temperature reaches 165°F(74ºC). Sprinkle on the parsley and serve.

Garlic Parmesan Drumsticks

Prep time: 5 minutes | Cook time: 25 minutes | Serves 4

8 (4-ounce / 113-g) chicken drumsticks	2 tablespoons salted butter, melted
½ teaspoon salt	½ cup grated Parmesan cheese
⅛ teaspoon ground black pepper	1 tablespoon dried parsley
½ teaspoon garlic powder	

1. Sprinkle drumsticks with salt, pepper, and garlic powder. Place drumsticks into ungreased air fryer basket. 2. Adjust the temperature to 400ºF (204ºC) and air fry for 25 minutes, turning drumsticks halfway through cooking. Drumsticks will be golden and have an internal temperature of at least 165ºF (74ºC) when done. 3. Transfer drumsticks to a large serving dish. Pour butter over drumsticks, and sprinkle with Parmesan and parsley. Serve warm.

Sweet and Spicy Turkey Meatballs

Prep time: 15 minutes | Cook time: 15 minutes | Serves 6

Olive oil	¼ cup plus 1 tablespoon hoisin sauce, divided
1 pound (454 g) lean ground turkey	2 teaspoons minced garlic
½ cup whole-wheat panko bread crumbs	⅛ teaspoon salt
1 egg, beaten	⅛ teaspoon freshly ground black pepper
1 tablespoon soy sauce	1 teaspoon Sriracha

1. Spray the air fryer basket lightly with olive oil. 2. In a large bowl, mix together the turkey, panko bread crumbs, egg, soy sauce, 1 tablespoon of hoisin sauce, garlic, salt, and black pepper. 3. Using a tablespoon, form 24 meatballs. 4. In a small bowl, combine the remaining ¼ cup of hoisin sauce and Sriracha to make a glaze and set aside. 5. Place the meatballs in the air fryer basket in a single layer. You may need to cook them in batches. 6. Air fry at 350ºF (177ºC) for 8 minutes. Brush the meatballs generously with the glaze and cook until cooked through, an additional 4 to 7 minutes.

Crispy Duck with Cherry Sauce

Prep time: 10 minutes | Cook time: 33 minutes | Serves 2 to 4

1 whole duck (up to 5 pounds / 2.3 kg), split in half, back and rib bones removed	½ cup sherry
1 teaspoon olive oil	¾ cup cherry preserves
Salt and freshly ground black pepper, to taste	1 cup chicken stock
Cherry Sauce:	1 teaspoon white wine vinegar
1 tablespoon butter	1 teaspoon fresh thyme leaves
1 shallot, minced	Salt and freshly ground black pepper, to taste

1. Preheat the air fryer to 400ºF (204ºC). 2. Trim some of the fat from the duck. Rub olive oil on the duck and season with salt and pepper. Place the duck halves in the air fryer basket, breast side up and facing the center of the basket. 3. Air fry the duck for 20 minutes. Turn the duck over and air fry for another 6 minutes. 4. While duck is air frying, make the cherry sauce. Melt the butter in a large sauté pan. Add the shallot and sauté until it is just starting to brown, about 2 to 3 minutes. Add the sherry and deglaze the pan by scraping up any brown bits from the bottom of the pan. Simmer the liquid for a few minutes, until it has reduced by half. Add the cherry preserves, chicken stock and white wine vinegar. Whisk well to combine all the ingredients. Simmer the sauce until it thickens and coats the back of a spoon, about 5 to 7 minutes. Season with salt and pepper and stir in the fresh thyme leaves. 5. When the air fryer timer goes off, spoon some cherry sauce over the duck and continue to air fry at 400ºF (204ºC) for 4 more minutes. Then, turn the duck halves back over so that the breast side is facing up. Spoon more cherry sauce over the top of the duck, covering the skin completely. Air fry for 3 more minutes and then remove the duck to a plate to rest for a few minutes. 6. Serve the duck in halves, or cut each piece in half again for a smaller serving. Spoon any additional sauce over the duck or serve it on the side.

Lemon-Basil Turkey Breasts

Prep time: 30 minutes | Cook time: 58 minutes | Serves 4

2 tablespoons olive oil	1 teaspoon fresh basil leaves, chopped
2 pounds (907 g) turkey breasts, bone-in, skin-on	2 tablespoons lemon zest, grated
Coarse sea salt and ground black pepper, to taste	

1. Rub olive oil on all sides of the turkey breasts; sprinkle with salt, pepper, basil, and lemon zest. 2. Place the turkey breasts skin side up on the parchment-lined air fryer basket. 3. Cook in the preheated air fryer at 330ºF (166ºC) for 30 minutes. Now, turn them over and cook an additional 28 minutes. 4. Serve with lemon wedges, if desired. Bon appétit!

Nice Goulash

Prep time: 5 minutes | Cook time: 17 minutes | Serves 2

2 red bell peppers, chopped 1 pound (454 g) ground chicken 2 medium tomatoes, diced	½ cup chicken broth Salt and ground black pepper, to taste Cooking spray

1. Preheat the air fryer to 365°F (185°C). Spritz a baking pan with cooking spray. 2. Set the bell pepper in the baking pan and put in the air fry to broil for 5 minutes or until the bell pepper is tender. Shake the basket halfway through. 3. Add the ground chicken and diced tomatoes in the baking pan and stir to mix well. Broil for 6 more minutes or until the chicken is lightly browned. 4. Pour the chicken broth over and sprinkle with salt and ground black pepper. Stir to mix well. Broil for an additional 6 minutes. 5. Serve immediately.

Lemon Chicken

Prep time: 5 minutes | Cook time: 20 to 25 minutes | Serves 4

8 bone-in chicken thighs, skin on 1 tablespoon olive oil 1½ teaspoons lemon-pepper seasoning	½ teaspoon paprika ½ teaspoon garlic powder ¼ teaspoon freshly ground black pepper Juice of ½ lemon

1. Preheat the air fryer to 360°F (182°C). 2. Place the chicken in a large bowl and drizzle with the olive oil. Top with the lemon-pepper seasoning, paprika, garlic powder, and freshly ground black pepper. Toss until thoroughly coated. 3. Working in batches if necessary, arrange the chicken in a single layer in the basket of the air fryer. Pausing halfway through the cooking time to turn the chicken, air fry for 20 to 25 minutes, until a thermometer inserted into the thickest piece registers 165°F (74°C). 4. Transfer the chicken to a serving platter and squeeze the lemon juice over the top.

Jalapeño Chicken Balls

Prep time: 10 minutes | Cook time: 25 minutes | Serves 4

1 medium red onion, minced 2 garlic cloves, minced 1 jalapeño pepper, minced 2 teaspoons extra-virgin olive oil 3 tablespoons ground	almonds 1 egg 1 teaspoon dried thyme 1 pound (454 g) ground chicken breast Cooking oil spray

1. Insert the crisper plate into the basket and the basket into the unit. Preheat the unit by selecting BAKE, setting the temperature to 400°F (204°C), and setting the time to 3 minutes. Select START/STOP to begin. 2. In a 6-by-2-inch round pan, combine the red onion, garlic, jalapeño, and olive oil. 3. Once the unit is preheated, place the pan into the basket. 4. Select BAKE, set the temperature to 400°F (204°C), and set the time to 4 minutes. Select START/STOP to begin. 5. When the cooking is complete, the vegetables should be crisp-tender. Transfer to a medium bowl. 6. Mix the almonds, egg, and thyme into the vegetable mixture. Add the chicken and mix until just combined. Form the chicken mixture into about 24 (1-inch) balls. 7. Insert the crisper plate into the basket and the basket into the unit. Preheat the unit by selecting BAKE, setting the temperature to 400°F (204°C), and setting the time to 3 minutes. Select START/STOP to begin. 8. Once the unit is preheated, spray the crisper plate with cooking oil. Working in batches, place half the meatballs in a single layer, not touching, into the basket. 9. Select BAKE, set the temperature to 400°F (204°C), and set the time to 10 minutes. Select START/STOP to begin. 10. When the cooking is complete, a food thermometer inserted into the meatballs should register at least 165°F (74°C). 11. Repeat steps 8 and 9 with the remaining meatballs. Serve warm.

Thai-Style Cornish Game Hens

Prep time: 30 minutes | Cook time: 20 minutes | Serves 4

1 cup chopped fresh cilantro leaves and stems ¼ cup fish sauce 1 tablespoon soy sauce 1 serrano chile, seeded and chopped 8 garlic cloves, smashed 2 tablespoons sugar 2 tablespoons lemongrass	paste 2 teaspoons black pepper 2 teaspoons ground coriander 1 teaspoon kosher salt 1 teaspoon ground turmeric 2 Cornish game hens, giblets removed, split in half lengthwise

1. In a blender, combine the cilantro, fish sauce, soy sauce, serrano, garlic, sugar, lemongrass, black pepper, coriander, salt, and turmeric. Blend until smooth. 2. Place the game hen halves in a large bowl. Pour the cilantro mixture over the hen halves and toss to coat. Marinate at room temperature for 30 minutes, or cover and refrigerate for up to 24 hours. 3. Arrange the hen halves in a single layer in the air fryer basket. Set the air fryer to 400°F (204°C) for 20 minutes. Use a meat thermometer to ensure the game hens have reached an internal temperature of 165°F (74°C).

Easy Chicken Fingers

Prep time: 20 minutes | Cook time: 30 minutes | Makes 12 chicken fingers

½ cup all-purpose flour 2 cups panko breadcrumbs 2 tablespoons canola oil 1 large egg 3 boneless and skinless	chicken breasts, each cut into 4 strips Kosher salt and freshly ground black pepper, to taste Cooking spray

1. Preheat the air fryer to 360°F (182°C). Spritz the air fryer basket with cooking spray. 2. Pour the flour in a large bowl. Combine the panko and canola oil on a shallow dish. Whisk the egg in a separate bowl. 3. Rub the chicken strips with salt and ground black pepper on a clean work surface, then dip the chicken in the bowl of flour. Shake the excess off and dunk the chicken strips in the bowl of whisked egg, then roll the strips over the panko to coat well. 4. Arrange 4 strips in the air fryer basket each time and air fry for 10 minutes or until crunchy and lightly browned. Flip the strips halfway through. Repeat with remaining ingredients. 5. Serve immediately.

Herbed Roast Chicken Breast

Prep time: 10 minutes | Cook time: 25 minutes | Serves 2 to 4

2 tablespoons salted butter or ghee, at room temperature 1 teaspoon dried Italian seasoning, crushed ½ teaspoon kosher salt ½ teaspoon smoked paprika	¼ teaspoon black pepper 2 bone-in, skin-on chicken breast halves (about 10 ounces / 283 g each) Lemon wedges, for serving

1. In a small bowl, stir together the butter, Italian seasoning, salt, paprika, and pepper until thoroughly combined. 2. Using a small sharp knife, carefully loosen the skin on each chicken breast half, starting at the thin end of each. Very carefully separate the skin from the flesh, leaving the skin attached at the thick end of each breast. Divide the herb butter into quarters. Rub one-quarter of the butter onto the flesh of each breast. Fold and lightly press the skin back onto each breast. Rub the remaining butter onto the skin of each breast. 3. Place the chicken in the air fryer basket. Set the air fryer to 375ºF (191ºC) for 25 minutes. Use a meat thermometer to ensure the chicken breasts have reached an internal temperature of 165ºF (74ºC). 4. Transfer the chicken to a cutting board. Lightly cover with aluminum foil and let rest for 5 to 10 minutes. 5. Serve with lemon wedges.

Spinach and Feta Stuffed Chicken Breasts

Prep time: 10 minutes | Cook time: 27 minutes | Serves 4

1 (10-ounce / 283-g) package frozen spinach, thawed and drained well 1 cup feta cheese, crumbled ½ teaspoon freshly ground	black pepper 4 boneless chicken breasts Salt and freshly ground black pepper, to taste 1 tablespoon olive oil

1. Prepare the filling. Squeeze out as much liquid as possible from the thawed spinach. Rough chop the spinach and transfer it to a mixing bowl with the feta cheese and the freshly ground black pepper. 2. Prepare the chicken breast. Place the chicken breast on a cutting board and press down on the chicken breast with one hand to keep it stabilized. Make an incision about 1-inch long in the fattest side of the breast. Move the knife up and down inside the chicken breast, without poking through either the top or the bottom, or the other side of the breast. The inside pocket should be about 3-inches long, but the opening should only be about 1-inch wide. If this is too difficult, you can make the incision longer, but you will have to be more careful when cooking the chicken breast since this will expose more of the stuffing. 3. Once you have prepared the chicken breasts, use your fingers to stuff the filling into each pocket, spreading the mixture down as far as you can. 4. Preheat the air fryer to 380ºF (193ºC). 5. Lightly brush or spray the air fryer basket and the chicken breasts with olive oil. Transfer two of the stuffed chicken breasts to the air fryer. Air fry for 12 minutes, turning the chicken breasts over halfway through the cooking time. Remove the chicken to a resting plate and air fry the second two breasts for 12 minutes. Return the first batch of chicken to the air fryer with the second batch and air fry for 3 more minutes. When the chicken is cooked, an instant read thermometer should register 165ºF (74ºC) in the thickest part of the chicken, as

well as in the stuffing. 6. Remove the chicken breasts and let them rest on a cutting board for 2 to 3 minutes. Slice the chicken on the bias and serve with the slices fanned out.

Crunchy Chicken with Roasted Carrots

Prep time: 10 minutes | Cook time: 22 minutes | Serves 4

4 bone-in, skin-on chicken thighs 2 carrots, cut into 2-inch pieces 2 tablespoons extra-virgin olive oil	2 teaspoons poultry spice 1 teaspoon sea salt, divided 2 teaspoons chopped fresh rosemary leaves Cooking oil spray 2 cups cooked white rice

1. Brush the chicken thighs and carrots with olive oil. Sprinkle both with the poultry spice, salt, and rosemary. 2. Insert the crisper plate into the basket and the basket into the unit. Preheat the unit by selecting AIR FRY, setting the temperature to 400ºF (204ºC), and setting the time to 3 minutes. Select START/STOP to begin. 3. Once the unit is preheated, spray the crisper plate with cooking oil. Place the carrots into the basket. Add the wire rack and arrange the chicken thighs on the rack. 4. Select AIR FRY, set the temperature to 400ºF (204ºC), and set the time to 20 minutes. Select START/STOP to begin. 5. When the cooking is complete, check the chicken temperature. If a food thermometer inserted into the chicken registers 165ºF (74ºC), remove the chicken from the air fryer, place it on a clean plate, and cover with aluminum foil to keep warm. Otherwise, resume cooking for 1 to 2 minutes longer. 6. The carrots can cook for 18 to 22 minutes and will be tender and caramelized; cooking time isn't as crucial for root vegetables. 7. Serve the chicken and carrots with the hot cooked rice.

Chicken Enchiladas

Prep time: 10 minutes | Cook time: 8 minutes | Serves 4

Oil, for spraying 3 cups shredded cooked chicken 1 package taco seasoning 8 flour tortillas, at room temperature ½ cup canned black beans,	rinsed and drained 1 (4-ounce / 113-g) can diced green chiles, drained 1 (10-ounce / 283-g) can red or green enchilada sauce 1 cup shredded Cheddar cheese

1. Line the air fryer basket with parchment and spray lightly with oil. (Do not skip the step of lining the basket; the parchment will keep the sauce and cheese from dripping through the holes.) 2. In a small bowl, mix together the chicken and taco seasoning. 3. Divide the mixture among the tortillas. Top with the black beans and green chiles. Carefully roll up each tortilla. 4. Place the enchiladas, seam-side down, in the prepared basket. You may need to work in batches, depending on the size of your air fryer. 5. Spoon the enchilada sauce over the enchiladas. Use just enough sauce to keep them from drying out. You can add more sauce when serving. Sprinkle the cheese on top. 6. Air fry at 360ºF (182ºC) for 5 to 8 minutes, or until heated through and the cheese is melted. 7. Place 2 enchiladas on each plate and top with more enchilada sauce, if desired.

Chicken Legs with Leeks

Prep time: 30 minutes | Cook time: 18 minutes | Serves 6

2 leeks, sliced 2 large-sized tomatoes, chopped 3 cloves garlic, minced ½ teaspoon dried oregano 6 chicken legs, boneless and	skinless ½ teaspoon smoked cayenne pepper 2 tablespoons olive oil A freshly ground nutmeg

1. In a mixing dish, thoroughly combine all ingredients, minus the leeks. Place in the refrigerator and let it marinate overnight. 2. Lay the leeks onto the bottom of the air fryer basket. Top with the chicken legs. 3. Roast chicken legs at 375°F (191°C) for 18 minutes, turning halfway through. Serve with hoisin sauce.

Chicken with Bacon and Tomato

Prep time: 25 minutes | Cook time: 10 minutes | Serves 4

4 medium-sized skin-on chicken drumsticks 1½ teaspoons herbs de Provence Salt and pepper, to taste 1 tablespoon rice vinegar 2 tablespoons olive oil	2 garlic cloves, crushed 12 ounces (340 g) crushed canned tomatoes 1 small-size leek, thinly sliced 2 slices smoked bacon, chopped

1. Sprinkle the chicken drumsticks with herbs de Provence, salt and pepper; then, drizzle them with rice vinegar and olive oil. 2. Cook in the baking pan at 360°F (182°C) for 8 to 10 minutes. Pause the air fryer; stir in the remaining ingredients and continue to cook for 15 minutes longer; make sure to check them periodically. Bon appétit!

Crunchy Chicken Tenders

Prep time: 5 minutes | Cook time: 12 minutes | Serves 4

1 egg ¼ cup unsweetened almond milk ¼ cup whole wheat flour ¼ cup whole wheat bread crumbs ½ teaspoon salt	½ teaspoon black pepper ½ teaspoon dried thyme ½ teaspoon dried sage ½ teaspoon garlic powder 1 pound (454 g) chicken tenderloins 1 lemon, quartered

1. Preheat the air fryer to 360°F(182°C). 2. In a shallow bowl, beat together the egg and almond milk until frothy. 3. In a separate shallow bowl, whisk together the flour, bread crumbs, salt, pepper, thyme, sage, and garlic powder. 4. Dip each chicken tenderloin into the egg mixture, then into the bread crumb mixture, coating the outside with the crumbs. Place the breaded chicken tenderloins into the bottom of the air fryer basket in an even layer, making sure that they don't touch each other. 5. Cook for 6 minutes, then turn and cook for an additional 5 to 6 minutes. Serve with lemon slices.

Cobb Salad

Prep time: 15 minutes | Cook time: 8 minutes | Serves 4

8 slices reduced-sodium bacon 8 chicken breast tenders (about 1½ pounds / 680 g) 8 cups chopped romaine lettuce 1 cup cherry tomatoes, halved ¼ red onion, thinly sliced 2 hard-boiled eggs, peeled and sliced	Avocado-Lime Dressing: ½ cup plain Greek yogurt ¼ cup almond milk ½ avocado Juice of ½ lime 3 scallions, coarsely chopped 1 clove garlic 2 tablespoons fresh cilantro ⅛ teaspoon ground cumin Salt and freshly ground black pepper, to taste

1. Preheat the air fryer to 400°F (204°C). 2. Wrap a piece of bacon around each piece of chicken and secure with a toothpick. Working in batches if necessary, arrange the bacon-wrapped chicken in a single layer in the air fryer basket. Air fry for 8 minutes until the bacon is browned and a thermometer inserted into the thickest piece of chicken register 165°F (74°C). Let cool for a few minutes, then slice into bite-size pieces. 3. To make the dressing: In a blender or food processor, combine the yogurt, milk, avocado, lime juice, scallions, garlic, cilantro, and cumin. Purée until smooth. Season to taste with salt and freshly ground pepper. 4. To assemble the salad, in a large bowl, combine the lettuce, tomatoes, and onion. Drizzle the dressing over the vegetables and toss gently until thoroughly combined. Arrange the chicken and eggs on top just before serving.

Bacon Lovers' Stuffed Chicken

Prep time: 10 minutes | Cook time: 20 minutes | Serves 4

4 (5-ounce / 142-g) boneless, skinless chicken breasts, pounded to ¼ inch thick 2 (5.2-ounce / 147-g) packages Boursin cheese (or Kite Hill brand chive cream	cheese style spread, softened, for dairy-free) 8 slices thin-cut bacon or beef bacon Sprig of fresh cilantro, for garnish (optional)

1. Spray the air fryer basket with avocado oil. Preheat the air fryer to 400°F (204°C). 2. Place one of the chicken breasts on a cutting board. With a sharp knife held parallel to the cutting board, make a 1-inch-wide incision at the top of the breast. Carefully cut into the breast to form a large pocket, leaving a ½-inch border along the sides and bottom. Repeat with the other 3 chicken breasts. 3. Snip the corner of a large resealable plastic bag to form a ¾-inch hole. Place the Boursin cheese in the bag and pipe the cheese into the pockets in the chicken breasts, dividing the cheese evenly among them. 4. Wrap 2 slices of bacon around each chicken breast and secure the ends with toothpicks. Place the bacon-wrapped chicken in the air fryer basket and air fry until the bacon is crisp and the chicken's internal temperature reaches 165°F (74°C), about 18 to 20 minutes, flipping after 10 minutes. Garnish with a sprig of cilantro before serving, if desired. 5. Store leftovers in an airtight container in the refrigerator for up to 4 days. Reheat in a preheated 400°F (204°C) air fryer for 5 minutes, or until warmed through.

Broccoli Cheese Chicken

Prep time: 10 minutes | Cook time: 19 to 24 minutes | Serves 6

1 tablespoon avocado oil ¼ cup chopped onion ½ cup finely chopped broccoli 4 ounces (113 g) cream cheese, at room temperature 2 ounces (57 g) Cheddar cheese, shredded 1 teaspoon garlic powder	½ teaspoon sea salt, plus additional for seasoning, divided ¼ freshly ground black pepper, plus additional for seasoning, divided 2 pounds (907 g) boneless, skinless chicken breasts 1 teaspoon smoked paprika

1. Heat a medium skillet over medium-high heat and pour in the avocado oil. Add the onion and broccoli and cook, stirring occasionally, for 5 to 8 minutes, until the onion is tender. 2. Transfer to a large bowl and stir in the cream cheese, Cheddar cheese, and garlic powder, and season to taste with salt and pepper. 3. Hold a sharp knife parallel to the chicken breast and cut a long pocket into one side. Stuff the chicken pockets with the broccoli mixture, using toothpicks to secure the pockets around the filling. 4. In a small dish, combine the paprika, ½ teaspoon salt, and ¼ teaspoon pepper. Sprinkle this over the outside of the chicken. 5. Set the air fryer to 400ºF (204ºC). Place the chicken in a single layer in the air fryer basket, cooking in batches if necessary, and cook for 14 to 16 minutes, until an instant-read thermometer reads 160ºF (71ºC). Place the chicken on a plate and tent a piece of aluminum foil over the chicken. Allow to rest for 5 to 10 minutes before serving.

Ranch Chicken Wings

Prep time: 10 minutes | Cook time: 40 minutes | Serves 4

2 tablespoons water 2 tablespoons hot pepper sauce 2 tablespoons unsalted butter, melted 2 tablespoons apple cider vinegar	1 (1-ounce / 28-g) envelope ranch salad dressing mix 1 teaspoon paprika 4 pounds (1.8 kg) chicken wings, tips removed Cooking oil spray

1. In a large bowl, whisk the water, hot pepper sauce, melted butter, vinegar, salad dressing mix, and paprika until combined. 2. Add the wings and toss to coat. At this point, you can cover the bowl and marinate the wings in the refrigerator for 4 to 24 hours for best results. However, you can just let the wings stand for 30 minutes in the refrigerator. 3. Insert the crisper plate into the basket and the basket into the unit. Preheat the unit by selecting AIR FRY, setting the temperature to 400ºF (204ºC), and setting the time to 3 minutes. Select START/STOP to begin. 4. Once the unit is preheated, spray the crisper plate with cooking oil. Working in batches, put half the wings into the basket; it is okay to stack them. Refrigerate the remaining wings. 5. Select AIR FRY, set the temperature to 400ºF (204ºC), and set the time to 20 minutes. Select START/STOP to begin. 6. After 5 minutes, remove the basket and shake it. Reinsert the basket to resume cooking. Remove and shake the basket every 5 minutes, three more times, until the chicken is browned and glazed and a food thermometer inserted into the wings registers 165ºF (74ºC). 7. Repeat steps 4, 5, and 6 with the remaining wings. 8. When the cooking is complete, serve warm.

Almond-Crusted Chicken

Prep time: 15 minutes | Cook time: 25 minutes | Serves 4

¼ cup slivered almonds 2 (6-ounce / 170-g) boneless, skinless chicken breasts	2 tablespoons full-fat mayonnaise 1 tablespoon Dijon mustard

1. Pulse the almonds in a food processor or chop until finely chopped. Place almonds evenly on a plate and set aside. 2. Completely slice each chicken breast in half lengthwise. 3. Mix the mayonnaise and mustard in a small bowl and then coat chicken with the mixture. 4. Lay each piece of chicken in the chopped almonds to fully coat. Carefully move the pieces into the air fryer basket. 5. Adjust the temperature to 350ºF (177ºC) and air fry for 25 minutes. 6. Chicken will be done when it has reached an internal temperature of 165ºF (74ºC) or more. Serve warm.

Blackened Cajun Chicken Tenders

Prep time: 10 minutes | Cook time: 17 minutes | Serves 4

2 teaspoons paprika 1 teaspoon chili powder ½ teaspoon garlic powder ½ teaspoon dried thyme ¼ teaspoon onion powder ⅛ teaspoon ground cayenne	pepper 2 tablespoons coconut oil 1 pound (454 g) boneless, skinless chicken tenders ¼ cup full-fat ranch dressing

1. In a small bowl, combine all seasonings. 2. Drizzle oil over chicken tenders and then generously coat each tender in the spice mixture. Place tenders into the air fryer basket. 3. Adjust the temperature to 375ºF (191ºC) and air fry for 17 minutes. 4. Tenders will be 165ºF (74ºC) internally when fully cooked. Serve with ranch dressing for dipping.

Lemon Thyme Roasted Chicken

Prep time: 10 minutes | Cook time: 60 minutes | Serves 6

1 (4-pound / 1.8-kg) chicken 2 teaspoons dried thyme 1 teaspoon garlic powder ½ teaspoon onion powder 2 teaspoons dried parsley	1 teaspoon baking powder 1 medium lemon 2 tablespoons salted butter, melted

1. Rub chicken with thyme, garlic powder, onion powder, parsley, and baking powder. 2. Slice lemon and place four slices on top of chicken, breast side up, and secure with toothpicks. Place remaining slices inside of the chicken. 3. Place entire chicken into the air fryer basket, breast side down. 4. Adjust the temperature to 350ºF (177ºC) and air fry for 60 minutes. 5. After 30 minutes, flip chicken so breast side is up. 6. When done, internal temperature should be 165ºF (74ºC) and the skin golden and crispy. To serve, pour melted butter over entire chicken.

Chicken Thighs with Cilantro

Prep time: 15 minutes | Cook time: 25 minutes | Serves 4

1 tablespoon olive oil	8 bone-in chicken thighs,
Juice of ½ lime	skin on
1 tablespoon coconut aminos	2 tablespoons chopped fresh
1½ teaspoons Montreal	cilantro
chicken seasoning	

1. In a gallon-size resealable bag, combine the olive oil, lime juice, coconut aminos, and chicken seasoning. Add the chicken thighs, seal the bag, and massage the bag to ensure the chicken is thoroughly coated. Refrigerate for at least 2 hours, preferably overnight. 2. Preheat the air fryer to 400ºF (204ºC). 3. Remove the chicken from the marinade (discard the marinade) and arrange in a single layer in the air fryer basket. Pausing halfway through the cooking time to flip the chicken, air fry for 20 to 25 minutes, until a thermometer inserted into the thickest part registers 165ºF (74ºC). 4. Transfer the chicken to a serving platter and top with the cilantro before serving.

Apricot-Glazed Turkey Tenderloin

Prep time: 20 minutes | Cook time: 30 minutes | Serves 4

Olive oil	1½ pounds (680 g) turkey
¼ cup sugar-free apricot	breast tenderloin
preserves	Salt and freshly ground black
½ tablespoon spicy brown	pepper, to taste
mustard	

1. Spray the air fryer basket lightly with olive oil. 2. In a small bowl, combine the apricot preserves and mustard to make a paste. 3. Season the turkey with salt and pepper. Spread the apricot paste all over the turkey. 4. Place the turkey in the air fryer basket and lightly spray with olive oil. 5. Air fry at 370ºF (188ºC) for 15 minutes. Flip the turkey over and lightly spray with olive oil. Air fry until the internal temperature reaches at least 170ºF (77ºC), an additional 10 to 15 minutes. 6. Let the turkey rest for 10 minutes before slicing and serving.

Garlic Soy Chicken Thighs

Prep time: 10 minutes | Cook time: 30 minutes | Serves 1 to 2

2 tablespoons chicken stock	2 large scallions, cut into 2-
2 tablespoons reduced-	to 3-inch batons, plus more,
sodium soy sauce	thinly sliced, for garnish
1½ tablespoons sugar	2 bone-in, skin-on chicken
4 garlic cloves, smashed and	thighs (7 to 8 ounces / 198 to
peeled	227 g each)

1. Preheat the air fryer to 375ºF (191ºC). 2. In a metal cake pan, combine the chicken stock, soy sauce, and sugar and stir until the sugar dissolves. Add the garlic cloves, scallions, and chicken thighs, turning the thighs to coat them in the marinade, then resting them skin-side up. Place the pan in the air fryer and bake, flipping the thighs every 5 minutes after the first 10 minutes, until the chicken is cooked through and the marinade is reduced to a sticky glaze over the chicken, about 30 minutes. 3. Remove the pan from the air fryer and serve the chicken thighs warm, with any remaining glaze spooned over top and sprinkled with more sliced scallions.

Buttermilk-Fried Drumsticks

Prep time: 10 minutes | Cook time: 25 minutes | Serves 2

1 egg	¼ teaspoon ground black
½ cup buttermilk	pepper (to mix into coating)
¾ cup self-rising flour	4 chicken drumsticks, skin
¾ cup seasoned panko bread	on
crumbs	Oil for misting or cooking
1 teaspoon salt	spray

1. Beat together egg and buttermilk in shallow dish. 2. In a second shallow dish, combine the flour, panko crumbs, salt, and pepper. 3. Sprinkle chicken legs with additional salt and pepper to taste. 4. Dip legs in buttermilk mixture, then roll in panko mixture, pressing in crumbs to make coating stick. Mist with oil or cooking spray. 5. Spray the air fryer basket with cooking spray. 6. Cook drumsticks at 360ºF (182ºC) for 10 minutes. Turn pieces over and cook an additional 10 minutes. 7. Turn pieces to check for browning. If you have any white spots that haven't begun to brown, spritz them with oil or cooking spray. Continue cooking for 5 more minutes or until crust is golden brown and juices run clear. Larger, meatier drumsticks will take longer to cook than small ones.

Gochujang Chicken Wings

Prep time: 15 minutes | Cook time: 25 minutes | Serves 4

Wings:	1 tablespoon toasted sesame
2 pounds (907 g) chicken	oil
wings	1 tablespoon minced fresh
1 teaspoon kosher salt	ginger
1 teaspoon black pepper	1 tablespoon minced garlic
or gochugaru (Korean red	1 teaspoon sugar
pepper)	1 teaspoon agave nectar or
Sauce:	honey
2 tablespoons gochujang	For Serving
(Korean chile paste)	1 teaspoon sesame seeds
1 tablespoon mayonnaise	¼ cup chopped scallions

1. For the wings: Season the wings with the salt and pepper and place in the air fryer basket. Set the air fryer to 400ºF (204ºC) for 20 minutes, turning the wings halfway through the cooking time. 2. Meanwhile, for the sauce: In a small bowl, combine the gochujang, mayonnaise, sesame oil, ginger, garlic, sugar, and agave; set aside. 3. As you near the 20-minute mark, use a meat thermometer to check the meat. When the wings reach 160ºF (71ºC), transfer them to a large bowl. Pour about half the sauce on the wings; toss to coat (serve the remaining sauce as a dip). 4. Return the wings to the air fryer basket and cook for 5 minutes, until the sauce has glazed. 5. Transfer the wings to a serving platter. Sprinkle with the sesame seeds and scallions. Serve with the reserved sauce on the side for dipping.

Bruschetta Chicken

Prep time: 10 minutes | Cook time: 20 minutes | Serves 4

Bruschetta Stuffing:	olive oil
1 tomato, diced	Chicken:
3 tablespoons balsamic	4 (4-ounce / 113-g) boneless,
vinegar	skinless chicken breasts, cut
1 teaspoon Italian seasoning	4 slits each
2 tablespoons chopped fresh	1 teaspoon Italian seasoning
basil	Chicken seasoning or rub,
3 garlic cloves, minced	to taste
2 tablespoons extra-virgin	Cooking spray

1. Preheat the air fryer to 370ºF (188ºC). Spritz the air fryer basket with cooking spray. 2. Combine the ingredients for the bruschetta stuffing in a bowl. Stir to mix well. Set aside. 3. Rub the chicken breasts with Italian seasoning and chicken seasoning on a clean work surface. 4. Arrange the chicken breasts, slits side up, in a single layer in the air fryer basket and spritz with cooking spray. You may need to work in batches to avoid overcrowding. 5. Air fry for 7 minutes, then open the air fryer and fill the slits in the chicken with the bruschetta stuffing. Cook for another 3 minutes or until the chicken is well browned. 6. Serve immediately.

Gold Livers

Prep time: 10 minutes | Cook time: 20 minutes | Serves 4

2 eggs	½ teaspoon ground black
2 tablespoons water	pepper
¾ cup flour	20 ounces (567 g) chicken
2 cups panko breadcrumbs	livers
1 teaspoon salt	Cooking spray

1. Preheat the air fryer to 390ºF (199ºC). Spritz the air fryer basket with cooking spray. 2. Whisk the eggs with water in a large bowl. Pour the flour in a separate bowl. Pour the panko on a shallow dish and sprinkle with salt and pepper. 3. Dredge the chicken livers in the flour. Shake the excess off, then dunk the livers in the whisked eggs, and then roll the livers over the panko to coat well. 4. Arrange the livers in the preheated air fryer and spritz with cooking spray. Work in batches to avoid overcrowding. 5. Air fry for 10 minutes or until the livers are golden and crispy. Flip the livers halfway through. Repeat with remaining livers. 6. Serve immediately.

Stuffed Turkey Roulade

Prep time: 10 minutes | Cook time: 45 minutes | Serves 4

1 (2-pound / 907-g) boneless	1 tablespoon fresh sage
turkey breast, skin removed	2 garlic cloves, minced
1 teaspoon salt	2 tablespoons olive oil
½ teaspoon black pepper	Fresh chopped parsley, for
4 ounces (113 g) goat cheese	garnish
1 tablespoon fresh thyme	

1. Preheat the air fryer to 380ºF(193ºC). 2. Using a sharp knife, butterfly the turkey breast, and season both sides with salt and pepper and set aside. 3. In a small bowl, mix together the goat cheese, thyme, sage, and garlic. 4. Spread the cheese mixture over the turkey breast, then roll it up tightly, tucking the ends underneath. 5. Place the turkey breast roulade onto a piece of aluminum foil, wrap it up, and place it into the air fryer. 6. Bake for 30 minutes. Remove the foil from the turkey breast and brush the top with oil, then continue cooking for another 10 to 15 minutes, or until the outside has browned and the internal temperature reaches 165ºF(74ºC). 7. Remove and cut into 1-inch-wide slices and serve with a sprinkle of parsley on top.

Turkish Chicken Kebabs

Prep time: 30 minutes | Cook time: 15 minutes | Serves 4

¼ cup plain Greek yogurt	1 teaspoon sweet Hungarian
1 tablespoon minced garlic	paprika
1 tablespoon tomato paste	½ teaspoon ground cinnamon
1 tablespoon fresh lemon	½ teaspoon black pepper
juice	½ teaspoon cayenne pepper
1 tablespoon vegetable oil	1 pound (454 g) boneless,
1 teaspoon kosher salt	skinless chicken thighs,
1 teaspoon ground cumin	quartered crosswise

1. In a large bowl, combine the yogurt, garlic, tomato paste, lemon juice, vegetable oil, salt, cumin, paprika, cinnamon, black pepper, and cayenne. Stir until the spices are blended into the yogurt. 2. Add the chicken to the bowl and toss until well coated. Marinate at room temperature for 30 minutes, or cover and refrigerate for up to 24 hours. 3. Arrange the chicken in a single layer in the air fryer basket. Set the air fryer to 375ºF (191ºC) for 10 minutes. Turn the chicken and cook for 5 minutes more. Use a meat thermometer to ensure the chicken has reached an internal temperature of 165ºF (74ºC).

Chapter 6

Fish and Seafood

Maple Balsamic Glazed Salmon

Prep time: 5 minutes | Cook time: 10 minutes | Serves 4

4 (6-ounce / 170-g) fillets of salmon Salt and freshly ground black pepper, to taste Vegetable oil	¼ cup pure maple syrup 3 tablespoons balsamic vinegar 1 teaspoon Dijon mustard

1. Preheat the air fryer to 400ºF (204ºC). 2. Season the salmon well with salt and freshly ground black pepper. Spray or brush the bottom of the air fryer basket with vegetable oil and place the salmon fillets inside. Air fry the salmon for 5 minutes. 3. While the salmon is air frying, combine the maple syrup, balsamic vinegar and Dijon mustard in a small saucepan over medium heat and stir to blend well. Let the mixture simmer while the fish is cooking. It should start to thicken slightly, but keep your eye on it so it doesn't burn. 4. Brush the glaze on the salmon fillets and air fry for an additional 5 minutes. The salmon should feel firm to the touch when finished and the glaze should be nicely browned on top. Brush a little more glaze on top before removing and serving with rice and vegetables, or a nice green salad.

Bacon Halibut Steak

Prep time: 15 minutes | Cook time: 10 minutes | Serves 4

24 ounces (680 g) halibut steaks (6 ounces / 170 g each fillet) 1 teaspoon avocado oil	1 teaspoon ground black pepper 4 ounces bacon, sliced

1. Sprinkle the halibut steaks with avocado oil and ground black pepper. 2. Then wrap the fish in the bacon slices and put in the air fryer. 3. Cook the fish at 390ºF (199ºC) for 5 minutes per side.

Shrimp Scampi

Prep time: 8 minutes | Cook time: 8 minutes | Serves 4

4 tablespoons (½ stick) salted butter or ghee 1 tablespoon fresh lemon juice 1 tablespoon minced garlic 2 teaspoons red pepper flakes 1 pound (454 g) shrimp (21 to 25 count), peeled and deveined	2 tablespoons chicken broth or dry white wine 2 tablespoons chopped fresh basil, plus more for sprinkling, or 1 teaspoon dried 1 tablespoon chopped fresh chives, or 1 teaspoon dried

1. Place a baking pan in the air fryer basket. Set the air fryer to 325ºF (163ºC) for 8 minutes (this will preheat the pan so the butter will melt faster). 2. Carefully remove the pan from the fryer and add the butter, lemon juice, garlic, and red pepper flakes. Place the pan back in the fryer. 3. Cook for 2 minutes, stirring once, until the butter has melted. (Do not skip this step; this is what infuses the butter with garlic flavor, which is what makes it all taste so good.) 4. Carefully remove the pan from the fryer and add the shrimp, broth, basil, and chives. Stir gently until the ingredients are well combined. 5. Return the pan to the air fryer and cook for 5 minutes, stirring once. 6. Thoroughly stir the shrimp mixture and let it rest for 1 minute on a wire rack. (This is so the shrimp cooks in the residual heat rather than getting overcooked and rubbery.) 7. Stir once more, sprinkle with additional chopped fresh basil, and serve.

Tandoori-Spiced Salmon and Potatoes

Prep time: 10 minutes | Cook time: 28 minutes | Serves 2

1 pound (454 g) fingerling potatoes 2 tablespoons vegetable oil, divided Kosher salt and freshly ground black pepper, to taste 1 teaspoon ground turmeric	1 teaspoon ground cumin 1 teaspoon ground ginger ½ teaspoon smoked paprika ¼ teaspoon cayenne pepper 2 (6-ounce / 170-g) skin-on salmon fillets

1. Preheat the air fryer to 375ºF (191ºC). 2. In a bowl, toss the potatoes with 1 tablespoon of the oil until evenly coated. Season with salt and pepper. Transfer the potatoes to the air fryer and air fry for 20 minutes. 3. Meanwhile, in a bowl, combine the remaining 1 tablespoon oil, the turmeric, cumin, ginger, paprika, and cayenne. Add the salmon fillets and turn in the spice mixture until fully coated all over. 4. After the potatoes have cooked for 20 minutes, place the salmon fillets, skin-side up, on top of the potatoes, and continue cooking until the potatoes are tender, the salmon is cooked, and the salmon skin is slightly crisp. 5. Transfer the salmon fillets to two plates and serve with the potatoes while both are warm.

Shrimp Pasta with Basil and Mushrooms

Prep time: 10 minutes | Cook time: 10 minutes | Serves 6

1 pound (454 g) small shrimp, peeled and deveined ¼ cup plus 1 tablespoon olive oil, divided ¼ teaspoon garlic powder ¼ teaspoon cayenne 1 pound (454 g) whole grain pasta	5 garlic cloves, minced 8 ounces (227 g) baby bella mushrooms, sliced ½ cup Parmesan, plus more for serving (optional) 1 teaspoon salt ½ teaspoon black pepper ½ cup fresh basil

1. Preheat the air fryer to 380ºF(193ºC). 2. In a small bowl, combine the shrimp, 1 tablespoon olive oil, garlic powder, and cayenne. Toss to coat the shrimp. 3. Place the shrimp into the air fryer basket and roast for 5 minutes. Remove the shrimp and set aside. 4. Cook the pasta according to package directions. Once done cooking, reserve ½ cup pasta water, then drain. 5. Meanwhile, in a large skillet, heat ¼ cup of olive oil over medium heat. Add the garlic and mushrooms and cook down for 5 minutes. 6. Pour the pasta, reserved pasta water, Parmesan, salt, pepper, and basil into the skillet with the vegetable-and-oil mixture, and stir to coat the pasta. 7. Toss in the shrimp and remove from heat, then let the mixture sit for 5 minutes before serving with additional Parmesan, if desired.

Tuna Casserole

Prep time: 15 minutes | Cook time: 15 minutes | Serves 4

2 tablespoons salted butter	mayonnaise
¼ cup diced white onion	¼ teaspoon xanthan gum
¼ cup chopped white mushrooms	½ teaspoon red pepper flakes
2 stalks celery, finely chopped	2 medium zucchini, spiralized
½ cup heavy cream	2 (5-ounce / 142-g) cans albacore tuna
½ cup vegetable broth	1 ounce (28 g) pork rinds, finely ground
2 tablespoons full-fat	

1. In a large saucepan over medium heat, melt butter. Add onion, mushrooms, and celery and sauté until fragrant, about 3 to 5 minutes. 2. Pour in heavy cream, vegetable broth, mayonnaise, and xanthan gum. Reduce heat and continue cooking an additional 3 minutes, until the mixture begins to thicken. 3. Add red pepper flakes, zucchini, and tuna. Turn off heat and stir until zucchini noodles are coated. 4. Pour into a round baking dish. Top with ground pork rinds and cover the top of the dish with foil. Place into the air fryer basket. 5. Adjust the temperature to 370°F (188°C) and set the timer for 15 minutes. 6. When 3 minutes remain, remove the foil to brown the top of the casserole. Serve warm.

Southern-Style Catfish

Prep time: 10 minutes | Cook time: 12 minutes | Serves 4

4 (7-ounce / 198-g) catfish fillets	2 teaspoons Old Bay seasoning
⅓ cup heavy whipping cream	½ teaspoon salt
1 tablespoon lemon juice	¼ teaspoon ground black pepper
1 cup blanched finely ground almond flour	

1. Place catfish fillets into a large bowl with cream and pour in lemon juice. Stir to coat. 2. In a separate large bowl, mix flour and Old Bay seasoning. 3. Remove each fillet and gently shake off excess cream. Sprinkle with salt and pepper. Press each fillet gently into flour mixture on both sides to coat. 4. Place fillets into ungreased air fryer basket. Adjust the temperature to 400°F (204°C) and air fry for 12 minutes, turning fillets halfway through cooking. Catfish will be golden brown and have an internal temperature of at least 145°F (63°C) when done. Serve warm.

Seasoned Breaded Shrimp

Prep time: 15 minutes | Cook time: 10 to 15 minutes | Serves 4

2 teaspoons Old Bay seasoning, divided	on
½ teaspoon garlic powder	2 large eggs
½ teaspoon onion powder	½ cup whole-wheat panko bread crumbs
1 pound (454 g) large shrimp, deveined, with tails	Cooking spray

1. Preheat the air fryer to 380°F (193°C). 2. Spray the air fryer basket lightly with cooking spray. 3. In a medium bowl, mix together 1 teaspoon of Old Bay seasoning, garlic powder, and onion powder. Add the shrimp and toss with the seasoning mix to lightly coat. 4. In a separate small bowl, whisk the eggs with 1 teaspoon water. 5. In a shallow bowl, mix together the remaining 1 teaspoon Old Bay seasoning and the panko bread crumbs. 6. Dip each shrimp in the egg mixture and dredge in the bread crumb mixture to evenly coat. 7. Place the shrimp in the air fryer basket, in a single layer. Lightly spray the shrimp with cooking spray. You many need to cook the shrimp in batches. 8. Air fry for 10 to 15 minutes, or until the shrimp is cooked through and crispy, shaking the basket at 5-minute intervals to redistribute and evenly cook. 9. Serve immediately.

Shrimp Kebabs

Prep time: 15 minutes | Cook time: 6 minutes | Serves 4

Oil, for spraying	1 tablespoon packed light brown sugar
1 pound (454 g) medium raw shrimp, peeled and deveined	1 teaspoon granulated garlic
4 tablespoons unsalted butter, melted	1 teaspoon onion powder
1 tablespoon Old Bay seasoning	½ teaspoon freshly ground black pepper

1. Line the air fryer basket with parchment and spray lightly with oil. 2. Thread the shrimp onto the skewers and place them in the prepared basket. 3. In a small bowl, mix together the butter, Old Bay, brown sugar, garlic, onion powder, and black pepper. Brush the sauce on the shrimp. 4. Air fry at 400°F (204°C) for 5 to 6 minutes, or until pink and firm. Serve immediately.

Fish Cakes

Prep time: 30 minutes | Cook time: 10 to 12 minutes | Serves 4

¾ cup mashed potatoes (about 1 large russet potato)	1 large egg
12 ounces (340 g) cod or other white fish	¼ cup potato starch
Salt and pepper, to taste	½ cup panko bread crumbs
Oil for misting or cooking spray	1 tablespoon fresh chopped chives
	2 tablespoons minced onion

1. Peel potatoes, cut into cubes, and cook on stovetop till soft. 2. Salt and pepper raw fish to taste. Mist with oil or cooking spray, and air fry at 360°F (182°C) for 6 to 8 minutes, until fish flakes easily. If fish is crowded, rearrange halfway through cooking to ensure all pieces cook evenly. 3. Transfer fish to a plate and break apart to cool. 4. Beat egg in a shallow dish. 5. Place potato starch in another shallow dish, and panko crumbs in a third dish. 6. When potatoes are done, drain in colander and rinse with cold water. 7. In a large bowl, mash the potatoes and stir in the chives and onion. Add salt and pepper to taste, then stir in the fish. 8. If needed, stir in a tablespoon of the beaten egg to help bind the mixture. 9. Shape into 8 small, fat patties. Dust lightly with potato starch, dip in egg, and roll in panko crumbs. Spray both sides with oil or cooking spray. 10. Air fry at 360°F (182°C) for 10 to 12 minutes, until golden brown and crispy.

Salmon with Cauliflower

Prep time: 10 minutes | Cook time: 25 minutes | Serves 4

1 pound (454 g) salmon fillet, diced	1 tablespoon coconut oil, melted
1 cup cauliflower, shredded	1 teaspoon ground turmeric
1 tablespoon dried cilantro	¼ cup coconut cream

1. Mix salmon with cauliflower, dried cilantro, ground turmeric, coconut cream, and coconut oil. 2. Transfer the salmon mixture into the air fryer and cook the meal at 350ºF (177ºC) for 25 minutes. Stir the meal every 5 minutes to avoid the burning.

Crab Cakes

Prep time: 10 minutes | Cook time: 10 minutes | Serves 4

2 (6-ounce / 170-g) cans lump crab meat	½ teaspoon Dijon mustard
¼ cup blanched finely ground almond flour	½ tablespoon lemon juice
1 large egg	½ medium green bell pepper, seeded and chopped
2 tablespoons full-fat mayonnaise	¼ cup chopped green onion
	½ teaspoon Old Bay seasoning

1. In a large bowl, combine all ingredients. Form into four balls and flatten into patties. Place patties into the air fryer basket. 2. Adjust the temperature to 350ºF (177ºC) and air fry for 10 minutes. 3. Flip patties halfway through the cooking time. Serve warm.

Crab Cakes with Lettuce and Apple Salad

Prep time: 10 minutes | Cook time: 13 minutes | Serves 2

8 ounces (227 g) lump crab meat, picked over for shells	olive oil, divided
2 tablespoons panko bread crumbs	1 teaspoon lemon juice, plus lemon wedges for serving
1 scallion, minced	⅛ teaspoon salt
1 large egg	Pinch of pepper
1 tablespoon mayonnaise	½ (3-ounce / 85-g) small head Bibb lettuce, torn into bite-size pieces
1½ teaspoons Dijon mustard	
Pinch of cayenne pepper	½ apple, cored and sliced thin
2 shallots, sliced thin	
1 tablespoon extra-virgin	

1. Preheat the air fryer to 400ºF (204ºC). 2. Line large plate with triple layer of paper towels. Transfer crab meat to prepared plate and pat dry with additional paper towels. Combine panko, scallion, egg, mayonnaise, mustard, and cayenne in a bowl. Using a rubber spatula, gently fold in crab meat until combined; discard paper towels. Divide crab mixture into 4 tightly packed balls, then flatten each into 1-inch-thick cake (cakes will be delicate). Transfer cakes to plate and refrigerate until firm, about 10 minutes. 3. Toss shallots with ½ teaspoon oil in separate bowl; transfer to air fryer basket. Air fry until shallots are browned, 5 to 7 minutes, tossing once halfway through cooking. Return shallots to now-empty bowl and set aside. 4. Arrange crab cakes in air fryer basket, spaced evenly apart. Return basket to air fryer and air fry until crab cakes are light golden brown on both sides, 8 to 10 minutes, flipping and rotating cakes halfway through cooking. 5. Meanwhile, whisk remaining 2½ teaspoons oil, lemon juice, salt, and pepper together in large bowl. Add lettuce, apple, and shallots and toss to coat. Serve crab cakes with salad, passing lemon wedges separately.

New Orleans-Style Crab Cakes

Prep time: 10 minutes | Cook time: 8 to 10 minutes | Serves 4

1¼ cups bread crumbs	1½ cups crab meat
2 teaspoons Creole Seasoning	2 large eggs, beaten
1 teaspoon dry mustard	1 teaspoon butter, melted
1 teaspoon salt	⅓ cup minced onion
1 teaspoon freshly ground black pepper	Cooking spray
	Pecan Tartar Sauce, for serving

1. Preheat the air fryer to 350ºF (177ºC). Line the air fryer basket with parchment paper. 2. In a medium bowl, whisk the bread crumbs, Creole Seasoning, dry mustard, salt, and pepper until blended. Add the crab meat, eggs, butter, and onion. Stir until blended. Shape the crab mixture into 8 patties. 3. Place the crab cakes on the parchment and spritz with oil. 4. Air fry for 4 minutes. Flip the cakes, spritz them with oil, and air fry for 4 to 6 minutes more until the outsides are firm and a fork inserted into the center comes out clean. Serve with the Pecan Tartar Sauce.

Air Fried Spring Rolls

Prep time: 10 minutes | Cook time: 17 to 22 minutes | Serves 4

2 teaspoons minced garlic	Salt and freshly ground black pepper, to taste
2 cups finely sliced cabbage	16 square spring roll wrappers
1 cup matchstick cut carrots	
2 (4-ounce / 113-g) cans tiny shrimp, drained	Cooking spray
4 teaspoons soy sauce	

1. Preheat the air fryer to 370ºF (188ºC). 2. Spray the air fryer basket lightly with cooking spray. Spray a medium sauté pan with cooking spray. 3. Add the garlic to the sauté pan and cook over medium heat until fragrant, 30 to 45 seconds. Add the cabbage and carrots and sauté until the vegetables are slightly tender, about 5 minutes. 4. Add the shrimp and soy sauce and season with salt and pepper, then stir to combine. Sauté until the moisture has evaporated, 2 more minutes. Set aside to cool. 5. Place a spring roll wrapper on a work surface so it looks like a diamond. Place 1 tablespoon of the shrimp mixture on the lower end of the wrapper. 6. Roll the wrapper away from you halfway, then fold in the right and left sides, like an envelope. Continue to roll to the very end, using a little water to seal the edge. Repeat with the remaining wrappers and filling. 7. Place the spring rolls in the air fryer basket in a single layer, leaving room between each roll. Lightly spray with cooking spray. You may need to cook them in batches. 8. Air fry for 5 minutes. Turn the rolls over, lightly spray with cooking spray, and air fry until heated through and the rolls start to brown, 5 to 10 more minutes. Cool for 5 minutes before serving.

Marinated Salmon Fillets

Prep time: 10 minutes | Cook time: 15 to 20 minutes | Serves 4

¼ cup soy sauce	½ teaspoon freshly ground
¼ cup rice wine vinegar	black pepper
1 tablespoon brown sugar	½ teaspoon minced garlic
1 tablespoon olive oil	4 (6-ounce / 170-g) salmon
1 teaspoon mustard powder	fillets, skin-on
1 teaspoon ground ginger	Cooking spray

1. In a small bowl, combine the soy sauce, rice wine vinegar, brown sugar, olive oil, mustard powder, ginger, black pepper, and garlic to make a marinade. 2. Place the fillets in a shallow baking dish and pour the marinade over them. Cover the baking dish and marinate for at least 1 hour in the refrigerator, turning the fillets occasionally to keep them coated in the marinade. 3. Preheat the air fryer to 370ºF (188ºC). Spray the air fryer basket lightly with cooking spray. 4. Shake off as much marinade as possible from the fillets and place them, skin-side down, in the air fryer basket in a single layer. You may need to cook the fillets in batches. 5. Air fry for 15 to 20 minutes for well done. The minimum internal temperature should be 145ºF (63ºC) at the thickest part of the fillets. 6. Serve hot.

Salmon Croquettes

Prep time: 10 minutes | Cook time: 7 to 8 minutes | Serves 4

1 tablespoon oil	saltine crackers (about 8
½ cup bread crumbs	crackers)
1 (14¾ -ounce / 418-g) can	½ teaspoon Old Bay
salmon, drained and all skin	Seasoning
and fat removed	½ teaspoon onion powder
1 egg, beaten	½ teaspoon Worcestershire
⅓ cup coarsely crushed	sauce

1. Preheat the air fryer to 390ºF (199ºC). 2. In a shallow dish, mix oil and bread crumbs until crumbly. 3. In a large bowl, combine the salmon, egg, cracker crumbs, Old Bay, onion powder, and Worcestershire. Mix well and shape into 8 small patties about ½-inch thick. 4. Gently dip each patty into bread crumb mixture and turn to coat well on all sides. 5. Cook for 7 to 8 minutes or until outside is crispy and browned.

Blackened Fish

Prep time: 15 minutes | Cook time: 8 minutes | Serves 4

1 large egg, beaten	sugar
Blackened seasoning, as	4 (4-ounce / 113- g) tilapia
needed	fillets
2 tablespoons light brown	Cooking spray

1. In a shallow bowl, place the beaten egg. In a second shallow bowl, stir together the Blackened seasoning and the brown sugar. 2. One at a time, dip the fish fillets in the egg, then the brown sugar mixture, coating thoroughly. 3. Preheat the air fryer to 300ºF (149ºC). Line the air fryer basket with parchment paper. 4. Place

the coated fish on the parchment and spritz with oil. 5. Bake for 4 minutes. Flip the fish, spritz it with oil, and bake for 4 to 6 minutes more until the fish is white inside and flakes easily with a fork. 6. Serve immediately.

Almond Catfish

Prep time: 10 minutes | Cook time: 12 minutes | Serves 4

2 pounds (907 g) catfish fillet	1 teaspoon salt
½ cup almond flour	1 teaspoon avocado oil
2 eggs, beaten	

1. Sprinkle the catfish fillet with salt and dip in the eggs. 2. Then coat the fish in the almond flour and put in the air fryer basket. Sprinkle the fish with avocado oil. 3. Cook the fish for 6 minutes per side at 380ºF (193ºC).

Shrimp Curry

Prep time: 30 minutes | Cook time: 10 minutes | Serves 4

¾ cup unsweetened full-fat	1 teaspoon salt
coconut milk	¼ to ½ teaspoon cayenne
¼ cup finely chopped yellow	pepper
onion	1 pound (454 g) raw shrimp
2 teaspoons garam masala	(21 to 25 count), peeled and
1 tablespoon minced fresh	deveined
ginger	2 teaspoons chopped fresh
1 tablespoon minced garlic	cilantro
1 teaspoon ground turmeric	

1. In a large bowl, stir together the coconut milk, onion, garam masala, ginger, garlic, turmeric, salt and cayenne, until well blended. 2. Add the shrimp and toss until coated with sauce on all sides. Marinate at room temperature for 30 minutes. 3. Transfer the shrimp and marinade to a baking pan. Place the pan in the air fryer basket. Set the air fryer to 375ºF (191ºC) for 10 minutes, stirring halfway through the cooking time. 4. Transfer the shrimp to a serving bowl or platter. Sprinkle with the cilantro and serve.

Garlic Lemon Scallops

Prep time: 5 minutes | Cook time: 10 minutes | Serves 4

4 tablespoons salted butter,	8 (1-ounce / 28-g) sea
melted	scallops, cleaned and patted
4 teaspoons peeled and finely	dry
minced garlic	¼ teaspoon salt
½ small lemon, zested and	¼ teaspoon ground black
juiced	pepper

1. In a small bowl, mix butter, garlic, lemon zest, and lemon juice. Place scallops in an ungreased round nonstick baking dish. Pour butter mixture over scallops, then sprinkle with salt and pepper. 2. Place dish into air fryer basket. Adjust the temperature to 360ºF (182ºC) and bake for 10 minutes. Scallops will be opaque and firm, and have an internal temperature of 135ºF (57ºC) when done. Serve warm.

Air Fryer Fish Fry

Prep time: 5 minutes | Cook time: 15 minutes | Serves 4

2 cups low-fat buttermilk	½ cup plain yellow cornmeal
½ teaspoon garlic powder	½ cup chickpea flour
½ teaspoon onion powder	¼ teaspoon cayenne pepper
4 (4-ounce) flounder fillets	Freshly ground black pepper

1. In a large bowl, combine the buttermilk, garlic powder, and onion powder. 2. Add the flounder, turning until well coated, and set aside to marinate for 20 minutes. 3. In a shallow bowl, stir the cornmeal, chickpea flour, cayenne, and pepper together. 4. Dredge the fillets in the meal mixture, turning until well coated. Place in the basket of an air fryer. 5. Set the air fryer to 380°F, close, and cook for 12 minutes.

Cod with Jalapeño

Prep time: 5 minutes | Cook time: 14 minutes | Serves 4

4 cod fillets, boneless	1 tablespoon avocado oil
1 jalapeño, minced	½ teaspoon minced garlic

1. In the shallow bowl, mix minced jalapeño, avocado oil, and minced garlic. 2. Put the cod fillets in the air fryer basket in one layer and top with minced jalapeño mixture. 3. Cook the fish at 365°F (185°C) for 7 minutes per side.

Crab Cakes with Mango Mayo

Prep time: 25 minutes | Cook time: 15 minutes | Serves 4

Crab Cakes:	½ teaspoon ground cumin
½ cup chopped red onion	½ teaspoon ground coriander
½ cup fresh cilantro leaves	¼ teaspoon kosher salt
1 small serrano chile or jalapeño, seeded and quartered	2 tablespoons fresh lemon juice
½ pound (227 g) lump crab meat	1½ cups panko bread crumbs
1 large egg	Vegetable oil spray
1 tablespoon mayonnaise	Mango Mayo:
1 tablespoon whole-grain mustard	½ cup diced fresh mango
2 teaspoons minced fresh ginger	½ cup mayonnaise
	½ teaspoon grated lime zest
	2 teaspoons fresh lime juice
	Pinch of cayenne pepper

1. For the crab cakes: Combine the onion, cilantro, and serrano in a food processor. Pulse until minced. 2. In a large bowl, combine the minced vegetable mixture with the crab meat, egg, mayonnaise, mustard, ginger, cumin, coriander, and salt. Add the lemon juice and mix gently until thoroughly combined. Add 1 cup of the bread crumbs. Mix gently again until well blended. 3. Form into four evenly sized patties. Put the remaining ½ cup bread crumbs in a shallow bowl and press both sides of each patty into the bread crumbs. 4. Arrange the patties in the air fryer basket. Spray with vegetable oil spray. Set the air fryer to 375°F (191°C) for 15 minutes, turning and spraying other side of the patties with vegetable oil spray halfway through the cooking time, until the crab cakes are golden brown and crisp. 5. Meanwhile, for the mayonnaise: In a blender, combine the mango, mayonnaise, lime zest, lime juice, and cayenne. Blend until smooth. 6. Serve the crab cakes warm, with the mango mayo.

Tandoori Shrimp

Prep time: 25 minutes | Cook time: 6 minutes | Serves 4

1 pound (454 g) jumbo raw shrimp (21 to 25 count), peeled and deveined	1 teaspoon ground turmeric
1 tablespoon minced fresh ginger	1 teaspoon garam masala
3 cloves garlic, minced	1 teaspoon smoked paprika
¼ cup chopped fresh cilantro or parsley, plus more for garnish	1 teaspoon kosher salt
	½ to 1 teaspoon cayenne pepper
	2 tablespoons olive oil (for Paleo) or melted ghee
	2 teaspoons fresh lemon juice

1. In a large bowl, combine the shrimp, ginger, garlic, cilantro, turmeric, garam masala, paprika, salt, and cayenne. Toss well to coat. Add the oil or ghee and toss again. Marinate at room temperature for 15 minutes, or cover and refrigerate for up to 8 hours. 2. Place the shrimp in a single layer in the air fryer basket. Set the air fryer to 325°F (163°C) for 6 minutes. Transfer the shrimp to a serving platter. Cover and let the shrimp finish cooking in the residual heat, about 5 minutes. 3. Sprinkle the shrimp with the lemon juice and toss to coat. Garnish with additional cilantro and serve.

Classic Shrimp Empanadas

Prep time: 10 minutes | Cook time: 8 minutes | Serves 5

½ pound (227g) raw shrimp, peeled, deveined and chopped	½ tablespoon fresh lime juice
¼ cup chopped red onion	¼ teaspoon sweet paprika
1 scallion, chopped	⅛ teaspoon kosher salt
2 garlic cloves, minced	⅛ teaspoon crushed red pepper flakes (optional)
2 tablespoons minced red bell pepper	1 large egg, beaten
2 tablespoons chopped fresh cilantro	10 frozen Goya Empanada Discos, thawed
	Cooking spray

1. In a medium bowl, combine the shrimp, red onion, scallion, garlic, bell pepper, cilantro, lime juice, paprika, salt, and pepper flakes (if using). 2. In a small bowl, beat the egg with 1 teaspoon water until smooth. 3. Place an empanada disc on a work surface and put 2 tablespoons of the shrimp mixture in the center. Brush the outer edges of the disc with the egg wash. Fold the disc over and gently press the edges to seal. Use a fork and press around the edges to crimp and seal completely. Brush the tops of the empanadas with the egg wash. 4. Preheat the air fryer to 380°F (193°C). 5. Spray the bottom of the air fryer basket with cooking spray to prevent sticking. Working in batches, arrange a single layer of the empanadas in the air fryer basket and air fry for about 8 minutes, flipping halfway, until golden brown and crispy. 6. Serve hot.

Tilapia with Pecans

Prep time: 20 minutes | Cook time: 16 minutes | Serves 5

2 tablespoons ground flaxseeds 1 teaspoon paprika Sea salt and white pepper, to taste 1 teaspoon garlic paste	2 tablespoons extra-virgin olive oil ½ cup pecans, ground 5 tilapia fillets, sliced into halves

1. Combine the ground flaxseeds, paprika, salt, white pepper, garlic paste, olive oil, and ground pecans in a Ziploc bag. Add the fish fillets and shake to coat well. 2. Spritz the air fryer basket with cooking spray. Cook in the preheated air fryer at 400°F (204°C) for 10 minutes; turn them over and cook for 6 minutes more. Work in batches. 3. Serve with lemon wedges, if desired. Enjoy!

Cornmeal-Crusted Trout Fingers

Prep time: 15 minutes | Cook time: 6 minutes | Serves 2

½ cup yellow cornmeal, medium or finely ground (not coarse) ⅓ cup all-purpose flour 1½ teaspoons baking powder 1 teaspoon kosher salt, plus more as needed ½ teaspoon freshly ground black pepper, plus more as needed ⅛ teaspoon cayenne pepper ¾ pound (340 g) skinless	trout fillets, cut into strips 1 inch wide and 3 inches long 3 large eggs, lightly beaten Cooking spray ½ cup mayonnaise 2 tablespoons capers, rinsed and finely chopped 1 tablespoon fresh tarragon 1 teaspoon fresh lemon juice, plus lemon wedges, for serving

1. Preheat the air fryer to 400°F (204°C). 2. In a large bowl, whisk together the cornmeal, flour, baking powder, salt, black pepper, and cayenne. Dip the trout strips in the egg, then toss them in the cornmeal mixture until fully coated. Transfer the trout to a rack set over a baking sheet and liberally spray all over with cooking spray. 3. Transfer half the fish to the air fryer and air fry until the fish is cooked through and golden brown, about 6 minutes. Transfer the fish sticks to a plate and repeat with the remaining fish. 4. Meanwhile, in a bowl, whisk together the mayonnaise, capers, tarragon, and lemon juice. Season the tartar sauce with salt and black pepper. 5. Serve the trout fingers hot along with the tartar sauce and lemon wedges.

Tuna Steak

Prep time: 10 minutes | Cook time: 12 minutes | Serves 4

1 pound (454 g) tuna steaks, boneless and cubed 1 tablespoon mustard	1 tablespoon avocado oil 1 tablespoon apple cider vinegar

1. Mix avocado oil with mustard and apple cider vinegar. 2. Then brush tuna steaks with mustard mixture and put in the air fryer basket. 3. Cook the fish at 360°F (182°C) for 6 minutes per side.

Baked Monkfish

Prep time: 20 minutes | Cook time: 12 minutes | Serves 2

2 teaspoons olive oil 1 cup celery, sliced 2 bell peppers, sliced 1 teaspoon dried thyme ½ teaspoon dried marjoram ½ teaspoon dried rosemary 2 monkfish fillets	1 tablespoon coconut aminos 2 tablespoons lime juice Coarse salt and ground black pepper, to taste 1 teaspoon cayenne pepper ½ cup Kalamata olives, pitted and sliced

1. In a nonstick skillet, heat the olive oil for 1 minute. Once hot, sauté the celery and peppers until tender, about 4 minutes. Sprinkle with thyme, marjoram, and rosemary and set aside. 2. Toss the fish fillets with the coconut aminos, lime juice, salt, black pepper, and cayenne pepper. Place the fish fillets in the lightly greased air fryer basket and bake at 390°F (199°C) for 8 minutes. 3. Turn them over, add the olives, and cook an additional 4 minutes. Serve with the sautéed vegetables on the side. Bon appétit!

Cilantro Lime Baked Salmon

Prep time: 10 minutes | Cook time: 12 minutes | Serves 2

2 (3-ounce / 85-g) salmon fillets, skin removed 1 tablespoon salted butter, melted 1 teaspoon chili powder ½ teaspoon finely minced	garlic ¼ cup sliced pickled jalapeños ½ medium lime, juiced 2 tablespoons chopped cilantro

1. Place salmon fillets into a round baking pan. Brush each with butter and sprinkle with chili powder and garlic. 2. Place jalapeño slices on top and around salmon. Pour half of the lime juice over the salmon and cover with foil. Place pan into the air fryer basket. 3. Adjust the temperature to 370°F (188°C) and bake for 12 minutes. 4. When fully cooked, salmon should flake easily with a fork and reach an internal temperature of at least 145°F (63°C). 5. To serve, spritz with remaining lime juice and garnish with cilantro.

Snapper with Fruit

Prep time: 15 minutes | Cook time: 9 to 13 minutes | Serves 4

4 (4-ounce / 113-g) red snapper fillets 2 teaspoons olive oil 3 nectarines, halved and pitted 3 plums, halved and pitted	1 cup red grapes 1 tablespoon freshly squeezed lemon juice 1 tablespoon honey ½ teaspoon dried thyme

1. Put the red snapper in the air fryer basket and drizzle with the olive oil. Air fry at 390°F (199°C) for 4 minutes. 2. Remove the basket and add the nectarines and plums. Scatter the grapes over all. 3. Drizzle with the lemon juice and honey and sprinkle with the thyme. 4. Return the basket to the air fryer and air fry for 5 to 9 minutes more, or until the fish flakes when tested with a fork and the fruit is tender. Serve immediately.

Fried Catfish with Dijon Sauce

Prep time: 20 minutes | Cook time: 7 minutes | Serves 4

4 tablespoons butter, melted 2 teaspoons Worcestershire sauce, divided 1 teaspoon lemon pepper 1 cup panko bread crumbs	4 (4-ounce / 113-g) catfish fillets Cooking spray ½ cup sour cream 1 tablespoon Dijon mustard

1. In a shallow bowl, stir together the melted butter, 1 teaspoon of Worcestershire sauce, and the lemon pepper. Place the bread crumbs in another shallow bowl. 2. One at a time, dip both sides of the fillets in the butter mixture, then the bread crumbs, coating thoroughly. 3. Preheat the air fryer to 300ºF (149ºC). Line the air fryer basket with parchment paper. 4. Place the coated fish on the parchment and spritz with oil. 5. Bake for 4 minutes. Flip the fish, spritz it with oil, and bake for 3 to 6 minutes more, depending on the thickness of the fillets, until the fish flakes easily with a fork. 6. In a small bowl, stir together the sour cream, Dijon, and remaining 1 teaspoon of Worcestershire sauce. This sauce can be made 1 day in advance and refrigerated before serving. Serve with the fried fish.

Honey-Glazed Salmon

Prep time: 5 minutes | Cook time: 12 minutes | Serves 4

¼ cup raw honey 4 garlic cloves, minced 1 tablespoon olive oil ½ teaspoon salt	Olive oil cooking spray 4 (1½-inch-thick) salmon fillets

1. Preheat the air fryer to 380ºF(193ºC). 2. In a small bowl, mix together the honey, garlic, olive oil, and salt. 3. Spray the bottom of the air fryer basket with olive oil cooking spray, and place the salmon in a single layer on the bottom of the air fryer basket. 4. Brush the top of each fillet with the honey-garlic mixture, and roast for 10 to 12 minutes, or until the internal temperature reaches 145°F(63ºC).

Scallops and Spinach with Cream Sauce

Prep time: 5 minutes | Cook time: 10 minutes | Serves 2

Vegetable oil spray 1 (10-ounce / 283-g) package frozen spinach, thawed and drained 8 jumbo sea scallops Kosher salt and black pepper,	to taste ¾ cup heavy cream 1 tablespoon tomato paste 1 tablespoon chopped fresh basil 1 teaspoon minced garlic

1. Spray a baking pan with vegetable oil spray. Spread the thawed spinach in an even layer in the bottom of the pan. 2. Spray both sides of the scallops with vegetable oil spray. Season lightly with salt and pepper. Arrange the scallops on top of the spinach. 3. In a small bowl, whisk together the cream, tomato paste, basil, garlic, ½ teaspoon salt, and ½ teaspoon pepper. Pour the sauce over the scallops and spinach. 4. Place the pan in the air fryer basket.

Set the air fryer to 350ºF (177ºC) for 10 minutes. Use a meat thermometer to ensure the scallops have an internal temperature of 135ºF (57ºC).

Garlic Shrimp

Prep time: 15 minutes | Cook time: 10 minutes | Serves 3

Shrimp: Oil, for spraying 1 pound (454 g) medium raw shrimp, peeled and deveined 6 tablespoons unsalted butter, melted 1 cup panko bread crumbs 2 tablespoons granulated garlic	1 teaspoon salt ½ teaspoon freshly ground black pepper Garlic Butter Sauce: ½ cup unsalted butter 2 teaspoons granulated garlic ¾ teaspoon salt (omit if using salted butter)

Make the Shrimp 1. Preheat the air fryer to 400ºF (204ºC). Line the air fryer basket with parchment and spray lightly with oil. 2. Place the shrimp and melted butter in a zip-top plastic bag, seal, and shake well, until evenly coated. 3. In a medium bowl, mix together the bread crumbs, garlic, salt, and black pepper. 4. Add the shrimp to the panko mixture and toss until evenly coated. Shake off any excess coating. 5. Place the shrimp in the prepared basket and spray lightly with oil. 6. Cook for 8 to 10 minutes, flipping and spraying with oil after 4 to 5 minutes, until golden brown and crispy. Make the Garlic Butter Sauce 7. In a microwave-safe bowl, combine the butter, garlic, and salt and microwave on 50% power for 30 to 60 seconds, stirring every 15 seconds, until completely melted. 8. Serve the shrimp immediately with the garlic butter sauce on the side for dipping.

Garlic Shrimp

Prep time: 15 minutes | Cook time: 10 minutes | Serves 3

Shrimp: Oil, for spraying 1 pound (454 g) medium raw shrimp, peeled and deveined 6 tablespoons unsalted butter, melted 1 cup panko bread crumbs 2 tablespoons granulated garlic	1 teaspoon salt ½ teaspoon freshly ground black pepper Garlic Butter Sauce: ½ cup unsalted butter 2 teaspoons granulated garlic ¾ teaspoon salt (omit if using salted butter)

Make the Shrimp 1. Preheat the air fryer to 400ºF (204ºC). Line the air fryer basket with parchment and spray lightly with oil. 2. Place the shrimp and melted butter in a zip-top plastic bag, seal, and shake well, until evenly coated. 3. In a medium bowl, mix together the bread crumbs, garlic, salt, and black pepper. 4. Add the shrimp to the panko mixture and toss until evenly coated. Shake off any excess coating. 5. Place the shrimp in the prepared basket and spray lightly with oil. 6. Cook for 8 to 10 minutes, flipping and spraying with oil after 4 to 5 minutes, until golden brown and crispy. Make the Garlic Butter Sauce 7. In a microwave-safe bowl, combine the butter, garlic, and salt and microwave on 50% power for 30 to 60 seconds, stirring every 15 seconds, until completely melted. 8. Serve the shrimp immediately with the garlic butter sauce on the side for dipping.

Crab Cake Sandwich

Prep time: 15 minutes | Cook time: 10 minutes | Serves 4

Crab Cakes:	to taste
½ cup panko bread crumbs	10 ounces (283 g) lump crab
1 large egg, beaten	meat
1 large egg white	Cooking spray
1 tablespoon mayonnaise	Cajun Mayo:
1 teaspoon Dijon mustard	¼ cup mayonnaise
¼ cup minced fresh parsley	1 tablespoon minced dill
1 tablespoon fresh lemon	pickle
juice	1 teaspoon fresh lemon juice
½ teaspoon Old Bay	¾ teaspoon Cajun seasoning
seasoning	For Serving:
⅛ teaspoon sweet paprika	4 Boston lettuce leaves
⅛ teaspoon kosher salt	4 whole wheat potato buns or
Freshly ground black pepper,	gluten-free buns

1. For the crab cakes: In a large bowl, combine the panko, whole egg, egg white, mayonnaise, mustard, parsley, lemon juice, Old Bay, paprika, salt, and pepper to taste and mix well. Fold in the crab meat, being careful not to over mix. Gently shape into 4 round patties, about ½ cup each, ¾ inch thick. Spray both sides with oil. 2. Preheat the air fryer to 370°F (188°C). 3. Working in batches, place the crab cakes in the air fryer basket. Air fry for about 10 minutes, flipping halfway, until the edges are golden. 4. Meanwhile, for the Cajun mayo: In a small bowl, combine the mayonnaise, pickle, lemon juice, and Cajun seasoning. 5. To serve: Place a lettuce leaf on each bun bottom and top with a crab cake and a generous tablespoon of Cajun mayonnaise. Add the bun top and serve.

Salmon with Provolone Cheese

Prep time: 5 minutes | Cook time: 15 minutes | Serves 4

1 pound (454 g) salmon	grated
fillet, chopped	1 teaspoon avocado oil
2 ounces (57 g) Provolone,	¼ teaspoon ground paprika

1. Sprinkle the salmon fillets with avocado oil and put in the air fryer. 2. Then sprinkle the fish with ground paprika and top with Provolone cheese. 3. Cook the fish at 360°F (182°C) for 15 minutes.

Almond Pesto Salmon

Prep time: 5 minutes | Cook time: 12 minutes | Serves 2

¼ cup pesto	fillets (about 4 ounces / 113
¼ cup sliced almonds,	g each)
roughly chopped	2 tablespoons unsalted butter,
2 (1½-inch-thick) salmon	melted

1. In a small bowl, mix pesto and almonds. Set aside. 2. Place fillets into a round baking dish. 3. Brush each fillet with butter and place half of the pesto mixture on the top of each fillet. Place dish into the air fryer basket. 4. Adjust the temperature to 390°F

(199°C) and set the timer for 12 minutes. 5. Salmon will easily flake when fully cooked and reach an internal temperature of at least 145°F (63°C). Serve warm.

Lime Lobster Tails

Prep time: 10 minutes | Cook time: 6 minutes | Serves 4

4 lobster tails, peeled	½ teaspoon coconut oil,
2 tablespoons lime juice	melted
½ teaspoon dried basil	

1. Mix lobster tails with lime juice, dried basil, and coconut oil. 2. Put the lobster tails in the air fryer and cook at 380°F (193°C) for 6 minutes.

Tortilla Shrimp Tacos

Prep time: 10 minutes | Cook time: 6 minutes | Serves 4

Spicy Mayo:	cilantro
3 tablespoons mayonnaise	Juice of 1 lime
1 tablespoon Louisiana-style	¼ teaspoon kosher salt
hot pepper sauce	Shrimp:
Cilantro-Lime Slaw:	1 large egg, beaten
2 cups shredded green	1 cup crushed tortilla chips
cabbage	24 jumbo shrimp (about 1
½ small red onion, thinly	pound / 454 g), peeled and
sliced	deveined
1 small jalapeño, thinly	⅛ teaspoon kosher salt
sliced	Cooking spray
2 tablespoons chopped fresh	8 corn tortillas, for serving

1. For the spicy mayo: In a small bowl, mix the mayonnaise and hot pepper sauce. 2. For the cilantro-lime slaw: In a large bowl, toss together the cabbage, onion, jalapeño, cilantro, lime juice, and salt to combine. Cover and refrigerate to chill. 3. For the shrimp: Place the egg in a shallow bowl and the crushed tortilla chips in another. Season the shrimp with the salt. Dip the shrimp in the egg, then in the crumbs, pressing gently to adhere. Place on a work surface and spray both sides with oil. 4. Preheat the air fryer to 360°F (182°C). 5. Working in batches, arrange a single layer of the shrimp in the air fryer basket. Air fry for 6 minutes, flipping halfway, until golden and cooked through in the center. 6. To serve, place 2 tortillas on each plate and top each with 3 shrimp. Top each taco with ¼ cup slaw, then drizzle with spicy mayo.

Oregano Tilapia Fingers

Prep time: 15 minutes | Cook time: 9 minutes | Serves 4

1 pound (454 g) tilapia fillet	½ teaspoon ground paprika
½ cup coconut flour	1 teaspoon dried oregano
2 eggs, beaten	1 teaspoon avocado oil

1. Cut the tilapia fillets into fingers and sprinkle with ground paprika and dried oregano. 2. Then dip the tilapia fingers in eggs and coat in the coconut flour. 3. Sprinkle fish fingers with avocado oil and cook in the air fryer at 370°F (188°C) for 9 minutes.

Paprika Crab Burgers

Prep time: 30 minutes | Cook time: 14 minutes | Serves 3

2 eggs, beaten 1 shallot, chopped 2 garlic cloves, crushed 1 tablespoon olive oil 1 teaspoon yellow mustard 1 teaspoon fresh cilantro, chopped	10 ounces (283 g) crab meat 1 teaspoon smoked paprika ½ teaspoon ground black pepper Sea salt, to taste ¾ cup Parmesan cheese

1. In a mixing bowl, thoroughly combine the eggs, shallot, garlic, olive oil, mustard, cilantro, crab meat, paprika, black pepper, and salt. Mix until well combined. 2. Shape the mixture into 6 patties. Roll the crab patties over grated Parmesan cheese, coating well on all sides. Place in your refrigerator for 2 hours. 3. Spritz the crab patties with cooking oil on both sides. Cook in the preheated air fryer at 360ºF (182ºC) for 14 minutes. Serve on dinner rolls if desired. Bon appétit!

BBQ Shrimp with Creole Butter Sauce

Prep time: 10 minutes | Cook time: 12 to 15 minutes | Serves 4

6 tablespoons unsalted butter ⅓ cup Worcestershire sauce 3 cloves garlic, minced Juice of 1 lemon 1 teaspoon paprika	1 teaspoon Creole seasoning 1½ pounds (680 g) large uncooked shrimp, peeled and deveined 2 tablespoons fresh parsley

1. Preheat the air fryer to 370ºF (188ºC). 2. In a large microwave-safe bowl, combine the butter, Worcestershire, and garlic. Microwave on high for 1 to 2 minutes until the butter is melted. Stir in the lemon juice, paprika, and Creole seasoning. Add the shrimp and toss until thoroughly coated. 3. Transfer the mixture to a casserole dish or pan that fits in your air fryer. Pausing halfway through the cooking time to turn the shrimp, air fry for 12 to 15 minutes, until the shrimp are cooked through. Top with the parsley just before serving.

Cajun and Lemon Pepper Cod

Prep time: 5 minutes | Cook time: 12 minutes | Makes 2 cod fillets

1 tablespoon Cajun seasoning 1 teaspoon salt ½ teaspoon lemon pepper ½ teaspoon freshly ground black pepper 2 (8-ounce / 227-g) cod	fillets, cut to fit into the air fryer basket Cooking spray 2 tablespoons unsalted butter, melted 1 lemon, cut into 4 wedges

1. Preheat the air fryer to 360ºF (182ºC). Spritz the air fryer basket with cooking spray. 2. Thoroughly combine the Cajun seasoning, salt, lemon pepper, and black pepper in a small bowl. Rub this mixture all over the cod fillets until completely coated. 3. Put the fillets in the air fryer basket and brush the melted butter over both sides of each fillet. 4. Bake in the preheated air fryer for 12 minutes, flipping the fillets halfway through, or until the fish flakes easily with a fork. 5. Remove the fillets from the basket and serve with fresh lemon wedges.

Almond-Crusted Fish

Prep time: 15 minutes | Cook time: 10 minutes | Serves 4

4 (4-ounce / 113-g) fish fillets ¾ cup bread crumbs ¼ cup sliced almonds, crushed 2 tablespoons lemon juice ⅛ teaspoon cayenne	Salt and pepper, to taste ¾ cup flour 1 egg, beaten with 1 tablespoon water Oil for misting or cooking spray

1. Split fish fillets lengthwise down the center to create 8 pieces. 2. Mix bread crumbs and almonds together and set aside. 3. Mix the lemon juice and cayenne together. Brush on all sides of fish. 4. Season fish to taste with salt and pepper. 5. Place the flour on a sheet of wax paper. 6. Roll fillets in flour, dip in egg wash, and roll in the crumb mixture. 7. Mist both sides of fish with oil or cooking spray. 8. Spray the air fryer basket and lay fillets inside. 9. Roast at 390ºF (199ºC) for 5 minutes, turn fish over, and cook for an additional 5 minutes or until fish is done and flakes easily.

Sea Bass with Roasted Root Vegetables

Prep time: 10 minutes | Cook time: 15 minutes | Serves 4

1 carrot, diced small 1 parsnip, diced small 1 rutabaga, diced small ¼ cup olive oil 1 teaspoon salt, divided	4 sea bass fillets ½ teaspoon onion powder 2 garlic cloves, minced 1 lemon, sliced, plus additional wedges for serving

1. Preheat the air fryer to 380°F(193°C). 2. In a small bowl, toss the carrot, parsnip, and rutabaga with olive oil and 1 teaspoon salt. 3. Lightly season the sea bass with the remaining 1 teaspoon of salt and the onion powder, then place it into the air fryer basket in a single layer. 4. Spread the garlic over the top of each fillet, then cover with lemon slices. 5. Pour the prepared vegetables into the basket around and on top of the fish. Roast for 15 minutes. 6. Serve with additional lemon wedges if desired.

Salmon Fritters with Zucchini

Prep time: 15 minutes | Cook time: 12 minutes | Serves 4

2 tablespoons almond flour 1 zucchini, grated 1 egg, beaten 6 ounces (170 g) salmon	fillet, diced 1 teaspoon avocado oil ½ teaspoon ground black pepper

1. Mix almond flour with zucchini, egg, salmon, and ground black pepper. 2. Then make the fritters from the salmon mixture. 3. Sprinkle the air fryer basket with avocado oil and put the fritters inside. 4. Cook the fritters at 375ºF (191ºC) for 6 minutes per side.

Chili Tilapia

Prep time: 5 minutes | Cook time: 20 minutes | Serves 4

4 tilapia fillets, boneless
1 teaspoon chili flakes
1 teaspoon dried oregano

1 tablespoon avocado oil
1 teaspoon mustard

1. Rub the tilapia fillets with chili flakes, dried oregano, avocado oil, and mustard and put in the air fryer. 2. Cook it for 10 minutes per side at 360°F (182°C).

Parmesan Mackerel with Coriander

Prep time: 10 minutes | Cook time: 7 minutes | Serves 2

12 ounces (340 g) mackerel fillet
2 ounces (57 g) Parmesan, grated

1 teaspoon ground coriander
1 tablespoon olive oil

1. Sprinkle the mackerel fillet with olive oil and put it in the air fryer basket. 2. Top the fish with ground coriander and Parmesan. 3. Cook the fish at 390°F (199°C) for 7 minutes.

Chapter 7
Snacks and Appetizers

Asiago Shishito Peppers

Prep time: 5 minutes | Cook time: 10 minutes | Serves 4

Oil, for spraying 6 ounces (170 g) shishito peppers 1 tablespoon olive oil	½ teaspoon salt ½ teaspoon lemon pepper ⅓ cup grated Asiago cheese, divided

1. Line the air fryer basket with parchment and spray lightly with oil. 2. Rinse the shishitos and pat dry with paper towels. 3. In a large bowl, mix together the shishitos, olive oil, salt, and lemon pepper. Place the shishitos in the prepared basket. 4. Roast at 350°F (177°C) for 10 minutes, or until blistered but not burned. 5. Sprinkle with half of the cheese and cook for 1 more minute. 6. Transfer to a serving plate. Immediately sprinkle with the remaining cheese and serve.

String Bean Fries

Prep time: 15 minutes | Cook time: 5 to 6 minutes | Serves 4

½ pound (227 g) fresh string beans 2 eggs 4 teaspoons water ½ cup white flour ½ cup bread crumbs ¼ teaspoon salt	¼ teaspoon ground black pepper ¼ teaspoon dry mustard (optional) Oil for misting or cooking spray

1. Preheat the air fryer to 360°F (182°C). 2. Trim stem ends from string beans, wash, and pat dry. 3. In a shallow dish, beat eggs and water together until well blended. 4. Place flour in a second shallow dish. 5. In a third shallow dish, stir together the bread crumbs, salt, pepper, and dry mustard if using. 6. Dip each string bean in egg mixture, flour, egg mixture again, then bread crumbs. 7. When you finish coating all the string beans, open air fryer and place them in basket. 8. Cook for 3 minutes. 9. Stop and mist string beans with oil or cooking spray. 10. Cook for 2 to 3 more minutes or until string beans are crispy and nicely browned.

Greek Yogurt Deviled Eggs

Prep time: 15 minutes | Cook time: 15 minutes | Serves 4

4 eggs ¼ cup nonfat plain Greek yogurt 1 teaspoon chopped fresh dill ⅛ teaspoon salt	⅛ teaspoon paprika ⅛ teaspoon garlic powder Chopped fresh parsley, for garnish

1. Preheat the air fryer to 260°F(127°C). 2. Place the eggs in a single layer in the air fryer basket and cook for 15 minutes. 3. Quickly remove the eggs from the air fryer and place them into a cold water bath. Let the eggs cool in the water for 10 minutes before removing and peeling them. 4. After peeling the eggs, cut them in half. 5. Spoon the yolk into a small bowl. Add the yogurt, dill, salt, paprika, and garlic powder and mix until smooth. 6. Spoon or pipe the yolk mixture into the halved egg whites. Serve with a sprinkle of fresh parsley on top.

Crunchy Basil White Beans

Prep time: 2 minutes | Cook time: 19 minutes | Serves 2

1 (15-ounce / 425-g) can cooked white beans 2 tablespoons olive oil 1 teaspoon fresh sage, chopped	¼ teaspoon garlic powder ¼ teaspoon salt, divided 1 teaspoon chopped fresh basil

1. Preheat the air fryer to 380°F(193°C). 2. In a medium bowl, mix together the beans, olive oil, sage, garlic, ⅛ teaspoon salt, and basil. 3. Pour the white beans into the air fryer and spread them out in a single layer. 4. Bake for 10 minutes. Stir and continue cooking for an additional 5 to 9 minutes, or until they reach your preferred level of crispiness. 5. Toss with the remaining ⅛ teaspoon salt before serving.

Pickle Chips

Prep time: 30 minutes | Cook time: 12 minutes | Serves 4

Oil, for spraying 2 cups sliced dill or sweet pickles, drained 1 cup buttermilk	2 cups all-purpose flour 2 large eggs, beaten 2 cups panko bread crumbs ¼ teaspoon salt

1. Line the air fryer basket with parchment and spray lightly with oil. 2. In a shallow bowl, combine the pickles and buttermilk and let soak for at least 1 hour, then drain. 3. Place the flour, beaten eggs, and bread crumbs in separate bowls. 4. Coat each pickle chip lightly in the flour, dip in the eggs, and dredge in the bread crumbs. Be sure each one is evenly coated. 5. Place the pickle chips in the prepared basket, sprinkle with the salt, and spray lightly with oil. You may need to work in batches, depending on the size of your air fryer. 6. Air fry at 390°F (199°C) for 5 minutes, flip, and cook for another 5 to 7 minutes, or until crispy. Serve hot.

Greek Street Tacos

Prep time: 10 minutes | Cook time: 3 minutes | Makes 8 small tacos

8 small flour tortillas (4-inch diameter) 8 tablespoons hummus 4 tablespoons crumbled feta cheese	4 tablespoons chopped kalamata or other olives (optional) Olive oil for misting

1. Place 1 tablespoon of hummus or tapenade in the center of each tortilla. Top with 1 teaspoon of feta crumbles and 1 teaspoon of chopped olives, if using. 2. Using your finger or a small spoon, moisten the edges of the tortilla all around with water. 3. Fold tortilla over to make a half-moon shape. Press center gently. Then press the edges firmly to seal in the filling. 4. Mist both sides with olive oil. 5. Place in air fryer basket very close but try not to overlap. 6. Air fry at 390°F (199°C) for 3 minutes, just until lightly browned and crispy.

Crispy Green Tomatoes with Horseradish

Prep time: 18 minutes | Cook time: 10 to 15 minutes | Serves 4

2 eggs ¼ cup buttermilk ½ cup bread crumbs ½ cup cornmeal ¼ teaspoon salt 1½ pounds (680 g) firm green tomatoes, cut into ¼-inch slices Cooking spray	Horseradish Sauce: ¼ cup sour cream ¼ cup mayonnaise 2 teaspoons prepared horseradish ½ teaspoon lemon juice ½ teaspoon Worcestershire sauce ⅛ teaspoon black pepper

1. Preheat air fryer to 390°F (199°C). Spritz the air fryer basket with cooking spray. 2. In a small bowl, whisk together all the ingredients for the horseradish sauce until smooth. Set aside. 3. In a shallow dish, beat the eggs and buttermilk. 4. In a separate shallow dish, thoroughly combine the bread crumbs, cornmeal, and salt. 5. Dredge the tomato slices, one at a time, in the egg mixture, then roll in the bread crumb mixture until evenly coated. 6. Working in batches, place the tomato slices in the air fryer basket in a single layer. Spray them with cooking spray. 7. Air fry for 10 to 15 minutes, flipping the slices halfway through, or until the tomato slices are nicely browned and crisp. 8. Remove from the basket to a platter and repeat with the remaining tomato slices. 9. Serve drizzled with the prepared horseradish sauce.

Pork and Cabbage Egg Rolls

Prep time: 15 minutes | Cook time: 12 minutes | Makes 12 egg rolls

Cooking oil spray 2 garlic cloves, minced 12 ounces (340 g) ground pork 1 teaspoon sesame oil ¼ cup soy sauce 2 teaspoons grated peeled	fresh ginger 2 cups shredded green cabbage 4 scallions, green parts (white parts optional), chopped 24 egg roll wrappers

1. Spray a skillet with the cooking oil and place it over medium-high heat. Add the garlic and cook for 1 minute until fragrant. 2. Add the ground pork to the skillet. Using a spoon, break the pork into smaller chunks. 3. In a small bowl, whisk the sesame oil, soy sauce, and ginger until combined. Add the sauce to the skillet. Stir to combine and continue cooking for about 5 minutes until the pork is browned and thoroughly cooked. 4. Stir in the cabbage and scallions. Transfer the pork mixture to a large bowl. 5. Lay the egg roll wrappers on a flat surface. Dip a basting brush in water and glaze each egg roll wrapper along the edges with the wet brush. This will soften the dough and make it easier to roll. 6. Stack 2 egg roll wrappers (it works best if you double-wrap the egg rolls). Scoop 1 to 2 tablespoons of the pork mixture into the center of each wrapper stack. 7. Roll one long side of the wrappers up over the filling. Press firmly on the area with the filling, tucking it in lightly to secure it in place. Fold in the left and right sides. Continue rolling to close. Use the basting brush to wet the seam and seal the egg roll. Repeat with the remaining ingredients. 8. Insert the crisper plate into the basket and the basket into the unit. Preheat the unit by selecting AIR FRY, setting the temperature to 400°F (204°C), and setting the time to 3 minutes. Select START/STOP to begin. 9. Once the unit is preheated, spray the crisper plate with cooking oil. Place the egg rolls into the basket. It is okay to stack them. Spray them with cooking oil. 10. Select AIR FRY, set the temperature to 400°F (204°C), and set the time to 12 minutes. Insert the basket into the unit. Select START/STOP to begin. 11. After 8 minutes, use tongs to flip the egg rolls. Reinsert the basket to resume cooking. 12. When the cooking is complete, serve the egg rolls hot.

Crispy Green Bean Fries with Lemon-Yogurt Sauce

Prep time: 5 minutes | Cook time: 5 minutes | Serves 4

Green Beans: 1 egg 2 tablespoons water 1 tablespoon whole wheat flour ¼ teaspoon paprika ½ teaspoon garlic powder ½ teaspoon salt ¼ cup whole wheat bread	crumbs ½ pound (227 g) whole green beans Lemon-Yogurt Sauce: ½ cup nonfat plain Greek yogurt 1 tablespoon lemon juice ¼ teaspoon salt ⅛ teaspoon cayenne pepper

Make the Green Beans: 1. Preheat the air fryer to 380°F(193°C). 2. In a medium shallow bowl, beat together the egg and water until frothy. 3. In a separate medium shallow bowl, whisk together the flour, paprika, garlic powder, and salt, then mix in the bread crumbs. 4. Spray the bottom of the air fryer with cooking spray. 5. Dip each green bean into the egg mixture, then into the bread crumb mixture, coating the outside with the crumbs. Place the green beans in a single layer in the bottom of the air fryer basket. 6. Fry in the air fryer for 5 minutes, or until the breading is golden brown. Make the Lemon-Yogurt Sauce: 7. In a small bowl, combine the yogurt, lemon juice, salt, and cayenne. 8. Serve the green bean fries alongside the lemon-yogurt sauce as a snack or appetizer.

Browned Ricotta with Capers and Lemon

Prep time: 10 minutes | Cook time: 8 to 10 minutes | Serves 4 to 6

1½ cups whole milk ricotta cheese 2 tablespoons extra-virgin olive oil 2 tablespoons capers, rinsed Zest of 1 lemon, plus more for garnish 1 teaspoon finely chopped	fresh rosemary Pinch crushed red pepper flakes Salt and freshly ground black pepper, to taste 1 tablespoon grated Parmesan cheese

1. Preheat the air fryer to 380°F (193°C). 2. In a mixing bowl, stir together the ricotta cheese, olive oil, capers, lemon zest, rosemary, red pepper flakes, salt, and pepper until well combined. 3. Spread the mixture evenly in a baking dish and place it in the air fryer basket. 4. Air fry for 8 to 10 minutes until the top is nicely browned. 5. Remove from the basket and top with a sprinkle of grated Parmesan cheese. 6. Garnish with the lemon zest and serve warm.

Greek Potato Skins with Olives and Feta

Prep time: 5 minutes | Cook time: 45 minutes | Serves 4

2 russet potatoes 3 tablespoons olive oil, divided, plus more for drizzling (optional) 1 teaspoon kosher salt, divided ¼ teaspoon black pepper	2 tablespoons fresh cilantro, chopped, plus more for serving ¼ cup Kalamata olives, diced ¼ cup crumbled feta Chopped fresh parsley, for garnish (optional)

1. Preheat the air fryer to 380°F(193°C). 2. Using a fork, poke 2 to 3 holes in the potatoes, then coat each with about ½ tablespoon olive oil and ½ teaspoon salt. 3. Place the potatoes into the air fryer basket and bake for 30 minutes. 4. Remove the potatoes from the air fryer, and slice in half. Using a spoon, scoop out the flesh of the potatoes, leaving a ½-inch layer of potato inside the skins, and set the skins aside. 5. In a medium bowl, combine the scooped potato middles with the remaining 2 tablespoons of olive oil, ½ teaspoon of salt, black pepper, and cilantro. Mix until well combined. 6. Divide the potato filling into the now-empty potato skins, spreading it evenly over them. Top each potato with a tablespoon each of the olives and feta. 7. Place the loaded potato skins back into the air fryer and bake for 15 minutes. 8. Serve with additional chopped cilantro or parsley and a drizzle of olive oil, if desired.

Homemade Sweet Potato Chips

Prep time: 5 minutes | Cook time: 15 minutes | Serves 2

1 large sweet potato, sliced thin	⅛ teaspoon salt 2 tablespoons olive oil

1. Preheat the air fryer to 380°F(193°C). 2. In a small bowl, toss the sweet potatoes, salt, and olive oil together until the potatoes are well coated. 3. Put the sweet potato slices into the air fryer and spread them out in a single layer. 4. Fry for 10 minutes. Stir, then air fry for 3 to 5 minutes more, or until the chips reach the preferred level of crispiness.

Red Pepper Tapenade

Prep time: 5 minutes | Cook time: 5 minutes | Serves 4

1 large red bell pepper 2 tablespoons plus 1 teaspoon olive oil, divided ½ cup Kalamata olives,	pitted and roughly chopped 1 garlic clove, minced ½ teaspoon dried oregano 1 tablespoon lemon juice

1. Preheat the air fryer to 380°F(193°C). 2. Brush the outside of a whole red pepper with 1 teaspoon olive oil and place it inside the air fryer basket. Roast for 5 minutes. 3. Meanwhile, in a medium bowl combine the remaining 2 tablespoons of olive oil with the olives, garlic, oregano, and lemon juice. 4. Remove the red pepper from the air fryer, then gently slice off the stem and remove the seeds. Roughly chop the roasted pepper into small pieces. 5. Add the red pepper to the olive mixture and stir all together until

combined. 6. Serve with pita chips, crackers, or crusty bread.

Veggie Shrimp Toast

Prep time: 15 minutes | Cook time: 3 to 6 minutes | Serves 4

8 large raw shrimp, peeled and finely chopped 1 egg white 2 garlic cloves, minced 3 tablespoons minced red bell pepper 1 medium celery stalk,	minced 2 tablespoons cornstarch ¼ teaspoon Chinese five-spice powder 3 slices firm thin-sliced no-sodium whole-wheat bread

1. Preheat the air fryer to 350°F (177°C). 2. In a small bowl, stir together the shrimp, egg white, garlic, red bell pepper, celery, cornstarch, and five-spice powder. Top each slice of bread with one-third of the shrimp mixture, spreading it evenly to the edges. With a sharp knife, cut each slice of bread into 4 strips. 3. Place the shrimp toasts in the air fryer basket in a single layer. You may need to cook them in batches. Air fry for 3 to 6 minutes, until crisp and golden brown. 4. Serve hot.

Roasted Grape Dip

Prep time: 10 minutes | Cook time: 8 to 12 minutes | Serves 6

2 cups seedless red grapes, rinsed and patted dry 1 tablespoon apple cider vinegar 1 tablespoon honey	1 cup low-fat Greek yogurt 2 tablespoons 2% milk 2 tablespoons minced fresh basil

1. In the air fryer basket, sprinkle the grapes with the cider vinegar and drizzle with the honey. Toss to coat. Roast the grapes at 380°F (193°C) for 8 to 12 minutes, or until shriveled but still soft. Remove from the air fryer. 2. In a medium bowl, stir together the yogurt and milk. 3. Gently blend in the grapes and basil. Serve immediately, or cover and chill for 1 to 2 hours.

Spicy Tortilla Chips

Prep time: 5 minutes | Cook time: 8 to 12 minutes | Serves 4

½ teaspoon ground cumin ½ teaspoon paprika ½ teaspoon chili powder ½ teaspoon salt	Pinch cayenne pepper 8 (6-inch) corn tortillas, each cut into 6 wedges Cooking spray

1. Preheat the air fryer to 375°F (191°C). Lightly spritz the air fryer basket with cooking spray. 2. Stir together the cumin, paprika, chili powder, salt, and pepper in a small bowl. 3. Working in batches, arrange the tortilla wedges in the air fryer basket in a single layer. Lightly mist them with cooking spray. Sprinkle some seasoning mixture on top of the tortilla wedges. 4. Air fry for 4 to 6 minutes, shaking the basket halfway through, or until the chips are lightly browned and crunchy. 5. Repeat with the remaining tortilla wedges and seasoning mixture. 6. Let the tortilla chips cool for 5 minutes and serve.

Bruschetta with Basil Pesto

Prep time: 10 minutes | Cook time: 5 to 11 minutes | Serves 4

8 slices French bread, ½ inch thick 2 tablespoons softened butter 1 cup shredded Mozzarella cheese	½ cup basil pesto 1 cup chopped grape tomatoes 2 green onions, thinly sliced

1. Preheat the air fryer to 350°F (177°C). 2. Spread the bread with the butter and place butter-side up in the air fryer basket. Bake for 3 to 5 minutes, or until the bread is light golden brown. 3. Remove the bread from the basket and top each piece with some of the cheese. Return to the basket in 2 batches and bake for 1 to 3 minutes, or until the cheese melts. 4. Meanwhile, combine the pesto, tomatoes, and green onions in a small bowl. 5. When the cheese has melted, remove the bread from the air fryer and place on a serving plate. Top each slice with some of the pesto mixture and serve.

Feta and Quinoa Stuffed Mushrooms

Prep time: 5 minutes | Cook time: 8 minutes | Serves 6

2 tablespoons finely diced red bell pepper 1 garlic clove, minced ¼ cup cooked quinoa ⅛ teaspoon salt ¼ teaspoon dried oregano 24 button mushrooms,	stemmed 2 ounces (57 g) crumbled feta 3 tablespoons whole wheat bread crumbs Olive oil cooking spray

1. Preheat the air fryer to 360°F(182°C). 2. In a small bowl, combine the bell pepper, garlic, quinoa, salt, and oregano. 3. Spoon the quinoa stuffing into the mushroom caps until just filled. 4. Add a small piece of feta to the top of each mushroom. 5. Sprinkle a pinch bread crumbs over the feta on each mushroom. 6. Spray the basket of the air fryer with olive oil cooking spray, then gently place the mushrooms into the basket, making sure that they don't touch each other. (Depending on the size of the air fryer, you may have to cook them in two batches.) 7. Place the basket into the air fryer and bake for 8 minutes. 8. Remove from the air fryer and serve.

Shrimp Pirogues

Prep time: 15 minutes | Cook time: 4 to 5 minutes | Serves 8

12 ounces (340 g) small, peeled, and deveined raw shrimp 3 ounces (85 g) cream cheese, room temperature 2 tablespoons plain yogurt 1 teaspoon lemon juice	1 teaspoon dried dill weed, crushed Salt, to taste 4 small hothouse cucumbers, each approximately 6 inches long

1. Pour 4 tablespoons water in bottom of air fryer drawer. 2. Place shrimp in air fryer basket in single layer and air fry at 390°F (199°C) for 4 to 5 minutes, just until done. Watch carefully because shrimp cooks quickly, and overcooking makes it tough. 3. Chop shrimp into small pieces, no larger than ½ inch. Refrigerate while mixing the remaining ingredients. 4. With a fork, mash and whip the cream cheese until smooth. 5. Stir in the yogurt and beat until smooth. Stir in lemon juice, dill weed, and chopped shrimp. 6. Taste for seasoning. If needed, add ¼ to ½ teaspoon salt to suit your taste. 7. Store in refrigerator until serving time. 8. When ready to serve, wash and dry cucumbers and split them lengthwise. Scoop out the seeds and turn cucumbers upside down on paper towels to drain for 10 minutes. 9. Just before filling, wipe centers of cucumbers dry. Spoon the shrimp mixture into the pirogues and cut in half crosswise. Serve immediately.

Hush Puppies

Prep time: 45 minutes | Cook time: 10 minutes | Serves 12

1 cup self-rising yellow cornmeal ½ cup all-purpose flour 1 teaspoon sugar 1 teaspoon salt 1 teaspoon freshly ground black pepper	1 large egg ⅓ cup canned creamed corn 1 cup minced onion 2 teaspoons minced jalapeño pepper 2 tablespoons olive oil, divided

1. Thoroughly combine the cornmeal, flour, sugar, salt, and pepper in a large bowl. 2. Whisk together the egg and corn in a small bowl. Pour the egg mixture into the bowl of cornmeal mixture and stir to combine. Stir in the minced onion and jalapeño. Cover the bowl with plastic wrap and place in the refrigerator for 30 minutes. 3. Preheat the air fryer to 375°F (191°C). Line the air fryer basket with parchment paper and lightly brush it with 1 tablespoon of olive oil. 4. Scoop out the cornmeal mixture and form into 24 balls, about 1 inch. 5. Arrange the balls in the parchment paper-lined basket, leaving space between each ball. 6. Air fry in batches for 5 minutes. Shake the basket and brush the balls with the remaining 1 tablespoon of olive oil. Continue cooking for 5 minutes until golden brown. 7. Remove the balls (hush puppies) from the basket and serve on a plate.

Peppery Chicken Meatballs

Prep time: 5 minutes | Cook time: 13 to 20 minutes | Makes 16 meatballs

2 teaspoons olive oil ¼ cup minced onion ¼ cup minced red bell pepper 2 vanilla wafers, crushed	1 egg white ½ teaspoon dried thyme ½ pound (227 g) ground chicken breast

1. Preheat the air fryer to 370°F (188°C). 2. In a baking pan, mix the olive oil, onion, and red bell pepper. Put the pan in the air fryer. Air fry for 3 to 5 minutes, or until the vegetables are tender. 3. In a medium bowl, mix the cooked vegetables, crushed wafers, egg white, and thyme until well combined 4. Mix in the chicken, gently but thoroughly, until everything is combined. 5. Form the mixture into 16 meatballs and place them in the air fryer basket. Air fry for 10 to 15 minutes, or until the meatballs reach an internal temperature of 165°F (74°C) on a meat thermometer. 6. Serve immediately.

Five-Ingredient Falafel with Garlic-Yogurt Sauce

Prep time: 5 minutes | Cook time: 15 minutes | Serves 4

Falafel:	Salt
1 (15-ounce / 425-g) can chickpeas, drained and rinsed	Garlic-Yogurt Sauce:
½ cup fresh parsley	1 cup nonfat plain Greek yogurt
2 garlic cloves, minced	1 garlic clove, minced
½ tablespoon ground cumin	1 tablespoon chopped fresh dill
1 tablespoon whole wheat flour	2 tablespoons lemon juice

Make the Falafel: 1. Preheat the air fryer to 360°F(182°C). 2. Put the chickpeas into a food processor. Pulse until mostly chopped, then add the parsley, garlic, and cumin and pulse for another 1 to 2 minutes, or until the ingredients are combined and turning into a dough. 3. Add the flour. Pulse a few more times until combined. The dough will have texture, but the chickpeas should be pulsed into small bits. 4. Using clean hands, roll the dough into 8 balls of equal size, then pat the balls down a bit so they are about ½-thick disks. 5. Spray the basket of the air fryer with olive oil cooking spray, then place the falafel patties in the basket in a single layer, making sure they don't touch each other. 6. Fry in the air fryer for 15 minutes. Make the garlic-yogurt sauce 7. In a small bowl, combine the yogurt, garlic, dill, and lemon juice. 8. Once the falafel are done cooking and nicely browned on all sides, remove them from the air fryer and season with salt. 9. Serve hot with a side of dipping sauce.

Zucchini Fries with Roasted Garlic Aïoli

Prep time: 20 minutes | Cook time: 12 minutes | Serves 4

1 tablespoon vegetable oil	Zucchini Fries:
½ head green or savoy cabbage, finely shredded	½ cup flour
Roasted Garlic Aïoli:	2 eggs, beaten
1 teaspoon roasted garlic	1 cup seasoned bread crumbs
½ cup mayonnaise	Salt and pepper, to taste
2 tablespoons olive oil	1 large zucchini, cut into ½-inch sticks
Juice of ½ lemon	Olive oil
Salt and pepper, to taste	

1. Make the aïoli: Combine the roasted garlic, mayonnaise, olive oil and lemon juice in a bowl and whisk well. Season the aïoli with salt and pepper to taste. 2. Prepare the zucchini fries. Create a dredging station with three shallow dishes. Place the flour in the first shallow dish and season well with salt and freshly ground black pepper. Put the beaten eggs in the second shallow dish. In the third shallow dish, combine the bread crumbs, salt and pepper. Dredge the zucchini sticks, coating with flour first, then dipping them into the eggs to coat, and finally tossing in bread crumbs. Shake the dish with the bread crumbs and pat the crumbs onto the zucchini sticks gently with your hands so they stick evenly. 3. Place the zucchini fries on a flat surface and let them sit at least 10 minutes before air frying to let them dry out a little. Preheat the air fryer to 400°F (204°C). 4. Spray the zucchini sticks with olive oil, and place them into the air fryer basket. You can air fry

the zucchini in two layers, placing the second layer in the opposite direction to the first. Air fry for 12 minutes turning and rotating the fries halfway through the cooking time. Spray with additional oil when you turn them over. 5. Serve zucchini fries warm with the roasted garlic aïoli.

Cheese-Stuffed Blooming Onion

Prep time: 10 minutes | Cook time: 15 minutes | Serves 2

1 large yellow onion (14 ounces / 397 g)	3 tablespoons mayonnaise
1 tablespoon olive oil	1 tablespoon fresh lemon juice
Kosher salt and freshly ground black pepper, to taste	1 tablespoon chopped fresh flat-leaf parsley
¼ cup plus 2 tablespoons panko bread crumbs	2 teaspoons whole-grain Dijon mustard
¼ cup grated Parmesan cheese	1 garlic clove, minced

1. Place the onion on a cutting board and trim the top off and peel off the outer skin. Turn the onion upside down and use a paring knife, cut vertical slits halfway through the onion at ½-inch intervals around the onion, keeping the root intact. When you turn the onion right side up, it should open up like the petals of a flower. Drizzle the cut sides of the onion with the olive oil and season with salt and pepper. Place petal-side up in the air fryer and air fry at 350°F (177°C) for 10 minutes. 2. Meanwhile, in a bowl, stir together the panko, Parmesan, mayonnaise, lemon juice, parsley, mustard, and garlic until incorporated into a smooth paste. 3. Remove the onion from the fryer and stuff the paste all over and in between the onion "petals." Return the onion to the air fryer and air fry at 375°F (191°C) until the onion is tender in the center and the bread crumb mixture is golden brown, about 5 minutes. Remove the onion from the air fryer, transfer to a plate, and serve hot.

Eggplant Fries

Prep time: 10 minutes | Cook time: 7 to 8 minutes per batch | Serves 4

1 medium eggplant	crumbs
1 teaspoon ground coriander	1 large egg
1 teaspoon cumin	2 tablespoons water
1 teaspoon garlic powder	Oil for misting or cooking spray
½ teaspoon salt	
1 cup crushed panko bread	

1. Peel and cut the eggplant into fat fries, ⅜- to ½-inch thick. 2. Preheat the air fryer to 390°F (199°C). 3. In a small cup, mix together the coriander, cumin, garlic, and salt. 4. Combine 1 teaspoon of the seasoning mix and panko crumbs in a shallow dish. 5. Place eggplant fries in a large bowl, sprinkle with remaining seasoning, and stir well to combine. 6. Beat eggs and water together and pour over eggplant fries. Stir to coat. 7. Remove eggplant from egg wash, shaking off excess, and roll in panko crumbs. 8. Spray with oil. 9. Place half of the fries in air fryer basket. You should have only a single layer, but it's fine if they overlap a little. 10. Cook for 5 minutes. Shake basket, mist lightly with oil, and cook 2 to 3 minutes longer, until browned and crispy. 11. Repeat step 10 to cook remaining eggplant.

Parmesan French Fries

Prep time: 10 minutes | Cook time: 25 minutes | Serves 2 to 3

2 to 3 large russet potatoes, peeled and cut into ½-inch sticks 2 teaspoons vegetable or canola oil ¾ cup grated Parmesan	cheese ½ teaspoon salt Freshly ground black pepper, to taste 1 teaspoon fresh chopped parsley

1. Bring a large saucepan of salted water to a boil on the stovetop while you peel and cut the potatoes. Blanch the potatoes in the boiling salted water for 4 minutes while you preheat the air fryer to 400ºF (204ºC). Strain the potatoes and rinse them with cold water. Dry them well with a clean kitchen towel. 2. Toss the dried potato sticks gently with the oil and place them in the air fryer basket. Air fry for 25 minutes, shaking the basket a few times while the fries cook to help them brown evenly. 3. Combine the Parmesan cheese, salt and pepper. With 2 minutes left on the air fryer cooking time, sprinkle the fries with the Parmesan cheese mixture. Toss the fries to coat them evenly with the cheese mixture and continue to air fry for the final 2 minutes, until the cheese has melted and just starts to brown. Sprinkle the finished fries with chopped parsley, a little more grated Parmesan cheese if you like, and serve.

Tortellini with Spicy Dipping Sauce

Prep time: 5 minutes | Cook time: 20 minutes | Serves 4

¾ cup mayonnaise 2 tablespoons mustard 1 egg ½ cup flour ½ teaspoon dried oregano	1½ cups bread crumbs 2 tablespoons olive oil 2 cups frozen cheese tortellini

1. Preheat the air fryer to 380ºF (193ºC). 2. In a small bowl, combine the mayonnaise and mustard and mix well. Set aside. 3. In a shallow bowl, beat the egg. In a separate bowl, combine the flour and oregano. In another bowl, combine the bread crumbs and olive oil, and mix well. 4. Drop the tortellini, a few at a time, into the egg, then into the flour, then into the egg again, and then into the bread crumbs to coat. Put into the air fryer basket, cooking in batches. 5. Air fry for about 10 minutes, shaking halfway through the cooking time, or until the tortellini are crisp and golden brown on the outside. Serve with the mayonnaise mixture.

Tangy Fried Pickle Spears

Prep time: 5 minutes | Cook time: 15 minutes | Serves 6

2 jars sweet and sour pickle spears, patted dry 2 medium-sized eggs ⅓ cup milk 1 teaspoon garlic powder	1 teaspoon sea salt ½ teaspoon shallot powder ⅓ teaspoon chili powder ⅓ cup all-purpose flour Cooking spray

1. Preheat the air fryer to 385ºF (196ºC). Spritz the air fryer basket with cooking spray. 2. In a bowl, beat together the eggs with milk. In another bowl, combine garlic powder, sea salt, shallot powder, chili powder and all-purpose flour until well blended. 3. One by one, roll the pickle spears in the powder mixture, then dredge them in the egg mixture. Dip them in the powder mixture a second time for additional coating. 4. Arrange the coated pickles in the prepared basket. Air fry for 15 minutes until golden and crispy, shaking the basket halfway through to ensure even cooking. 5. Transfer to a plate and let cool for 5 minutes before serving.

Crispy Mozzarella Sticks

Prep time: 8 minutes | Cook time: 5 minutes | Serves 4

½ cup all-purpose flour 1 egg, beaten ½ cup panko bread crumbs ½ cup grated Parmesan cheese	1 teaspoon Italian seasoning ½ teaspoon garlic salt 6 Mozzarella sticks, halved crosswise Olive oil spray

1. Put the flour in a small bowl. 2. Put the beaten egg in another small bowl. 3. In a medium bowl, stir together the panko, Parmesan cheese, Italian seasoning, and garlic salt. 4. Roll a Mozzarella-stick half in the flour, dip it into the egg, and then roll it in the panko mixture to coat. Press the coating lightly to make sure the bread crumbs stick to the cheese. Repeat with the remaining 11 Mozzarella sticks. 5. Insert the crisper plate into the basket and the basket into the unit. Preheat the unit by selecting AIR FRY, setting the temperature to 400ºF (204ºC), and setting the time to 3 minutes. Select START/STOP to begin. 6. Once the unit is preheated, spray the crisper plate with olive oil and place a parchment paper liner in the basket. Place the Mozzarella sticks into the basket and lightly spray them with olive oil. 7. Select AIR FRY, set the temperature to 400ºF (204ºC), and set the time to 5 minutes. Select START/STOP to begin. 8. When the cooking is complete, the Mozzarella sticks should be golden and crispy. Let the sticks stand for 1 minute before transferring them to a serving plate. Serve warm.

Cheese Wafers

Prep time: 30 minutes | Cook time: 5 to 6 minutes per batch | Makes 4 dozen

4 ounces (113 g) sharp Cheddar cheese, grated ¼ cup butter ½ cup flour	¼ teaspoon salt ½ cup crisp rice cereal Oil for misting or cooking spray

1. Cream the butter and grated cheese together. You can do it by hand, but using a stand mixer is faster and easier. 2. Sift flour and salt together. Add it to the cheese mixture and mix until well blended. 3. Stir in cereal. 4. Place dough on wax paper and shape into a long roll about 1 inch in diameter. Wrap well with the wax paper and chill for at least 4 hours. 5. When ready to cook, preheat the air fryer to 360ºF (182ºC). 6. Cut cheese roll into ¼-inch slices. 7. Spray the air fryer basket with oil or cooking spray and place slices in a single layer, close but not touching. 8. Cook for 5 to 6 minutes or until golden brown. When done, place them on paper towels to cool. 9. Repeat previous step to cook remaining cheese bites.

Onion Pakoras

Prep time: 30 minutes | Cook time: 10 minutes per batch | Serves 2

2 medium yellow or white onions, sliced (2 cups)	tablespoons chickpea flour
½ cup chopped fresh cilantro	1 teaspoon ground turmeric
2 tablespoons vegetable oil	1 teaspoon cumin seeds
1 tablespoon chickpea flour	1 teaspoon kosher salt
1 tablespoon rice flour, or 2	½ teaspoon cayenne pepper
	Vegetable oil spray

1. In a large bowl, combine the onions, cilantro, oil, chickpea flour, rice flour, turmeric, cumin seeds, salt, and cayenne. Stir to combine. Cover and let stand for 30 minutes or up to overnight. (This allows the onions to release moisture, creating a batter.) Mix well before using. 2. Spray the air fryer basket generously with vegetable oil spray. Drop half of the batter in 6 heaping tablespoons into the basket. Set the air fryer to 350ºF (177ºC) for 8 minutes. Carefully turn the pakoras over and spray with oil spray. Set the air fryer for 2 minutes, or until the batter is cooked through and crisp. 3. Repeat with remaining batter to make 6 more pakoras, checking at 6 minutes for doneness. Serve hot.

Crispy Cajun Dill Pickle Chips

Prep time: 5 minutes | Cook time: 10 minutes | Makes 16 slices

¼ cup all-purpose flour	2 large dill pickles, sliced
½ cup panko bread crumbs	into 8 rounds each
1 large egg, beaten	Cooking spray
2 teaspoons Cajun seasoning	

1. Preheat the air fryer to 390ºF (199ºC). 2. Place the all-purpose flour, panko bread crumbs, and egg into 3 separate shallow bowls, then stir the Cajun seasoning into the flour. 3. Dredge each pickle chip in the flour mixture, then the egg, and finally the bread crumbs. Shake off any excess, then place each coated pickle chip on a plate. 4. Spritz the air fryer basket with cooking spray, then place 8 pickle chips in the basket and air fry for 5 minutes, or until crispy and golden brown. Repeat this process with the remaining pickle chips. 5. Remove the chips and allow to slightly cool on a wire rack before serving.

Spiralized Potato Nest with Tomato Ketchup

Prep time: 10 minutes | Cook time: 15 minutes | Serves 2

1 large russet potato (about 12 ounces / 340 g)	tomatoes
2 tablespoons vegetable oil	2 tablespoons apple cider vinegar
1 tablespoon hot smoked paprika	1 tablespoon dark brown sugar
½ teaspoon garlic powder	1 tablespoon Worcestershire sauce
Kosher salt and freshly ground black pepper, to taste	1 teaspoon mild hot sauce
½ cup canned crushed	

1. Using a spiralizer, spiralize the potato, then place in a large colander. (If you don't have a spiralizer, cut the potato into thin ⅛-inch-thick matchsticks.) Rinse the potatoes under cold running water until the water runs clear. Spread the potatoes out on a double-thick layer of paper towels and pat completely dry. 2. In a large bowl, combine the potatoes, oil, paprika, and garlic powder. Season with salt and pepper and toss to combine. Transfer the potatoes to the air fryer and air fry at 400ºF (204ºC) until the potatoes are browned and crisp, 15 minutes, shaking the basket halfway through. 3. Meanwhile, in a small blender, purée the tomatoes, vinegar, brown sugar, Worcestershire, and hot sauce until smooth. Pour into a small saucepan or skillet and simmer over medium heat until reduced by half, 3 to 5 minutes. Pour the homemade ketchup into a bowl and let cool. 4. Remove the spiralized potato nest from the air fryer and serve hot with the ketchup.

Cinnamon Apple Chips

Prep time: 5 minutes | Cook time: 7 to 8 hours | Serves 4

4 medium apples, any type, cored and cut into ⅓-inch-thick slices (thin slices yield	crunchy chips)
	¼ teaspoon ground cinnamon
	¼ teaspoon ground nutmeg

1. Place the apple slices in a large bowl. Sprinkle the cinnamon and nutmeg onto the apple slices and toss to coat. 2. Insert the crisper plate into the basket and the basket into the unit. Preheat the unit by selecting DEHYDRATE, setting the temperature to 135ºF (57ºC), and setting the time to 3 minutes. Select START/STOP to begin. 3. Once the unit is preheated, place the apple chips into the basket. It is okay to stack them. 4. Select DEHYDRATE, set the temperature to 135ºF (57ºC), and set the time to 7 or 8 hours. Select START/STOP to begin. 5. When the cooking is complete, cool the apple chips. Serve or store at room temperature in an airtight container for up to 1 week.

Shishito Peppers with Herb Dressing

Prep time: 10 minutes | Cook time: 6 minutes | Serves 2 to 4

6 ounces (170 g) shishito peppers	1 tablespoon finely chopped fresh tarragon
1 tablespoon vegetable oil	1 tablespoon finely chopped fresh chives
Kosher salt and freshly ground black pepper, to taste	Finely grated zest of ½ lemon
½ cup mayonnaise	1 tablespoon fresh lemon juice
2 tablespoons finely chopped fresh basil leaves	Flaky sea salt, for serving
2 tablespoons finely chopped fresh flat-leaf parsley	

1. Preheat the air fryer to 400ºF (204ºC). 2. In a bowl, toss together the shishitos and oil to evenly coat and season with kosher salt and black pepper. Transfer to the air fryer and air fry for 6 minutes, shaking the basket halfway through, or until the shishitos are blistered and lightly charred. 3. Meanwhile, in a small bowl, whisk together the mayonnaise, basil, parsley, tarragon, chives, lemon zest, and lemon juice. 4. Pile the peppers on a plate, sprinkle with flaky sea salt, and serve hot with the dressing.

Crunchy Chickpeas

Prep time: 5 minutes | Cook time: 15 to 20 minutes | Serves 4

½ teaspoon chili powder ½ teaspoon ground cumin ¼ teaspoon cayenne pepper ¼ teaspoon salt	1 (19-ounce / 539-g) can chickpeas, drained and rinsed Cooking spray

1. Preheat the air fryer to 390ºF (199ºC). Lightly spritz the air fryer basket with cooking spray. 2. Mix the chili powder, cumin, cayenne pepper, and salt in a small bowl. 3. Place the chickpeas in a medium bowl and lightly mist with cooking spray. 4. Add the spice mixture to the chickpeas and toss until evenly coated. 5. Place the chickpeas in the air fryer basket and air fry for 15 to 20 minutes, or until the chickpeas are cooked to your preferred crunchiness. Shake the basket three or four times during cooking. 6. Let the chickpeas cool for 5 minutes before serving.

Black Bean Corn Dip

Prep time: 10 minutes | Cook time: 10 minutes | Serves 4

½ (15-ounce / 425-g) can black beans, drained and rinsed ½ (15-ounce / 425-g) can corn, drained and rinsed ¼ cup chunky salsa 2 ounces (57 g) reduced-fat	cream cheese, softened ¼ cup shredded reduced-fat Cheddar cheese ½ teaspoon ground cumin ½ teaspoon paprika Salt and freshly ground black pepper, to taste

1. Preheat the air fryer to 325ºF (163ºC). 2. In a medium bowl, mix together the black beans, corn, salsa, cream cheese, Cheddar cheese, cumin, and paprika. Season with salt and pepper and stir until well combined. 3. Spoon the mixture into a baking dish. 4. Place baking dish in the air fryer basket and bake until heated through, about 10 minutes. 5. Serve hot.

Fried Peaches

Prep time: 15 minutes | Cook time: 6 to 8 minutes | Serves 4

2 egg whites 1 tablespoon water ¼ cup sliced almonds 2 tablespoons brown sugar ½ teaspoon almond extract 1 cup crisp rice cereal	2 medium, very firm peaches, peeled and pitted ¼ cup cornstarch Oil for misting or cooking spray

1. Preheat the air fryer to 390ºF (199ºC). 2. Beat together egg whites and water in a shallow dish. 3. In a food processor, combine the almonds, brown sugar, and almond extract. Process until ingredients combine well and the nuts are finely chopped. 4. Add cereal and pulse just until cereal crushes. Pour crumb mixture into a shallow dish or onto a plate. 5. Cut each peach into eighths and place in a plastic bag or container with lid. Add cornstarch, seal, and shake to coat. 6. Remove peach slices from bag or container, tapping them hard to shake off the excess cornstarch. Dip in egg wash and roll in crumbs. Spray with oil. 7. Place in air fryer basket and cook for 5 minutes. Shake basket, separate any that have stuck together, and spritz a little oil on any spots that aren't browning. 8. Cook for 1 to 3 minutes longer, until golden brown and crispy.

Taco-Spiced Chickpeas

Prep time: 5 minutes | Cook time: 17 minutes | Serves 3

Oil, for spraying 1 (15½-ounce / 439-g) can chickpeas, drained 1 teaspoon chili powder	½ teaspoon ground cumin ½ teaspoon salt ½ teaspoon granulated garlic 2 teaspoons lime juice

1. Line the air fryer basket with parchment and spray lightly with oil. Place the chickpeas in the prepared basket. 2. Air fry at 390ºF (199ºC) for 17 minutes, shaking or stirring the chickpeas and spraying lightly with oil every 5 to 7 minutes. 3. In a small bowl, mix together the chili powder, cumin, salt, and garlic. 4. When 2 to 3 minutes of cooking time remain, sprinkle half of the seasoning mix over the chickpeas. Finish cooking. 5. Transfer the chickpeas to a medium bowl and toss with the remaining seasoning mix and the lime juice. Serve immediately.

Veggie Salmon Nachos

Prep time: 10 minutes | Cook time: 9 to 12 minutes | Serves 6

2 ounces (57 g) baked no-salt corn tortilla chips 1 (5-ounce / 142-g) baked salmon fillet, flaked ½ cup canned low-sodium black beans, rinsed and drained	1 red bell pepper, chopped ½ cup grated carrot 1 jalapeño pepper, minced ⅓ cup shredded low-sodium low-fat Swiss cheese 1 tomato, chopped

1. Preheat the air fryer to 360ºF (182ºC). 2. In a baking pan, layer the tortilla chips. Top with the salmon, black beans, red bell pepper, carrot, jalapeño, and Swiss cheese. 3. Bake in the air fryer for 9 to 12 minutes, or until the cheese is melted and starts to brown. 4. Top with the tomato and serve.

Artichoke and Olive Pita Flatbread

Prep time: 5 minutes | Cook time: 10 minutes | Serves 4

2 whole wheat pitas 2 tablespoons olive oil, divided 2 garlic cloves, minced ¼ teaspoon salt ½ cup canned artichoke	hearts, sliced ¼ cup Kalamata olives ¼ cup shredded Parmesan ¼ cup crumbled feta Chopped fresh parsley, for garnish (optional)

1. Preheat the air fryer to 380°F(193ºC). 2. Brush each pita with 1 tablespoon olive oil, then sprinkle the minced garlic and salt over the top. 3. Distribute the artichoke hearts, olives, and cheeses evenly between the two pitas, and place both into the air fryer to bake for 10 minutes. 4. Remove the pitas and cut them into 4 pieces each before serving. Sprinkle parsley over the top, if desired.

Apple Wedges

Prep time: 10 minutes | Cook time: 8 to 9 minutes | Serves 4

¼ cup panko bread crumbs	1 egg white
¼ cup pecans	2 teaspoons water
1½ teaspoons cinnamon	1 medium apple
1½ teaspoons brown sugar	Oil for misting or cooking
¼ cup cornstarch	spray

1. In a food processor, combine panko, pecans, cinnamon, and brown sugar. Process to make small crumbs. 2. Place cornstarch in a plastic bag or bowl with lid. In a shallow dish, beat together the egg white and water until slightly foamy. 3. Preheat the air fryer to 390°F (199°C). 4. Cut apple into small wedges. The thickest edge should be no more than ⅜- to ½-inch thick. Cut away the core, but do not peel. 5. Place apple wedges in cornstarch, reseal bag or bowl, and shake to coat. 6. Dip wedges in egg wash, shake off excess, and roll in crumb mixture. Spray with oil. 7. Place apples in air fryer basket in single layer and cook for 5 minutes. Shake basket and break apart any apples that have stuck together. Mist lightly with oil and cook 3 to 4 minutes longer, until crispy.

Fried Artichoke Hearts

Prep time: 10 minutes | Cook time: 12 minutes | Serves 10

Oil, for spraying	1 cup panko bread crumbs
3 (14-ounce / 397-g) cans quartered artichokes, drained and patted dry	⅓ cup grated Parmesan cheese
½ cup mayonnaise	Salt and freshly ground black pepper, to taste

1. Line the air fryer basket with parchment and spray lightly with oil. 2. Place the artichokes on a plate. Put the mayonnaise and bread crumbs in separate bowls. 3. Working one at a time, dredge each artichoke piece in the mayonnaise, then in the bread crumbs to cover. 4. Place the artichokes in the prepared basket. You may need to work in batches, depending on the size of your air fryer. 5. Air fry at 370°F (188°C) for 10 to 12 minutes, or until crispy and golden brown. 6. Sprinkle with the Parmesan cheese and season with salt and black pepper. Serve immediately.

Lemony Pear Chips

Prep time: 15 minutes | Cook time: 9 to 13 minutes | Serves 4

2 firm Bosc pears, cut crosswise into ⅛-inch-thick slices	squeezed lemon juice
	½ teaspoon ground cinnamon
1 tablespoon freshly	⅛ teaspoon ground cardamom

1. Preheat the air fryer to 380°F (193°C). 2. Separate the smaller stem-end pear rounds from the larger rounds with seeds. Remove the core and seeds from the larger slices. Sprinkle all slices with lemon juice, cinnamon, and cardamom. 3. Put the smaller chips into the air fryer basket. Air fry for 3 to 5 minutes, or until light golden brown, shaking the basket once during cooking. Remove from the air fryer. 4. Repeat with the larger slices, air frying for 6 to 8 minutes, or until light golden brown, shaking the basket once during cooking. 5. Remove the chips from the air fryer. Cool and serve or store in an airtight container at room temperature up for to 2 days.

Air Fryer Popcorn with Garlic Salt

Prep time: 3 minutes | Cook time: 10 minutes | Serves 2

2 tablespoons olive oil	1 teaspoon garlic salt
¼ cup popcorn kernels	

1. Preheat the air fryer to 380°F (193°C). 2. Tear a square of aluminum foil the size of the bottom of the air fryer and place into the air fryer. 3. Drizzle olive oil over the top of the foil, and then pour in the popcorn kernels. 4. Roast for 8 to 10 minutes, or until the popcorn stops popping. 5. Transfer the popcorn to a large bowl and sprinkle with garlic salt before serving.

Parmesan Cauliflower

Prep time: 15 minutes | Cook time: 15 minutes | Makes 5 cups

8 cups small cauliflower florets (about 1¼ pounds / 567 g)	½ teaspoon salt
	½ teaspoon turmeric
3 tablespoons olive oil	¼ cup shredded Parmesan cheese
1 teaspoon garlic powder	

1. Preheat the air fryer to 390°F (199°C). 2. In a bowl, combine the cauliflower florets, olive oil, garlic powder, salt, and turmeric and toss to coat. 3. Transfer to the air fryer basket and air fry for 15 minutes, or until the florets are crisp-tender. Shake the basket twice during cooking. 4. Remove from the basket to a plate. Sprinkle with the shredded Parmesan cheese and toss well. Serve warm.

Polenta Fries with Chili-Lime Mayo

Prep time: 10 minutes | Cook time: 28 minutes | Serves 4

Polenta Fries:	Chili-Lime Mayo:
2 teaspoons vegetable or olive oil	½ cup mayonnaise
	1 teaspoon chili powder
¼ teaspoon paprika	1 teaspoon chopped fresh cilantro
1 pound (454 g) prepared polenta, cut into 3-inch × ½-inch strips	¼ teaspoon ground cumin
	Juice of ½ lime

Salt and freshly ground black pepper, to taste

1. Preheat the air fryer to 400°F (204°C). 2. Mix the oil and paprika in a bowl. Add the polenta strips and toss until evenly coated. 3. Transfer the polenta strips to the air fry basket and air fry for 28 minutes until the fries are golden brown, shaking the basket once during cooking. Season as desired with salt and pepper. 4. Meanwhile, whisk together all the ingredients for the chili-lime mayo in a small bowl. 5. Remove the polenta fries from the air fryer to a plate and serve alongside the chili-lime mayo as a dipping sauce.

Sweet Potato Fries with Mayonnaise

Prep time: 5 minutes | Cook time: 20 minutes | Serves 2 to 3

1 large sweet potato (about 1 pound / 454 g), scrubbed 1 teaspoon vegetable or canola oil Salt, to taste Dipping Sauce:	¼ cup light mayonnaise ½ teaspoon sriracha sauce 1 tablespoon spicy brown mustard 1 tablespoon sweet Thai chili sauce

1. Preheat the air fryer to 200°F (93°C). 2. On a flat work surface, cut the sweet potato into fry-shaped strips about ¼ inch wide and ¼ inch thick. You can use a mandoline to slice the sweet potato quickly and uniformly. 3. In a medium bowl, drizzle the sweet potato strips with the oil and toss well. 4. Transfer to the air fryer basket and air fry for 10 minutes, shaking the basket twice during cooking. 5. Remove the air fryer basket and sprinkle with the salt and toss to coat. 6. Increase the air fryer temperature to 400°F (204°C) and air fry for an additional 10 minutes, or until the fries are crispy and tender. Shake the basket a few times during cooking. 7. Meanwhile, whisk together all the ingredients for the sauce in a small bowl. 8. Remove the sweet potato fries from the basket to a plate and serve warm alongside the dipping sauce.

Corn Dog Muffins

Prep time: 10 minutes | Cook time: 8 to 10 minutes per batch | Makes 8 muffins

1¼ cups sliced kosher hotdogs (3 or 4, depending on size) ½ cup flour ½ cup yellow cornmeal 2 teaspoons baking powder ½ cup skim milk	1 egg 2 tablespoons canola oil 8 foil muffin cups, paper liners removed Cooking spray Mustard or your favorite dipping sauce

1. Slice each hotdog in half lengthwise, then cut in ¼-inch half-moon slices. Set aside. 2. Preheat the air fryer to 390°F (199°C). 3. In a large bowl, stir together flour, cornmeal, and baking powder. 4. In a small bowl, beat together the milk, egg, and oil until just blended. 5. Pour egg mixture into dry ingredients and stir with a spoon to mix well. 6. Stir in sliced hot dogs. 7. Spray the foil cups lightly with cooking spray. 8. Divide mixture evenly into muffin cups. 9. Place 4 muffin cups in the air fryer basket and cook for 5 minutes. 10. Reduce temperature to 360°F (182°C) and cook 3 to 5 minutes or until toothpick inserted in center of muffin comes out clean. 11. Repeat steps 9 and 10 to bake remaining corn dog muffins. 12. Serve with mustard or other sauces for dipping.

Lemony Endive in Curried Yogurt

Prep time: 5 minutes | Cook time: 10 minutes | Serves 6

6 heads endive ½ cup plain and fat-free yogurt 3 tablespoons lemon juice	1 teaspoon garlic powder ½ teaspoon curry powder Salt and ground black pepper, to taste

1. Wash the endives, and slice them in half lengthwise. 2. In a bowl, mix together the yogurt, lemon juice, garlic powder, curry powder, salt and pepper. 3. Brush the endive halves with the marinade, coating them completely. Allow to sit for at least 30 minutes or up to 24 hours. 4. Preheat the air fryer to 320°F (160°C). 5. Put the endives in the air fryer basket and air fry for 10 minutes. 6. Serve hot.

Chapter 8
Vegetables and Sides

Sweet-and-Sour Brussels Sprouts

Prep time: 10 minutes | Cook time: 20 minutes | Serves 2

¼ cup Thai sweet chili sauce	sprouts halved)
2 tablespoons black vinegar or balsamic vinegar	2 small shallots, cut into ¼-inch-thick slices
½ teaspoon hot sauce, such as Tabasco	Kosher salt and freshly ground black pepper, to taste
8 ounces (227 g) Brussels sprouts, trimmed (large	2 teaspoons lightly packed fresh cilantro leaves

1. In a large bowl, whisk together the chili sauce, vinegar, and hot sauce. Add the Brussels sprouts and shallots, season with salt and pepper, and toss to combine. Scrape the Brussels sprouts and sauce into a cake pan. 2. Place the pan in the air fryer and roast at 375°F (191°C), stirring every 5 minutes, until the Brussels sprouts are tender and the sauce is reduced to a sticky glaze, about 20 minutes. 3. Remove the pan from the air fryer and transfer the Brussels sprouts to plates. Sprinkle with the cilantro and serve warm.

Lemon-Thyme Asparagus

Prep time: 5 minutes | Cook time: 4 to 8 minutes | Serves 4

1 pound (454 g) asparagus, woody ends trimmed off	black pepper, to taste
1 tablespoon avocado oil	2 ounces (57 g) goat cheese, crumbled
½ teaspoon dried thyme or ½ tablespoon chopped fresh thyme	Zest and juice of 1 lemon
Sea salt and freshly ground	Flaky sea salt, for serving (optional)

1. In a medium bowl, toss together the asparagus, avocado oil, and thyme, and season with sea salt and pepper. 2. Place the asparagus in the air fryer basket in a single layer. Set the air fryer to 400°F (204°C) and air fry for 4 to 8 minutes, to your desired doneness. 3. Transfer to a serving platter. Top with the goat cheese, lemon zest, and lemon juice. If desired, season with a pinch of flaky salt.

Broccoli-Cheddar Twice-Baked Potatoes

Prep time: 10 minutes | Cook time: 46 minutes | Serves 4

Oil, for spraying	1 teaspoon granulated garlic
2 medium russet potatoes	1 teaspoon onion powder
1 tablespoon olive oil	½ cup shredded Cheddar cheese
¼ cup broccoli florets	
1 tablespoon sour cream	

1. Line the air fryer basket with parchment and spray lightly with oil. 2. Rinse the potatoes and pat dry with paper towels. Rub the outside of the potatoes with the olive oil and place them in the prepared basket. 3. Air fry at 400°F (204°C) for 40 minutes, or until easily pierced with a fork. Let cool just enough to handle, then cut the potatoes in half lengthwise. 4. Meanwhile, place the broccoli in a microwave-safe bowl, cover with water, and microwave on high for 5 to 8 minutes. Drain and set aside. 5. Scoop out most of the potato flesh and transfer to a medium bowl. 6. Add the sour cream, garlic, and onion powder and stir until the potatoes are mashed. 7. Spoon the potato mixture back into the hollowed potato skins, mounding it to fit, if necessary. Top with the broccoli and cheese. Return the potatoes to the basket. You may need to work in batches, depending on the size of your air fryer. 8. Air fry at 400°F (204°C) for 3 to 6 minutes, or until the cheese has melted. Serve immediately.

Spinach and Sweet Pepper Poppers

Prep time: 10 minutes | Cook time: 8 minutes | Makes 16 poppers

4 ounces (113 g) cream cheese, softened	½ teaspoon garlic powder
1 cup chopped fresh spinach leaves	8 mini sweet bell peppers, tops removed, seeded, and halved lengthwise

1. In a medium bowl, mix cream cheese, spinach, and garlic powder. Place 1 tablespoon mixture into each sweet pepper half and press down to smooth. 2. Place poppers into ungreased air fryer basket. Adjust the temperature to 400°F (204°C) and air fry for 8 minutes. Poppers will be done when cheese is browned on top and peppers are tender-crisp. Serve warm.

Simple Zucchini Crisps

Prep time: 5 minutes | Cook time: 14 minutes | Serves 4

2 zucchini, sliced into ¼- to ½-inch-thick rounds (about 2 cups)	⅛ teaspoon sea salt
¼ teaspoon garlic granules	Freshly ground black pepper, to taste (optional)
	Cooking spray

1. Preheat the air fryer to 392°F (200°C). Spritz the air fryer basket with cooking spray. 2. Put the zucchini rounds in the air fryer basket, spreading them out as much as possible. Top with a sprinkle of garlic granules, sea salt, and black pepper (if desired). Spritz the zucchini rounds with cooking spray. 3. Roast for 14 minutes, flipping the zucchini rounds halfway through, or until the zucchini rounds are crisp-tender. 4. Let them rest for 5 minutes and serve.

Mediterranean Zucchini Boats

Prep time: 5 minutes | Cook time: 10 minutes | Serves 4

1 large zucchini, ends removed, halved lengthwise	¼ cup feta cheese
6 grape tomatoes, quartered	1 tablespoon balsamic vinegar
¼ teaspoon salt	1 tablespoon olive oil

1. Use a spoon to scoop out 2 tablespoons from center of each zucchini half, making just enough space to fill with tomatoes and feta. 2. Place tomatoes evenly in centers of zucchini halves and sprinkle with salt. Place into ungreased air fryer basket. Adjust the temperature to 350°F (177°C) and roast for 10 minutes. When done, zucchini will be tender. 3. Transfer boats to a serving tray and sprinkle with feta, then drizzle with vinegar and olive oil. Serve warm.

Roasted Brussels Sprouts with Orange and Garlic

Prep time: 5 minutes | Cook time: 10 minutes | Serves 4

1 pound (454 g) Brussels sprouts, quartered	2 tablespoons olive oil
2 garlic cloves, minced	½ teaspoon salt
	1 orange, cut into rings

1. Preheat the air fryer to 360°F(182°C). 2. In a large bowl, toss the quartered Brussels sprouts with the garlic, olive oil, and salt until well coated. 3. Pour the Brussels sprouts into the air fryer, lay the orange slices on top of them, and roast for 10 minutes. 4. Remove from the air fryer and set the orange slices aside. Toss the Brussels sprouts before serving.

Zucchini Balls

Prep time: 5 minutes | Cook time: 10 minutes | Serves 4

4 zucchinis	cheese
1 egg	1 tablespoon Italian herbs
½ cup grated Parmesan	1 cup grated coconut

1. Thinly grate the zucchinis and dry with a cheesecloth, ensuring to remove all the moisture. 2. In a bowl, combine the zucchinis with the egg, Parmesan, Italian herbs, and grated coconut, mixing well to incorporate everything. Using the hands, mold the mixture into balls. 3. Preheat the air fryer to 400°F (204°C). 4. Lay the zucchini balls in the air fryer basket and air fry for 10 minutes. 5. Serve hot.

Parsnip Fries with Romesco Sauce

Prep time: 20 minutes | Cook time: 24 minutes | Serves 4

Romesco Sauce:	and seeded (or ⅓ cup canned crushed tomatoes)
1 red bell pepper, halved and seeded	1 tablespoon red wine vinegar
1 (1-inch) thick slice of Italian bread, torn into pieces (about 1 to 1½ cups)	¼ teaspoon smoked paprika
1 cup almonds, toasted	½ teaspoon salt
Olive oil	¾ cup olive oil
½ Jalapeño pepper, seeded	3 parsnips, peeled and cut into long strips
1 tablespoon fresh parsley leaves	2 teaspoons olive oil
1 clove garlic	Salt and freshly ground black pepper, to taste
2 Roma tomatoes, peeled	

1. Preheat the air fryer to 400°F (204°C). 2. Place the red pepper halves, cut side down, in the air fryer basket and air fry for 8 to 10 minutes, or until the skin turns black all over. Remove the pepper from the air fryer and let it cool. When it is cool enough to handle, peel the pepper. 3. Toss the torn bread and almonds with a little olive oil and air fry for 4 minutes, shaking the basket a couple times throughout the cooking time. When the bread and almonds are nicely toasted, remove them from the air fryer and let them cool for just a minute or two. 4. Combine the toasted bread, almonds, roasted red pepper, Jalapeño pepper, parsley, garlic, tomatoes, vinegar, smoked paprika and salt in a food processor or blender. Process until smooth. With the processor running, add the olive oil through the feed tube until the sauce comes together in a smooth paste that is barely pourable. 5. Toss the parsnip strips with the olive oil, salt and freshly ground black pepper and air fry at 400°F (204°C) for 10 minutes, shaking the basket a couple times during the cooking process so they brown and cook evenly. Serve the parsnip fries warm with the Romesco sauce to dip into.

Roasted Radishes with Sea Salt

Prep time: 5 minutes | Cook time: 18 minutes | Serves 4

1 pound (454 g) radishes, ends trimmed if needed	2 tablespoons olive oil
	½ teaspoon sea salt

1. Preheat the air fryer to 360°F(182°C). 2. In a large bowl, combine the radishes with olive oil and sea salt. 3. Pour the radishes into the air fryer and roast for 10 minutes. Stir or turn the radishes over and roast for 8 minutes more, then serve.

Parmesan Mushrooms

Prep time: 5 minutes | Cook time: 15 minutes | Serves 4

Oil, for spraying	mix
1 pound (454 g) cremini mushrooms, stems trimmed	½ teaspoon salt
2 tablespoons olive oil	¼ teaspoon freshly ground black pepper
2 teaspoons granulated garlic	⅓ cup grated Parmesan cheese, divided
1 teaspoon dried onion soup	

1. Line the air fryer basket with parchment and spray lightly with oil. 2. In a large bowl, toss the mushrooms with the olive oil, garlic, onion soup mix, salt, and black pepper until evenly coated. 3. Place the mushrooms in the prepared basket. 4. Roast at 370°F (188°C) for 13 minutes. 5. Sprinkle half of the cheese over the mushrooms and cook for another 2 minutes. 6. Transfer the mushrooms to a serving bowl, add the remaining Parmesan cheese, and toss until evenly coated. Serve immediately.

Tingly Chili-Roasted Broccoli

Prep time: 5 minutes | Cook time: 10 minutes | Serves 2

12 ounces (340 g) broccoli florets	2 garlic cloves, finely chopped
2 tablespoons Asian hot chili oil	1 (2-inch) piece fresh ginger, peeled and finely chopped
1 teaspoon ground Sichuan peppercorns (or black pepper)	Kosher salt and freshly ground black pepper, to taste

1. In a bowl, toss together the broccoli, chili oil, Sichuan peppercorns, garlic, ginger, and salt and black pepper to taste. 2. Transfer to the air fryer and roast at 375°F (191°C), shaking the basket halfway through, until lightly charred and tender, about 10 minutes. Remove from the air fryer and serve warm.

Cauliflower Rice Balls

Prep time: 10 minutes | Cook time: 8 minutes | Serves 4

1 (10-ounce / 283-g) steamer bag cauliflower rice, cooked according to package instructions ½ cup shredded Mozzarella cheese	1 large egg 2 ounces (57 g) plain pork rinds, finely crushed ¼ teaspoon salt ½ teaspoon Italian seasoning

1. Place cauliflower into a large bowl and mix with Mozzarella. 2. Whisk egg in a separate medium bowl. Place pork rinds into another large bowl with salt and Italian seasoning. 3. Separate cauliflower mixture into four equal sections and form each into a ball. Carefully dip a ball into whisked egg, then roll in pork rinds. Repeat with remaining balls. 4. Place cauliflower balls into ungreased air fryer basket. Adjust the temperature to 400ºF (204ºC) and air fry for 8 minutes. Rice balls will be golden when done. 5. Use a spatula to carefully move cauliflower balls to a large dish for serving. Serve warm.

Five-Spice Roasted Sweet Potatoes

Prep time: 10 minutes | Cook time: 12 minutes | Serves 4

½ teaspoon ground cinnamon ¼ teaspoon ground cumin ¼ teaspoon paprika 1 teaspoon chile powder ⅛ teaspoon turmeric ½ teaspoon salt (optional)	Freshly ground black pepper, to taste 2 large sweet potatoes, peeled and cut into ¾-inch cubes (about 3 cups) 1 tablespoon olive oil

1. In a large bowl, mix together cinnamon, cumin, paprika, chile powder, turmeric, salt, and pepper to taste. 2. Add potatoes and stir well. 3. Drizzle the seasoned potatoes with the olive oil and stir until evenly coated. 4. Place seasoned potatoes in a baking pan or an ovenproof dish that fits inside your air fryer basket. 5. Cook for 6 minutes at 390ºF (199ºC), stop, and stir well. 6. Cook for an additional 6 minutes.

Citrus Sweet Potatoes and Carrots

Prep time: 5 minutes | Cook time: 20 to 25 minutes | Serves 4

2 large carrots, cut into 1-inch chunks 1 medium sweet potato, peeled and cut into 1-inch cubes ½ cup chopped onion	2 garlic cloves, minced 2 tablespoons honey 1 tablespoon freshly squeezed orange juice 2 teaspoons butter, melted

1. Insert the crisper plate into the basket and the basket into the unit. Preheat the unit by selecting AIR ROAST, setting the temperature to 400ºF (204ºC), and setting the time to 3 minutes. Select START/STOP to begin. 2. In a 6-by-2-inch round pan, toss together the carrots, sweet potato, onion, garlic, honey, orange juice, and melted butter to coat. 3. Once the unit is preheated, place the pan into the basket. 4. Select AIR ROAST, set the temperature to 400ºF (204ºC), and set the time to 25 minutes. Select START/STOP to begin. 5. After 15 minutes, remove the basket and shake the vegetables. Reinsert the basket to resume cooking. After 5 minutes, if the vegetables are tender and glazed, they are done. If not, resume cooking. 6. When the cooking is complete, serve immediately.

Scalloped Potatoes

Prep time: 5 minutes | Cook time: 20 minutes | Serves 4

2 cup sliced frozen potatoes, thawed 3 cloves garlic, minced Pinch salt	Freshly ground black pepper, to taste ¾ cup heavy cream

1. Preheat the air fryer to 380ºF (193ºC). 2. Toss the potatoes with the garlic, salt, and black pepper in a baking pan until evenly coated. Pour the heavy cream over the top. 3. Place the baking pan in the air fryer basket and bake for 15 minutes, or until the potatoes are tender and top is golden brown. Check for doneness and bake for another 5 minutes as needed. 4. Serve hot.

Tofu Bites

Prep time: 15 minutes | Cook time: 30 minutes | Serves 4

1 packaged firm tofu, cubed and pressed to remove excess water 1 tablespoon soy sauce 1 tablespoon ketchup 1 tablespoon maple syrup ½ teaspoon vinegar	1 teaspoon liquid smoke 1 teaspoon hot sauce 2 tablespoons sesame seeds 1 teaspoon garlic powder Salt and ground black pepper, to taste Cooking spray

1. Preheat the air fryer to 375ºF (191ºC). 2. Spritz a baking dish with cooking spray. 3. Combine all the ingredients to coat the tofu completely and allow the marinade to absorb for half an hour. 4. Transfer the tofu to the baking dish, then air fry for 15 minutes. Flip the tofu over and air fry for another 15 minutes on the other side. 5. Serve immediately.

Ratatouille

Prep time: 15 minutes | Cook time: 20 minutes | Serves 2 to 3

2 cups ¾-inch cubed peeled eggplant 1 small red, yellow, or orange bell pepper, stemmed, seeded, and diced 1 cup cherry tomatoes 6 to 8 cloves garlic, peeled	and halved lengthwise 3 tablespoons olive oil 1 teaspoon dried oregano ½ teaspoon dried thyme 1 teaspoon kosher salt ½ teaspoon black pepper

1. In a medium bowl, combine the eggplant, bell pepper, tomatoes, garlic, oil, oregano, thyme, salt, and pepper. Toss to combine. 2. Place the vegetables in the air fryer basket. Set the air fryer to 400ºF (204ºC) for 20 minutes, or until the vegetables are crisp-tender.

Herbed Shiitake Mushrooms

Prep time: 10 minutes | Cook time: 5 minutes | Serves 4

8 ounces (227 g) shiitake mushrooms, stems removed and caps roughly chopped 1 tablespoon olive oil ½ teaspoon salt Freshly ground black pepper, to taste	1 teaspoon chopped fresh thyme leaves 1 teaspoon chopped fresh oregano 1 tablespoon chopped fresh parsley

1. Preheat the air fryer to 400ºF (204ºC). 2. Toss the mushrooms with the olive oil, salt, pepper, thyme and oregano. Air fry for 5 minutes, shaking the basket once or twice during the cooking process. The mushrooms will still be somewhat chewy with a meaty texture. If you'd like them a little more tender, add a couple of minutes to this cooking time. 3. Once cooked, add the parsley to the mushrooms and toss. Season again to taste and serve.

Crispy Lemon Artichoke Hearts

Prep time: 10 minutes | Cook time: 15 minutes | Serves 2

1 (15-ounce / 425-g) can artichoke hearts in water, drained 1 egg 1 tablespoon water	¼ cup whole wheat bread crumbs ¼ teaspoon salt ¼ teaspoon paprika ½ lemon

1. Preheat the air fryer to 380°F(193°C). 2. In a medium shallow bowl, beat together the egg and water until frothy. 3. In a separate medium shallow bowl, mix together the bread crumbs, salt, and paprika. 4. Dip each artichoke heart into the egg mixture, then into the bread crumb mixture, coating the outside with the crumbs. Place the artichokes hearts in a single layer of the air fryer basket. 5. Fry the artichoke hearts for 15 minutes. 6. Remove the artichokes from the air fryer, and squeeze fresh lemon juice over the top before serving.

Lebanese Baba Ghanoush

Prep time: 15 minutes | Cook time: 20 minutes | Serves 4

1 medium eggplant 2 tablespoons vegetable oil 2 tablespoons tahini (sesame paste) 2 tablespoons fresh lemon juice	½ teaspoon kosher salt 1 tablespoon extra-virgin olive oil ½ teaspoon smoked paprika 2 tablespoons chopped fresh parsley

1. Rub the eggplant all over with the vegetable oil. Place the eggplant in the air fryer basket. Set the air fryer to 400ºF (204ºC) for 20 minutes, or until the eggplant skin is blistered and charred. 2. Transfer the eggplant to a resealable plastic bag, seal, and set aside for 15 minutes (the eggplant will finish cooking in the residual heat trapped in the bag). 3. Transfer the eggplant to a large bowl. Peel off and discard the charred skin. Roughly mash the eggplant flesh. Add the tahini, lemon juice, and salt. Stir to combine. 4.

Transfer the mixture to a serving bowl. Drizzle with the olive oil. Sprinkle with the paprika and parsley and serve.

Super Cheesy Gold Eggplant

Prep time: 15 minutes | Cook time: 30 minutes | Serves 4

1 medium eggplant, peeled and cut into ½-inch-thick rounds 1 teaspoon salt, plus more for seasoning ½ cup all-purpose flour 2 eggs ¾ cup Italian bread crumbs 2 tablespoons grated	Parmesan cheese Freshly ground black pepper, to taste Cooking oil spray ¾ cup marinara sauce ½ cup shredded Parmesan cheese, divided ½ cup shredded Mozzarella cheese, divided

1. Blot the eggplant with paper towels to dry completely. You can also sprinkle with 1 teaspoon of salt to sweat out the moisture; if you do this, rinse the eggplant slices and blot dry again. 2. Place the flour in a shallow bowl. 3. In another shallow bowl, beat the eggs. 4. In a third shallow bowl, stir together the bread crumbs and grated Parmesan cheese and season with salt and pepper. 5. Dip each eggplant round in the flour, in the eggs, and into the bread crumbs to coat. 6. Insert the crisper plate into the basket and the basket into the unit. Preheat the unit by selecting AIR FRY, setting the temperature to 400ºF (204ºC), and setting the time to 3 minutes. Select START/STOP to begin. 7. Once the unit is preheated, spray the crisper plate and the basket with cooking oil. Working in batches, place the eggplant rounds into the basket. Do not stack them. Spray the eggplant with the cooking oil. 8. Select AIR FRY, set the temperature to 400ºF (204ºC), and set the time to 10 minutes. Select START/STOP to begin. 9. After 7 minutes, open the unit and top each round with 1 teaspoon of marinara sauce and ½ tablespoon each of shredded Parmesan and Mozzarella cheese. Resume cooking for 2 to 3 minutes until the cheese melts. 10. Repeat steps 5, 6, 7, 8, and 9 with the remaining eggplant. 11. When the cooking is complete, serve immediately.

Stuffed Red Peppers with Herbed Ricotta and Tomatoes

Prep time: 10 minutes | Cook time: 20 minutes | Serves 4

2 red bell peppers 1 cup cooked brown rice 2 Roma tomatoes, diced 1 garlic clove, minced ¼ teaspoon salt ¼ teaspoon black pepper 4 ounces (113 g) ricotta	3 tablespoons fresh basil, chopped 3 tablespoons fresh oregano, chopped ¼ cup shredded Parmesan, for topping

1. Preheat the air fryer to 360°F(182°C). 2. Cut the bell peppers in half and remove the seeds and stem. 3. In a medium bowl, combine the brown rice, tomatoes, garlic, salt, and pepper. 4. Distribute the rice filling evenly among the four bell pepper halves. 5. In a small bowl, combine the ricotta, basil, and oregano. Put the herbed cheese over the top of the rice mixture in each bell pepper. 6. Place the bell peppers into the air fryer and roast for 20 minutes. 7. Remove and serve with shredded Parmesan on top.

Bacon-Wrapped Asparagus

Prep time: 10 minutes | Cook time: 10 minutes | Serves 4

8 slices reduced-sodium bacon, cut in half 16 thick (about 1 pound / 454	g) asparagus spears, trimmed of woody ends

1. Preheat the air fryer to 350ºF (177ºC). 2. Wrap a half piece of bacon around the center of each stalk of asparagus. 3. Working in batches, if necessary, arrange seam-side down in a single layer in the air fryer basket. Air fry for 10 minutes until the bacon is crisp and the stalks are tender.

Glazed Sweet Potato Bites

Prep time: 10 minutes | Cook time: 25 minutes | Serves 4

Oil, for spraying 3 medium sweet potatoes, peeled and cut into 1-inch pieces	2 tablespoons honey 1 tablespoon olive oil 2 teaspoons ground cinnamon

1. Line the air fryer basket with parchment and spray lightly with oil. 2. In a large bowl, toss together the sweet potatoes, honey, olive oil, and cinnamon until evenly coated. 3. Place the potatoes in the prepared basket. 4. Air fry at 400ºF (204ºC) for 20 to 25 minutes, or until crispy and easily pierced with a fork.

Butter and Garlic Fried Cabbage

Prep time: 5 minutes | Cook time: 9 minutes | Serves 2

Oil, for spraying ½ head cabbage, cut into bite-size pieces 2 tablespoons unsalted butter, melted	1 teaspoon granulated garlic ½ teaspoon coarse sea salt ¼ teaspoon freshly ground black pepper

1. Line the air fryer basket with parchment and spray lightly with oil. 2. In a large bowl, mix together the cabbage, butter, garlic, salt, and black pepper until evenly coated. 3. Transfer the cabbage to the prepared basket and spray lightly with oil. 4. Air fry at 375ºF (191ºC) for 5 minutes, toss, and cook for another 3 to 4 minutes, or until lightly crispy.

Dijon Roast Cabbage

Prep time: 10 minutes | Cook time: 10 minutes | Serves 4

1 small head cabbage, cored and sliced into 1-inch-thick slices 2 tablespoons olive oil, divided	½ teaspoon salt 1 tablespoon Dijon mustard 1 teaspoon apple cider vinegar 1 teaspoon granular erythritol

1. Drizzle each cabbage slice with 1 tablespoon olive oil, then sprinkle with salt. Place slices into ungreased air fryer basket, working in batches if needed. Adjust the temperature to 350ºF (177ºC) and air fry for 10 minutes. Cabbage will be tender and edges will begin to brown when done. 2. In a small bowl, whisk remaining olive oil with mustard, vinegar, and erythritol. Drizzle over cabbage in a large serving dish. Serve warm.

Burger Bun for One

Prep time: 2 minutes | Cook time: 5 minutes | Serves 1

2 tablespoons salted butter, melted ¼ cup blanched finely ground almond flour	¼ teaspoon baking powder ⅛ teaspoon apple cider vinegar 1 large egg, whisked

1. Pour butter into an ungreased ramekin. Add flour, baking powder, and vinegar to ramekin and stir until combined. Add egg and stir until batter is mostly smooth. 2. Place ramekin into air fryer basket. Adjust the temperature to 350ºF (177ºC) and bake for 5 minutes. When done, the center will be firm and the top slightly browned. Let cool, about 5 minutes, then remove from ramekin and slice in half. Serve.

Fig, Chickpea, and Arugula Salad

Prep time: 15 minutes | Cook time: 20 minutes | Serves 4

8 fresh figs, halved 1½ cups cooked chickpeas 1 teaspoon crushed roasted cumin seeds 4 tablespoons balsamic vinegar 2 tablespoons extra-virgin	olive oil, plus more for greasing Salt and ground black pepper, to taste 3 cups arugula rocket, washed and dried

1. Preheat the air fryer to 375ºF (191ºC). 2. Cover the air fryer basket with aluminum foil and grease lightly with oil. Put the figs in the air fryer basket and air fry for 10 minutes. 3. In a bowl, combine the chickpeas and cumin seeds. 4. Remove the air fried figs from the air fryer and replace with the chickpeas. Air fry for 10 minutes. Leave to cool. 5. In the meantime, prepare the dressing. Mix the balsamic vinegar, olive oil, salt and pepper. 6. In a salad bowl, combine the arugula rocket with the cooled figs and chickpeas. 7. Toss with the sauce and serve.

Curried Fruit

Prep time: 10 minutes | Cook time: 20 minutes | Serves 6 to 8

1 cup cubed fresh pineapple 1 cup cubed fresh pear (firm, not overly ripe) 8 ounces (227 g) frozen peaches, thawed	1 (15-ounce / 425-g) can dark, sweet, pitted cherries with juice 2 tablespoons brown sugar 1 teaspoon curry powder

1. Combine all ingredients in large bowl. Stir gently to mix in the sugar and curry. 2. Pour into a baking pan and bake at 360ºF (182ºC) for 10 minutes. 3. Stir fruit and cook 10 more minutes. 4. Serve hot.

Garlic Herb Radishes

Prep time: 10 minutes | Cook time: 10 minutes | Serves 4

1 pound (454 g) radishes 2 tablespoons unsalted butter, melted ½ teaspoon garlic powder	½ teaspoon dried parsley ¼ teaspoon dried oregano ¼ teaspoon ground black pepper

1. Remove roots from radishes and cut into quarters. 2. In a small bowl, add butter and seasonings. Toss the radishes in the herb butter and place into the air fryer basket. 3. Adjust the temperature to 350ºF (177ºC) and set the timer for 10 minutes. 4. Halfway through the cooking time, toss the radishes in the air fryer basket. Continue cooking until edges begin to turn brown. 5. Serve warm.

Green Tomato Salad

Prep time: 10 minutes | Cook time: 8 to 10 minutes | Serves 4

4 green tomatoes ½ teaspoon salt 1 large egg, lightly beaten ½ cup peanut flour 1 tablespoon Creole seasoning 1 (5-ounce / 142-g) bag arugula Buttermilk Dressing: 1 cup mayonnaise	½ cup sour cream 2 teaspoons fresh lemon juice 2 tablespoons finely chopped fresh parsley 1 teaspoon dried dill 1 teaspoon dried chives ½ teaspoon salt ½ teaspoon garlic powder ½ teaspoon onion powder

1. Preheat the air fryer to 400ºF (204ºC). 2. Slice the tomatoes into ½-inch slices and sprinkle with the salt. Let sit for 5 to 10 minutes. 3. Place the egg in a small shallow bowl. In another small shallow bowl, combine the peanut flour and Creole seasoning. Dip each tomato slice into the egg wash, then dip into the peanut flour mixture, turning to coat evenly. 4. Working in batches if necessary, arrange the tomato slices in a single layer in the air fryer basket and spray both sides lightly with olive oil. Air fry until browned and crisp, 8 to 10 minutes. 5. To make the buttermilk dressing: In a small bowl, whisk together the mayonnaise, sour cream, lemon juice, parsley, dill, chives, salt, garlic powder, and onion powder. 6. Serve the tomato slices on top of a bed of the arugula with the dressing on the side.

Mexican Corn in a Cup

Prep time: 5 minutes | Cook time: 10 minutes | Serves 4

4 cups frozen corn kernels (do not thaw) Vegetable oil spray 2 tablespoons butter ¼ cup sour cream ¼ cup mayonnaise ¼ cup grated Parmesan cheese (or feta, cotija, or	queso fresco) 2 tablespoons fresh lemon or lime juice 1 teaspoon chili powder Chopped fresh green onion (optional) Chopped fresh cilantro (optional)

1. Place the corn in the bottom of the air fryer basket and spray with vegetable oil spray. Set the air fryer to 350ºF (177ºC) for 10 minutes. 2. Transfer the corn to a serving bowl. Add the butter and stir until melted. Add the sour cream, mayonnaise, cheese, lemon juice, and chili powder; stir until well combined. Serve immediately with green onion and cilantro (if using).

Garlic Roasted Broccoli

Prep time: 8 minutes | Cook time: 10 to 14 minutes | Serves 6

1 head broccoli, cut into bite-size florets 1 tablespoon avocado oil 2 teaspoons minced garlic ⅛ teaspoon red pepper flakes	Sea salt and freshly ground black pepper, to taste 1 tablespoon freshly squeezed lemon juice ½ teaspoon lemon zest

1. In a large bowl, toss together the broccoli, avocado oil, garlic, red pepper flakes, salt, and pepper. 2. Set the air fryer to 375ºF (191ºC). Arrange the broccoli in a single layer in the air fryer basket, working in batches if necessary. Roast for 10 to 14 minutes, until the broccoli is lightly charred. 3. Place the florets in a medium bowl and toss with the lemon juice and lemon zest. Serve.

Creamed Spinach

Prep time: 10 minutes | Cook time: 15 minutes | Serves 4

Vegetable oil spray 1 (10-ounce / 283-g) package frozen spinach, thawed and squeezed dry ½ cup chopped onion 2 cloves garlic, minced 4 ounces (113 g) cream	cheese, diced ½ teaspoon ground nutmeg 1 teaspoon kosher salt 1 teaspoon black pepper ½ cup grated Parmesan cheese

1. Spray a baking pan with vegetable oil spray. 2. In a medium bowl, combine the spinach, onion, garlic, cream cheese, nutmeg, salt, and pepper. Transfer to the prepared pan. 3. Place the pan in the air fryer basket. Set the air fryer to 350ºF (177ºC) for 10 minutes. Open and stir to thoroughly combine the cream cheese and spinach. 4. Sprinkle the Parmesan cheese on top. Set the air fryer to 400ºF (204ºC) for 5 minutes, or until the cheese has melted and browned.

Buttery Mushrooms

Prep time: 10 minutes | Cook time: 10 minutes | Serves 4

8 ounces (227 g) cremini mushrooms, halved 2 tablespoons salted butter, melted	¼ teaspoon salt ¼ teaspoon ground black pepper

1. In a medium bowl, toss mushrooms with butter, then sprinkle with salt and pepper. Place into ungreased air fryer basket. Adjust the temperature to 400ºF (204ºC) and air fry for 10 minutes, shaking the basket halfway through cooking. Mushrooms will be tender when done. Serve warm.

Asparagus Fries

Prep time: 15 minutes | Cook time: 5 to 7 minutes per batch | Serves 4

12 ounces (340 g) fresh asparagus spears with tough ends trimmed off 2 egg whites ¼ cup water ¾ cup panko bread crumbs	¼ cup grated Parmesan cheese, plus 2 tablespoons ¼ teaspoon salt Oil for misting or cooking spray

1. Preheat the air fryer to 390ºF (199ºC). 2. In a shallow dish, beat egg whites and water until slightly foamy. 3. In another shallow dish, combine panko, Parmesan, and salt. 4. Dip asparagus spears in egg, then roll in crumbs. Spray with oil or cooking spray. 5. Place a layer of asparagus in air fryer basket, leaving just a little space in between each spear. Stack another layer on top, crosswise. Air fry at 390ºF (199ºC) for 5 to 7 minutes, until crispy and golden brown. 6. Repeat to cook remaining asparagus.

Spiced Butternut Squash

Prep time: 10 minutes | Cook time: 15 minutes | Serves 4

4 cups 1-inch-cubed butternut squash 2 tablespoons vegetable oil 1 to 2 tablespoons brown	sugar 1 teaspoon Chinese five-spice powder

1. In a medium bowl, combine the squash, oil, sugar, and five-spice powder. Toss to coat. 2. Place the squash in the air fryer basket. Set the air fryer to 400ºF (204ºC) for 15 minutes or until tender.

Shishito Pepper Roast

Prep time: 4 minutes | Cook time: 9 minutes | Serves 4

Cooking oil spray (sunflower, safflower, or refined coconut) 1 pound (454 g) shishito, Anaheim, or bell peppers,	rinsed 1 tablespoon soy sauce 2 teaspoons freshly squeezed lime juice 2 large garlic cloves, pressed

1. Insert the crisper plate into the basket and the basket into the unit. Preheat the unit by selecting AIR ROAST, setting the temperature to 390ºF (199ºC), and setting the time to 3 minutes. Select START/STOP to begin. 2. Once the unit is preheated, spray the crisper plate and the basket with cooking oil. Place the peppers into the basket and spray them with oil. 3. Select AIR ROAST, set the temperature to 390ºF (199ºC), and set the time to 9 minutes. Select START/STOP to begin. 4. After 3 minutes, remove the basket and shake the peppers. Spray the peppers with more oil. Reinsert the basket to resume cooking. Repeat this step again after 3 minutes. 5. While the peppers roast, in a medium bowl, whisk the soy sauce, lime juice, and garlic until combined. Set aside. 6. When the cooking is complete, several of the peppers should have lots of nice browned spots on them. If using Anaheim or bell peppers, cut a slit in the side of each pepper and remove the seeds, which can be bitter. 7. Place the roasted peppers in the bowl with the sauce. Toss to coat the peppers evenly and serve.

Cauliflower with Lime Juice

Prep time: 10 minutes | Cook time: 7 minutes | Serves 4

2 cups chopped cauliflower florets 2 tablespoons coconut oil, melted 2 teaspoons chili powder	½ teaspoon garlic powder 1 medium lime 2 tablespoons chopped cilantro

1. In a large bowl, toss cauliflower with coconut oil. Sprinkle with chili powder and garlic powder. Place seasoned cauliflower into the air fryer basket. 2. Adjust the temperature to 350ºF (177ºC) and set the timer for 7 minutes. 3. Cauliflower will be tender and begin to turn golden at the edges. Place into a serving bowl. 4. Cut the lime into quarters and squeeze juice over cauliflower. Garnish with cilantro.

Flatbread

Prep time: 5 minutes | Cook time: 7 minutes | Serves 2

1 cup shredded Mozzarella cheese ¼ cup blanched finely	ground almond flour 1 ounce (28 g) full-fat cream cheese, softened

1. In a large microwave-safe bowl, melt Mozzarella in the microwave for 30 seconds. Stir in almond flour until smooth and then add cream cheese. Continue mixing until dough forms, gently kneading it with wet hands if necessary. 2. Divide the dough into two pieces and roll out to ¼-inch thickness between two pieces of parchment. Cut another piece of parchment to fit your air fryer basket. 3. Place a piece of flatbread onto your parchment and into the air fryer, working in two batches if needed. 4. Adjust the temperature to 320ºF (160ºC) and air fry for 7 minutes. 5. Halfway through the cooking time flip the flatbread. Serve warm.

Caramelized Eggplant with Harissa Yogurt

Prep time: 10 minutes | Cook time: 15 minutes | Serves 2

1 medium eggplant (about ¾ pound / 340 g), cut crosswise into ½-inch-thick slices and quartered 2 tablespoons vegetable oil Kosher salt and freshly	ground black pepper, to taste ½ cup plain yogurt (not Greek) 2 tablespoons harissa paste 1 garlic clove, grated 2 teaspoons honey

1. In a bowl, toss together the eggplant and oil, season with salt and pepper, and toss to coat evenly. Transfer to the air fryer and air fry at 400ºF (204ºC), shaking the basket every 5 minutes, until the eggplant is caramelized and tender, about 15 minutes. 2. Meanwhile, in a small bowl, whisk together the yogurt, harissa, and garlic, then spread onto a serving plate. 3. Pile the warm eggplant over the yogurt and drizzle with the honey just before serving.

Spinach and Cheese Stuffed Tomatoes

Prep time: 20 minutes | Cook time: 15 minutes | Serves 2

4 ripe beefsteak tomatoes ¾ teaspoon black pepper ½ teaspoon kosher salt 1 (10-ounce / 283-g) package frozen chopped spinach, thawed and squeezed dry	1 (5.2-ounce / 147-g) package garlic-and-herb Boursin cheese 3 tablespoons sour cream ½ cup finely grated Parmesan cheese

1. Cut the tops off the tomatoes. Using a small spoon, carefully remove and discard the pulp. Season the insides with ½ teaspoon of the black pepper and ¼ teaspoon of the salt. Invert the tomatoes onto paper towels and allow to drain while you make the filling. 2. Meanwhile, in a medium bowl, combine the spinach, Boursin cheese, sour cream, ¼ cup of the Parmesan, and the remaining ¼ teaspoon salt and ¼ teaspoon pepper. Stir until ingredients are well combined. Divide the filling among the tomatoes. Top with the remaining ¼ cup Parmesan. 3. Place the tomatoes in the air fryer basket. Set the air fryer to 350°F (177°C) for 15 minutes, or until the filling is hot.

Curry Roasted Cauliflower

Prep time: 10 minutes | Cook time: 20 minutes | Serves 4

¼ cup olive oil 2 teaspoons curry powder ½ teaspoon salt ¼ teaspoon freshly ground black pepper 1 head cauliflower, cut into	bite-size florets ½ red onion, sliced 2 tablespoons freshly chopped parsley, for garnish (optional)

1. Preheat the air fryer to 400°F (204°C). 2. In a large bowl, combine the olive oil, curry powder, salt, and pepper. Add the cauliflower and onion. Toss gently until the vegetables are completely coated with the oil mixture. Transfer the vegetables to the basket of the air fryer. 3. Pausing about halfway through the cooking time to shake the basket, air fry for 20 minutes until the cauliflower is tender and beginning to brown. Top with the parsley, if desired, before serving.

Grits Casserole

Prep time: 5 minutes | Cook time: 28 to 30 minutes | Serves 4

10 fresh asparagus spears, cut into 1-inch pieces 2 cups cooked grits, cooled to room temperature 1 egg, beaten 2 teaspoons Worcestershire Oil for misting or cooking spray	sauce ½ teaspoon garlic powder ¼ teaspoon salt 2 slices provolone cheese (about 1½ ounces / 43 g)

1. Mist asparagus spears with oil and air fry at 390°F (199°C) for 5 minutes, until crisp-tender. 2. In a medium bowl, mix together the grits, egg, Worcestershire, garlic powder, and salt. 3. Spoon half of grits mixture into a baking pan and top with asparagus. 4. Tear cheese slices into pieces and layer evenly on top of asparagus. 5. Top with remaining grits. 6. Bake at 360°F (182°C) for 23 to 25 minutes. The casserole will rise a little as it cooks. When done, the top will have browned lightly with just a hint of crispiness.

Corn on the Cob

Prep time: 5 minutes | Cook time: 12 to 15 minutes | Serves 4

2 large ears fresh corn Olive oil for misting	Salt, to taste (optional)

1. Shuck corn, remove silks, and wash. 2. Cut or break each ear in half crosswise. 3. Spray corn with olive oil. 4. Air fry at 390°F (199°C) for 12 to 15 minutes or until browned as much as you like. 5. Serve plain or with coarsely ground salt.

Garlic-Parmesan Crispy Baby Potatoes

Prep time: 10 minutes | Cook time: 15 minutes | Serves 4

Oil, for spraying 1 pound (454 g) baby potatoes ½ cup grated Parmesan cheese, divided 3 tablespoons olive oil 2 teaspoons granulated garlic	½ teaspoon onion powder ½ teaspoon salt ¼ teaspoon freshly ground black pepper ¼ teaspoon paprika 2 tablespoons chopped fresh parsley, for garnish

1. Line the air fryer basket with parchment and spray lightly with oil. 2. Rinse the potatoes, pat dry with paper towels, and place in a large bowl. 3. In a small bowl, mix together ¼ cup of Parmesan cheese, the olive oil, garlic, onion powder, salt, black pepper, and paprika. Pour the mixture over the potatoes and toss to coat. 4. Transfer the potatoes to the prepared basket and spread them out in an even layer, taking care to keep them from touching. You may need to work in batches, depending on the size of your air fryer. 5. Air fry at 400°F (204°C) for 15 minutes, stirring after 7 to 8 minutes, or until easily pierced with a fork. Continue to cook for another 1 to 2 minutes, if needed. 6. Sprinkle with the parsley and the remaining Parmesan cheese and serve.

Glazed Carrots

Prep time: 10 minutes | Cook time: 8 to 10 minutes | Serves 4

2 teaspoons honey 1 teaspoon orange juice ½ teaspoon grated orange rind	⅛ teaspoon ginger 1 pound (454 g) baby carrots 2 teaspoons olive oil ¼ teaspoon salt

1. Combine honey, orange juice, grated rind, and ginger in a small bowl and set aside. 2. Toss the carrots, oil, and salt together to coat well and pour them into the air fryer basket. 3. Roast at 390°F (199°C) for 5 minutes. Shake basket to stir a little and cook for 2 to 4 minutes more, until carrots are barely tender. 4. Pour carrots into a baking pan. 5. Stir the honey mixture to combine well, pour glaze over carrots, and stir to coat. 6. Roast at 360°F (182°C) for 1 minute or just until heated through.

Garlic and Thyme Tomatoes

Prep time: 10 minutes | Cook time: 15 minutes | Serves 2 to 4

4 Roma tomatoes
1 tablespoon olive oil
Salt and freshly ground black pepper, to taste

1 clove garlic, minced
½ teaspoon dried thyme

1. Preheat the air fryer to 390°F (199°C). 2. Cut the tomatoes in half and scoop out the seeds and any pithy parts with your fingers. Place the tomatoes in a bowl and toss with the olive oil, salt, pepper, garlic and thyme. 3. Transfer the tomatoes to the air fryer, cut side up. Air fry for 15 minutes. The edges should just start to brown. Let the tomatoes cool to an edible temperature for a few minutes and then use in pastas, on top of crostini, or as an accompaniment to any poultry, meat or fish.

Parmesan-Thyme Butternut Squash

Prep time: 15 minutes | Cook time: 20 minutes | Serves 4

2½ cups butternut squash, cubed into 1-inch pieces
(approximately 1 medium)
2 tablespoons olive oil
¼ teaspoon salt

¼ teaspoon garlic powder
¼ teaspoon black pepper
1 tablespoon fresh thyme
¼ cup grated Parmesan

1. Preheat the air fryer to 360°F (182°C). 2. In a large bowl, combine the cubed squash with the olive oil, salt, garlic powder, pepper, and thyme until the squash is well coated. 3. Pour this mixture into the air fryer basket, and roast for 10 minutes. Stir and roast another 8 to 10 minutes more. 4. Remove the squash from the air fryer and toss with freshly grated Parmesan before serving.

Chapter 9

Vegetarian Mains

Potato and Broccoli with Tofu Scramble

Prep time: 15 minutes | Cook time: 30 minutes | Serves 3

2½ cups chopped red potato	1 teaspoon turmeric powder
2 tablespoons olive oil, divided	½ teaspoon onion powder
1 block tofu, chopped finely	½ teaspoon garlic powder
2 tablespoons tamari	½ cup chopped onion
	4 cups broccoli florets

1. Preheat the air fryer to 400ºF (204ºC). 2. Toss together the potatoes and 1 tablespoon of the olive oil. 3. Air fry the potatoes in a baking dish for 15 minutes, shaking once during the cooking time to ensure they fry evenly. 4. Combine the tofu, the remaining 1 tablespoon of the olive oil, turmeric, onion powder, tamari, and garlic powder together, stirring in the onions, followed by the broccoli. 5. Top the potatoes with the tofu mixture and air fry for an additional 15 minutes. Serve warm.

Parmesan Artichokes

Prep time: 10 minutes | Cook time: 10 minutes | Serves 4

2 medium artichokes, trimmed and quartered, center removed	Parmesan cheese
2 tablespoons coconut oil	¼ cup blanched finely ground almond flour
1 large egg, beaten	½ teaspoon crushed red pepper flakes
½ cup grated vegetarian	

1. In a large bowl, toss artichokes in coconut oil and then dip each piece into the egg. 2. Mix the Parmesan and almond flour in a large bowl. Add artichoke pieces and toss to cover as completely as possible, sprinkle with pepper flakes. Place into the air fryer basket. 3. Adjust the temperature to 400ºF (204ºC) and air fry for 10 minutes. 4. Toss the basket two times during cooking. Serve warm.

Cayenne Tahini Kale

Prep time: 5 minutes | Cook time: 15 minutes | Serves 2 to 4

Dressing:	Kale:
¼ cup tahini	4 cups packed torn kale leaves (stems and ribs removed and leaves torn into palm-size pieces)
¼ cup fresh lemon juice	
2 tablespoons olive oil	
1 teaspoon sesame seeds	
½ teaspoon garlic powder	Kosher salt and freshly ground black pepper, to taste
¼ teaspoon cayenne pepper	

1. Preheat the air fryer to 350ºF (177ºC). 2. Make the dressing: Whisk together the tahini, lemon juice, olive oil, sesame seeds, garlic powder, and cayenne pepper in a large bowl until well mixed. 3. Add the kale and massage the dressing thoroughly all over the leaves. Sprinkle the salt and pepper to season. 4. Place the kale in the air fryer basket in a single layer and air fry for about 15 minutes, or until the leaves are slightly wilted and crispy. 5. Remove from the basket and serve on a plate.

Roasted Veggie Bowl

Prep time: 10 minutes | Cook time: 15 minutes | Serves 2

1 cup broccoli florets	½ medium green bell pepper, seeded and sliced ¼ inch thick
1 cup quartered Brussels sprouts	
½ cup cauliflower florets	1 tablespoon coconut oil
¼ medium white onion, peeled and sliced ¼ inch thick	2 teaspoons chili powder
	½ teaspoon garlic powder
	½ teaspoon cumin

1. Toss all ingredients together in a large bowl until vegetables are fully coated with oil and seasoning. 2. Pour vegetables into the air fryer basket. 3. Adjust the temperature to 360ºF (182ºC) and roast for 15 minutes. 4. Shake two or three times during cooking. Serve warm.

Baked Zucchini

Prep time: 10 minutes | Cook time: 8 minutes | Serves 4

2 tablespoons salted butter	cream cheese
¼ cup diced white onion	1 cup shredded sharp Cheddar cheese
½ teaspoon minced garlic	
½ cup heavy whipping cream	2 medium zucchini, spiralized
2 ounces (57 g) full-fat	

1. In a large saucepan over medium heat, melt butter. Add onion and sauté until it begins to soften, 1 to 3 minutes. Add garlic and sauté for 30 seconds, then pour in cream and add cream cheese. 2. Remove the pan from heat and stir in Cheddar. Add the zucchini and toss in the sauce, then put into a round baking dish. Cover the dish with foil and place into the air fryer basket. 3. Adjust the temperature to 370ºF (188ºC) and set the timer for 8 minutes. 4. After 6 minutes remove the foil and let the top brown for remaining cooking time. Stir and serve.

Three-Cheese Zucchini Boats

Prep time: 15 minutes | Cook time: 20 minutes | Serves 2

2 medium zucchini	cheese
1 tablespoon avocado oil	¼ teaspoon dried oregano
¼ cup low-carb, no-sugar-added pasta sauce	¼ teaspoon garlic powder
	½ teaspoon dried parsley
¼ cup full-fat ricotta cheese	2 tablespoons grated vegetarian Parmesan cheese
¼ cup shredded Mozzarella	

1. Cut off 1 inch from the top and bottom of each zucchini. Slice zucchini in half lengthwise and use a spoon to scoop out a bit of the inside, making room for filling. Brush with oil and spoon 2 tablespoons pasta sauce into each shell. 2. In a medium bowl, mix ricotta, Mozzarella, oregano, garlic powder, and parsley. Spoon the mixture into each zucchini shell. Place stuffed zucchini shells into the air fryer basket. 3. Adjust the temperature to 350ºF (177ºC) and air fry for 20 minutes. 4. To remove from the basket, use tongs or a spatula and carefully lift out. Top with Parmesan. Serve immediately.

Caprese Eggplant Stacks

Prep time: 5 minutes | Cook time: 12 minutes | Serves 4

1 medium eggplant, cut into ¼-inch slices 2 large tomatoes, cut into ¼-inch slices 4 ounces (113 g) fresh	Mozzarella, cut into ½-ounce / 14-g slices 2 tablespoons olive oil ¼ cup fresh basil, sliced

1. In a baking dish, place four slices of eggplant on the bottom. Place a slice of tomato on top of each eggplant round, then Mozzarella, then eggplant. Repeat as necessary. 2. Drizzle with olive oil. Cover dish with foil and place dish into the air fryer basket. 3. Adjust the temperature to 350°F (177°C) and bake for 12 minutes. 4. When done, eggplant will be tender. Garnish with fresh basil to serve.

Russet Potato Gratin

Prep time: 10 minutes | Cook time: 35 minutes | Serves 6

½ cup milk 7 medium russet potatoes, peeled Salt, to taste 1 teaspoon black pepper	½ cup heavy whipping cream ½ cup grated semi-mature cheese ½ teaspoon nutmeg

1. Preheat the air fryer to 390°F (199°C). 2. Cut the potatoes into wafer-thin slices. 3. In a bowl, combine the milk and cream and sprinkle with salt, pepper, and nutmeg. 4. Use the milk mixture to coat the slices of potatoes. Put in a baking dish. Top the potatoes with the rest of the milk mixture. 5. Put the baking dish into the air fryer basket and bake for 25 minutes. 6. Pour the cheese over the potatoes. 7. Bake for an additional 10 minutes, ensuring the top is nicely browned before serving.

Crispy Eggplant Slices with Parsley

Prep time: 5 minutes | Cook time: 10 to 12 minutes | Serves 4

1 cup flour 4 eggs Salt, to taste 2 cups bread crumbs 1 teaspoon Italian seasoning	2 eggplants, sliced 2 garlic cloves, sliced 2 tablespoons chopped parsley Cooking spray

1. Preheat the air fryer to 390°F (199°C). Spritz the air fryer basket with cooking spray. 2. On a plate, place the flour. In a shallow bowl, whisk the eggs with salt. In another shallow bowl, combine the bread crumbs and Italian seasoning. 3. Dredge the eggplant slices, one at a time, in the flour, then in the whisked eggs, finally in the bread crumb mixture to coat well. 4. Arrange the coated eggplant slices in the air fryer basket and air fry for 10 to 12 minutes until golden brown and crispy. Flip the eggplant slices halfway through the cooking time. 5. Transfer the eggplant slices to a plate and sprinkle the garlic and parsley on top before serving.

Spaghetti Squash Alfredo

Prep time: 10 minutes | Cook time: 15 minutes | Serves 2

½ large cooked spaghetti squash 2 tablespoons salted butter, melted ½ cup low-carb Alfredo sauce ¼ cup grated vegetarian	Parmesan cheese ½ teaspoon garlic powder 1 teaspoon dried parsley ¼ teaspoon ground peppercorn ½ cup shredded Italian blend cheese

1. Using a fork, remove the strands of spaghetti squash from the shell. Place into a large bowl with butter and Alfredo sauce. Sprinkle with Parmesan, garlic powder, parsley, and peppercorn. 2. Pour into a 4-cup round baking dish and top with shredded cheese. Place dish into the air fryer basket. 3. Adjust the temperature to 320°F (160°C) and bake for 15 minutes. When finished, cheese will be golden and bubbling. Serve immediately.

Loaded Cauliflower Steak

Prep time: 5 minutes | Cook time: 7 minutes | Serves 4

1 medium head cauliflower ¼ cup hot sauce 2 tablespoons salted butter,	melted ¼ cup blue cheese crumbles ¼ cup full-fat ranch dressing

1. Remove cauliflower leaves. Slice the head in ½-inch-thick slices. 2. In a small bowl, mix hot sauce and butter. Brush the mixture over the cauliflower. 3. Place each cauliflower steak into the air fryer, working in batches if necessary. 4. Adjust the temperature to 400°F (204°C) and air fry for 7 minutes. 5. When cooked, edges will begin turning dark and caramelized. 6. To serve, sprinkle steaks with crumbled blue cheese. Drizzle with ranch dressing.

Rosemary Beets with Balsamic Glaze

Prep time: 5 minutes | Cook time: 10 minutes | Serves 2

Beet: 2 beets, cubed 2 tablespoons olive oil 2 springs rosemary, chopped Salt and black pepper, to	taste Balsamic Glaze: ⅓ cup balsamic vinegar 1 tablespoon honey

1. Preheat the air fryer to 400°F (204°C). 2. Combine the beets, olive oil, rosemary, salt, and pepper in a mixing bowl and toss until the beets are completely coated. 3. Place the beets in the air fryer basket and air fry for 10 minutes until the beets are crisp and browned at the edges. Shake the basket halfway through the cooking time. 4. Meanwhile, make the balsamic glaze: Place the balsamic vinegar and honey in a small saucepan and bring to a boil over medium heat. When the sauce starts to boil, reduce the heat to medium-low heat and simmer until the liquid is reduced by half. 5. When ready, remove the beets from the basket to a platter. Pour the balsamic glaze over the top and serve immediately.

Spinach Cheese Casserole

Prep time: 15 minutes | Cook time: 15 minutes | Serves 4

1 tablespoon salted butter, melted ¼ cup diced yellow onion 8 ounces (227 g) full-fat cream cheese, softened ⅓ cup full-fat mayonnaise ⅓ cup full-fat sour cream ¼ cup chopped pickled	jalapeños 2 cups fresh spinach, chopped 2 cups cauliflower florets, chopped 1 cup artichoke hearts, chopped

1. In a large bowl, mix butter, onion, cream cheese, mayonnaise, and sour cream. Fold in jalapeños, spinach, cauliflower, and artichokes. 2. Pour the mixture into a round baking dish. Cover with foil and place into the air fryer basket. 3. Adjust the temperature to 370°F (188°C) and set the timer for 15 minutes. In the last 2 minutes of cooking, remove the foil to brown the top. Serve warm.

Pesto Spinach Flatbread

Prep time: 10 minutes | Cook time: 8 minutes | Serves 4

1 cup blanched finely ground almond flour 2 ounces (57 g) cream cheese 2 cups shredded Mozzarella	cheese 1 cup chopped fresh spinach leaves 2 tablespoons basil pesto

1. Place flour, cream cheese, and Mozzarella in a large microwave-safe bowl and microwave on high 45 seconds, then stir. 2. Fold in spinach and microwave an additional 15 seconds. Stir until a soft dough ball forms. 3. Cut two pieces of parchment paper to fit air fryer basket. Separate dough into two sections and press each out on ungreased parchment to create 6-inch rounds. 4. Spread 1 tablespoon pesto over each flatbread and place rounds on parchment into ungreased air fryer basket. Adjust the temperature to 350°F (177°C) and air fry for 8 minutes, turning crusts halfway through cooking. Flatbread will be golden when done. 5. Let cool 5 minutes before slicing and serving.

Basmati Risotto

Prep time: 10 minutes | Cook time: 30 minutes | Serves 2

1 onion, diced 1 small carrot, diced 2 cups vegetable broth, boiling ½ cup grated Cheddar cheese	1 clove garlic, minced ¾ cup long-grain basmati rice 1 tablespoon olive oil 1 tablespoon unsalted butter

1. Preheat the air fryer to 390°F (199°C). 2. Grease a baking tin with oil and stir in the butter, garlic, carrot, and onion. 3. Put the tin in the air fryer and bake for 4 minutes. 4. Pour in the rice and bake for a further 4 minutes, stirring three times throughout the baking time. 5. Turn the temperature down to 320°F (160°C). 6. Add the vegetable broth and give the dish a gentle stir. Bake for 22 minutes, leaving the air fryer uncovered. 7. Pour in the cheese, stir once more and serve.

Roasted Vegetables with Rice

Prep time: 5 minutes | Cook time: 12 minutes | Serves 4

2 teaspoons melted butter 1 cup chopped mushrooms 1 cup cooked rice 1 cup peas 1 carrot, chopped 1 red onion, chopped	1 garlic clove, minced Salt and black pepper, to taste 2 hard-boiled eggs, grated 1 tablespoon soy sauce

1. Preheat the air fryer to 380°F (193°C). Coat a baking dish with melted butter. 2. Stir together the mushrooms, cooked rice, peas, carrot, onion, garlic, salt, and pepper in a large bowl until well mixed. 3. Pour the mixture into the prepared baking dish and transfer to the air fryer basket. 4. Roast in the preheated air fryer for 12 minutes until the vegetables are tender. 5. Divide the mixture among four plates. Serve warm with a sprinkle of grated eggs and a drizzle of soy sauce.

Broccoli Crust Pizza

Prep time: 15 minutes | Cook time: 12 minutes | Serves 4

3 cups riced broccoli, steamed and drained well 1 large egg ½ cup grated vegetarian Parmesan cheese	3 tablespoons low-carb Alfredo sauce ½ cup shredded Mozzarella cheese

1. In a large bowl, mix broccoli, egg, and Parmesan. 2. Cut a piece of parchment to fit your air fryer basket. Press out the pizza mixture to fit on the parchment, working in two batches if necessary. Place into the air fryer basket. 3. Adjust the temperature to 370°F (188°C) and air fry for 5 minutes. 4. The crust should be firm enough to flip. If not, add 2 additional minutes. Flip crust. 5. Top with Alfredo sauce and Mozzarella. Return to the air fryer basket and cook an additional 7 minutes or until cheese is golden and bubbling. Serve warm.

Stuffed Portobellos

Prep time: 10 minutes | Cook time: 8 minutes | Serves 4

3 ounces (85 g) cream cheese, softened ½ medium zucchini, trimmed and chopped ¼ cup seeded and chopped red bell pepper 1½ cups chopped fresh	spinach leaves 4 large portobello mushrooms, stems removed 2 tablespoons coconut oil, melted ½ teaspoon salt

1. In a medium bowl, mix cream cheese, zucchini, pepper, and spinach. 2. Drizzle mushrooms with coconut oil and sprinkle with salt. Scoop ¼ zucchini mixture into each mushroom. 3. Place mushrooms into ungreased air fryer basket. Adjust the temperature to 400°F (204°C) and air fry for 8 minutes. Portobellos will be tender and tops will be browned when done. Serve warm.

Basic Spaghetti Squash

Prep time: 10 minutes | Cook time: 45 minutes | Serves 2

½ large spaghetti squash
1 tablespoon coconut oil
2 tablespoons salted butter, melted

½ teaspoon garlic powder
1 teaspoon dried parsley

1. Brush shell of spaghetti squash with coconut oil. Place the skin side down and brush the inside with butter. Sprinkle with garlic powder and parsley. 2. Place squash with the skin side down into the air fryer basket. 3. Adjust the temperature to 350ºF (177ºC) and air fry for 30 minutes. 4. Flip the squash so skin side is up and cook an additional 15 minutes or until fork tender. Serve warm.

Cheese Stuffed Peppers

Prep time: 20 minutes | Cook time: 15 minutes | Serves 2

1 red bell pepper, top and seeds removed
1 yellow bell pepper, top and seeds removed
Salt and pepper, to taste

1 cup Cottage cheese
4 tablespoons mayonnaise
2 pickles, chopped

1. Arrange the peppers in the lightly greased air fryer basket. Cook in the preheated air fryer at 400ºF (204ºC) for 15 minutes, turning them over halfway through the cooking time. 2. Season with salt and pepper. Then, in a mixing bowl, combine the cream cheese with the mayonnaise and chopped pickles. Stuff the pepper with the cream cheese mixture and serve. Enjoy!

Chapter 10
Desserts

Honeyed Roasted Apples with Walnuts

Prep time: 5 minutes | Cook time: 12 to 15 minutes | Serves 4

2 Granny Smith apples ¼ cup certified gluten-free rolled oats 2 tablespoons honey ½ teaspoon ground cinnamon	2 tablespoons chopped walnuts Pinch salt 1 tablespoon olive oil

1. Preheat the air fryer to 380°F(193°C). 2. Core the apples and slice them in half. 3. In a medium bowl, mix together the oats, honey, cinnamon, walnuts, salt, and olive oil. 4. Scoop a quarter of the oat mixture onto the top of each half apple. 5. Place the apples in the air fryer basket, and roast for 12 to 15 minutes, or until the apples are fork-tender.

Pumpkin Cookie with Cream Cheese Frosting

Prep time: 10 minutes | Cook time: 7 minutes | Serves 6

½ cup blanched finely ground almond flour ½ cup powdered erythritol, divided 2 tablespoons butter, softened 1 large egg ½ teaspoon unflavored gelatin ½ teaspoon baking powder ½ teaspoon vanilla extract	½ teaspoon pumpkin pie spice 2 tablespoons pure pumpkin purée ½ teaspoon ground cinnamon, divided ¼ cup low-carb, sugar-free chocolate chips 3 ounces (85 g) full-fat cream cheese, softened

1. In a large bowl, mix almond flour and ¼ cup erythritol. Stir in butter, egg, and gelatin until combined. 2. Stir in baking powder, vanilla, pumpkin pie spice, pumpkin purée, and ¼ teaspoon cinnamon, then fold in chocolate chips. 3. Pour batter into a round baking pan. Place pan into the air fryer basket. 4. Adjust the temperature to 300°F (149°C) and bake for 7 minutes. 5. When fully cooked, the top will be golden brown and a toothpick inserted in center will come out clean. Let cool at least 20 minutes. 6. To make the frosting: mix cream cheese, remaining ¼ teaspoon cinnamon, and remaining ¼ cup erythritol in a large bowl. Using an electric mixer, beat until it becomes fluffy. Spread onto the cooled cookie. Garnish with additional cinnamon if desired.

Funnel Cake

Prep time: 10 minutes | Cook time: 5 minutes | Serves 4

Oil, for spraying 1 cup self-rising flour, plus more for dusting 1 cup fat-free vanilla Greek	yogurt ½ teaspoon ground cinnamon ¼ cup confectioners' sugar

1. Preheat the air fryer to 375°F (191°C). Line the air fryer basket with parchment and spray lightly with oil. 2. In a large bowl, mix together the flour, yogurt, and cinnamon until the mixture forms a ball. 3. Place the dough on a lightly floured work surface and knead for about 2 minutes. 4. Cut the dough into 4 equal pieces, then cut each of those into 6 pieces. You should have 24 total pieces. 5. Roll the pieces into 8- to 10-inch-long ropes. Loosely mound the ropes into 4 piles of 6 ropes. 6. Place the dough piles in the prepared basket and spray liberally with oil. You may need to work in batches, depending on the size of your air fryer. 7. Cook for 5 minutes, or until lightly browned. 8. Dust with the confectioners' sugar before serving.

Cream Cheese Danish

Prep time: 20 minutes | Cook time: 15 minutes | Serves 6

¾ cup blanched finely ground almond flour 1 cup shredded Mozzarella cheese 5 ounces (142 g) full-fat cream cheese, divided	2 large egg yolks ¾ cup powdered erythritol, divided 2 teaspoons vanilla extract, divided

1. In a large microwave-safe bowl, add almond flour, Mozzarella, and 1 ounce (28 g) cream cheese. Mix and then microwave for 1 minute. 2. Stir and add egg yolks to the bowl. Continue stirring until soft dough forms. Add ½ cup erythritol to dough and 1 teaspoon vanilla. 3. Cut a piece of parchment to fit your air fryer basket. Wet your hands with warm water and press out the dough into a ¼-inch-thick rectangle. 4. In a medium bowl, mix remaining cream cheese, erythritol, and vanilla. Place this cream cheese mixture on the right half of the dough rectangle. Fold over the left side of the dough and press to seal. Place into the air fryer basket. 5. Adjust the temperature to 330°F (166°C) and bake for 15 minutes. 6. After 7 minutes, flip over the Danish. 7. When done, remove the Danish from parchment and allow to completely cool before cutting.

Chocolate Bread Pudding

Prep time: 10 minutes | Cook time: 10 to 12 minutes | Serves 4

Nonstick flour-infused baking spray 1 egg 1 egg yolk ¾ cup chocolate milk 2 tablespoons cocoa powder	3 tablespoons light brown sugar 3 tablespoons peanut butter 1 teaspoon vanilla extract 5 slices firm white bread, cubed

1. Spray a 6-by-2-inch round baking pan with the baking spray. Set aside. 2. In a medium bowl, whisk the egg, egg yolk, chocolate milk, cocoa powder, brown sugar, peanut butter, and vanilla until thoroughly combined. Stir in the bread cubes and let soak for 10 minutes. Spoon this mixture into the prepared pan. 3. Insert the crisper plate into the basket and the basket into the unit. Preheat the unit by selecting BAKE, setting the temperature to 325°F (163°C), and setting the time to 3 minutes. Select START/STOP to begin. 4. Once the unit is preheated, place the pan into the basket. Select BAKE, set the temperature to 325°F (163°C), and set the time to 12 minutes. Select START/STOP to begin. 5. Check the pudding after about 10 minutes. It is done when it is firm to the touch. If not, resume cooking. 6. When the cooking is complete, let the pudding cool for 5 minutes. Serve warm.

Vanilla Scones

Prep time: 20 minutes | Cook time: 10 minutes | Serves 6

4 ounces (113 g) coconut flour ½ teaspoon baking powder 1 teaspoon apple cider vinegar	2 teaspoons mascarpone ¼ cup heavy cream 1 teaspoon vanilla extract 1 tablespoon erythritol Cooking spray

1. In the mixing bowl, mix coconut flour with baking powder, apple cider vinegar, mascarpone, heavy cream, vanilla extract, and erythritol. 2. Knead the dough and cut into scones. 3. Then put them in the air fryer basket and sprinkle with cooking spray. 4. Cook the vanilla scones at 365ºF (185ºC) for 10 minutes.

Cream Cheese Shortbread Cookies

Prep time: 30 minutes | Cook time: 20 minutes | Makes 12 cookies

¼ cup coconut oil, melted 2 ounces (57 g) cream cheese, softened ½ cup granular erythritol	1 large egg, whisked 2 cups blanched finely ground almond flour 1 teaspoon almond extract

1. Combine all ingredients in a large bowl to form a firm ball. 2. Place dough on a sheet of plastic wrap and roll into a 12-inch-long log shape. Roll log in plastic wrap and place in refrigerator 30 minutes to chill. 3. Remove log from plastic and slice into twelve equal cookies. Cut two sheets of parchment paper to fit air fryer basket. Place six cookies on each ungreased sheet. Place one sheet with cookies into air fryer basket. Adjust the temperature to 320ºF (160ºC) and bake for 10 minutes, turning cookies halfway through cooking. They will be lightly golden when done. Repeat with remaining cookies. 4. Let cool 15 minutes before serving to avoid crumbling.

Pretzels

Prep time: 10 minutes | Cook time: 10 minutes | Serves 6

1½ cups shredded Mozzarella cheese 1 cup blanched finely ground almond flour 2 tablespoons salted butter,	melted, divided ¼ cup granular erythritol, divided 1 teaspoon ground cinnamon

1. Place Mozzarella, flour, 1 tablespoon butter, and 2 tablespoons erythritol in a large microwave-safe bowl. Microwave on high 45 seconds, then stir with a fork until a smooth dough ball forms. 2. Separate dough into six equal sections. Gently roll each section into a 12-inch rope, then fold into a pretzel shape. 3. Place pretzels into ungreased air fryer basket. Adjust the temperature to 370ºF (188ºC) and set the timer for 8 minutes, turning pretzels halfway through cooking. 4. In a small bowl, combine remaining butter, remaining erythritol, and cinnamon. Brush ½ mixture on both sides of pretzels. 5. Place pretzels back into air fryer and cook an additional 2 minutes at 370ºF (188ºC). 6. Transfer pretzels to a large plate. Brush on both sides with remaining butter mixture,

then let cool 5 minutes before serving.

Chocolate Cake

Prep time: 10 minutes | Cook time: 20 to 23 minutes | Serves 8

½ cup sugar ¼ cup flour, plus 3 tablespoons 3 tablespoons cocoa ½ teaspoon baking powder ½ teaspoon baking soda	¼ teaspoon salt 1 egg 2 tablespoons oil ½ cup milk ½ teaspoon vanilla extract

1. Preheat the air fryer to 330ºF (166ºC). 2. Grease and flour a baking pan. 3. In a medium bowl, stir together the sugar, flour, cocoa, baking powder, baking soda, and salt. 4. Add all other ingredients and beat with a wire whisk until smooth. 5. Pour batter into prepared pan and bake at 330ºF (166ºC) for 20 to 23 minutes, until toothpick inserted in center comes out clean or with crumbs clinging to it.

Oatmeal Raisin Bars

Prep time: 15 minutes | Cook time: 15 minutes | Serves 8

⅓ cup all-purpose flour ¼ teaspoon kosher salt ¼ teaspoon baking powder ¼ teaspoon ground cinnamon ¼ cup light brown sugar, lightly packed	¼ cup granulated sugar ½ cup canola oil 1 large egg 1 teaspoon vanilla extract 1⅓ cups quick-cooking oats ⅓ cup raisins

1. Preheat the air fryer to 360ºF (182ºC). 2. In a large bowl, combine the all-purpose flour, kosher salt, baking powder, ground cinnamon, light brown sugar, granulated sugar, canola oil, egg, vanilla extract, quick-cooking oats, and raisins. 3. Spray a baking pan with nonstick cooking spray, then pour the oat mixture into the pan and press down to evenly distribute. Place the pan in the air fryer and bake for 15 minutes or until golden brown. 4. Remove from the air fryer and allow to cool in the pan on a wire rack for 20 minutes before slicing and serving.

Fried Oreos

Prep time: 7 minutes | Cook time: 6 minutes per batch | Makes 12 cookies

Oil for misting or nonstick spray 1 cup complete pancake and waffle mix 1 teaspoon vanilla extract ½ cup water, plus 2	tablespoons 12 Oreos or other chocolate sandwich cookies 1 tablespoon confectioners' sugar

1. Spray baking pan with oil or nonstick spray and place in basket. 2. Preheat the air fryer to 390ºF (199ºC). 3. In a medium bowl, mix together the pancake mix, vanilla, and water. 4. Dip 4 cookies in batter and place in baking pan. 5. Cook for 6 minutes, until browned. 6. Repeat steps 4 and 5 for the remaining cookies. 7. Sift sugar over warm cookies.

Fried Cheesecake Bites

Prep time: 30 minutes | Cook time: 2 minutes | Makes 16 bites

8 ounces (227 g) cream cheese, softened ½ cup plus 2 tablespoons Swerve, divided	4 tablespoons heavy cream, divided ½ teaspoon vanilla extract ½ cup almond flour

1. In a stand mixer fitted with a paddle attachment, beat the cream cheese, ½ cup of the Swerve, 2 tablespoons of the heavy cream, and the vanilla until smooth. Using a small ice-cream scoop, divide the mixture into 16 balls and arrange them on a rimmed baking sheet lined with parchment paper. Freeze for 45 minutes until firm. 2. Line the air fryer basket with parchment paper and preheat the air fryer to 350ºF (177ºC). 3. In a small shallow bowl, combine the almond flour with the remaining 2 tablespoons Swerve. 4. In another small shallow bowl, place the remaining 2 tablespoons cream. 5. One at a time, dip the frozen cheesecake balls into the cream and then roll in the almond flour mixture, pressing lightly to form an even coating. Arrange the balls in a single layer in the air fryer basket, leaving room between them. Air fry for 2 minutes until the coating is lightly browned.

Zucchini Bread

Prep time: 10 minutes | Cook time: 40 minutes | Serves 12

2 cups coconut flour 2 teaspoons baking powder ¾ cup erythritol ½ cup coconut oil, melted 1 teaspoon apple cider	vinegar 1 teaspoon vanilla extract 3 eggs, beaten 1 zucchini, grated 1 teaspoon ground cinnamon

1. In the mixing bowl, mix coconut flour with baking powder, erythritol, coconut oil, apple cider vinegar, vanilla extract, eggs, zucchini, and ground cinnamon. 2. Transfer the mixture into the air fryer basket and flatten it in the shape of the bread. 3. Cook the bread at 350ºF (177ºC) for 40 minutes.

Gingerbread

Prep time: 5 minutes | Cook time: 20 minutes | Makes 1 loaf

Cooking spray 1 cup flour 2 tablespoons sugar ¾ teaspoon ground ginger ¼ teaspoon cinnamon 1 teaspoon baking powder ½ teaspoon baking soda	⅛ teaspoon salt 1 egg ¼ cup molasses ½ cup buttermilk 2 tablespoons oil 1 teaspoon pure vanilla extract

1. Preheat the air fryer to 330ºF (166ºC). 2. Spray a baking dish lightly with cooking spray. 3. In a medium bowl, mix together all the dry ingredients. 4. In a separate bowl, beat the egg. Add molasses, buttermilk, oil, and vanilla and stir until well mixed. 5. Pour liquid mixture into dry ingredients and stir until well blended. 6. Pour batter into baking dish and bake at 330ºF (166ºC) for 20 minutes or until toothpick inserted in center of loaf comes

out clean.

Strawberry Pecan Pie

Prep time: 15 minutes | Cook time: 10 minutes | Serves 6

1½ cups whole shelled pecans 1 tablespoon unsalted butter, softened	1 cup heavy whipping cream 12 medium fresh strawberries, hulled 2 tablespoons sour cream

1. Place pecans and butter into a food processor and pulse ten times until a dough forms. Press dough into the bottom of an ungreased round nonstick baking dish. 2. Place dish into air fryer basket. Adjust the temperature to 320ºF (160ºC) and set the timer for 10 minutes. Crust will be firm and golden when done. Let cool 20 minutes. 3. In a large bowl, whisk cream until fluffy and doubled in size, about 2 minutes. 4. In a separate large bowl, mash strawberries until mostly liquid. Fold strawberries and sour cream into whipped cream. 5. Spoon mixture into cooled crust, cover, and place in refrigerator for at least 30 minutes to set. Serve chilled.

Pecan Butter Cookies

Prep time: 5 minutes | Cook time: 24 minutes | Makes 12 cookies

1 cup chopped pecans ½ cup salted butter, melted ½ cup coconut flour	¾ cup erythritol, divided 1 teaspoon vanilla extract

1. In a food processor, blend together pecans, butter, flour, ½ cup erythritol, and vanilla 1 minute until a dough forms. 2. Form dough into twelve individual cookie balls, about 1 tablespoon each. 3. Cut three pieces of parchment to fit air fryer basket. Place four cookies on each ungreased parchment and place one piece parchment with cookies into air fryer basket. Adjust air fryer temperature to 325ºF (163ºC) and set the timer for 8 minutes. Repeat cooking with remaining batches. 4. When the timer goes off, allow cookies to cool 5 minutes on a large serving plate until cool enough to handle. While still warm, dust cookies with remaining erythritol. Allow to cool completely, about 15 minutes, before serving.

Apple Wedges with Apricots

Prep time: 5 minutes | Cook time: 15 to 18 minutes | Serves 4

4 large apples, peeled and sliced into 8 wedges 2 tablespoons olive oil ½ cup dried apricots,	chopped 1 to 2 tablespoons sugar ½ teaspoon ground cinnamon

1. Preheat the air fryer to 350ºF (180ºC). 2. Toss the apple wedges with the olive oil in a mixing bowl until well coated. 3. Place the apple wedges in the air fryer basket and air fry for 12 to 15 minutes. 4. Sprinkle with the dried apricots and air fry for another 3 minutes. 5. Meanwhile, thoroughly combine the sugar and cinnamon in a small bowl. 6. Remove the apple wedges from the basket to a plate. Serve sprinkled with the sugar mixture.

New York Cheesecake

Prep time: 1 hour | Cook time: 37 minutes | Serves 8

1½ cups almond flour	½ cup heavy cream
3 ounces (85 g) Swerve	1¼ cups granulated Swerve
½ stick butter, melted	3 eggs, at room temperature
20 ounces (567 g) full-fat cream cheese	1 tablespoon vanilla essence
	1 teaspoon grated lemon zest

1. Coat the sides and bottom of a baking pan with a little flour. 2. In a mixing bowl, combine the almond flour and Swerve. Add the melted butter and mix until your mixture looks like bread crumbs. 3. Press the mixture into the bottom of the prepared pan to form an even layer. Bake at 330ºF (166ºC) for 7 minutes until golden brown. Allow it to cool completely on a wire rack. 4. Meanwhile, in a mixer fitted with the paddle attachment, prepare the filling by mixing the soft cheese, heavy cream, and granulated Swerve; beat until creamy and fluffy. 5. Crack the eggs into the mixing bowl, one at a time; add the vanilla and lemon zest and continue to mix until fully combined. 6. Pour the prepared topping over the cooled crust and spread evenly. 7. Bake in the preheated air fryer at 330ºF (166ºC) for 25 to 30 minutes; leave it in the air fryer to keep warm for another 30 minutes. 8. Cover your cheesecake with plastic wrap. Place in your refrigerator and allow it to cool at least 6 hours or overnight. Serve well chilled.

Vanilla Cookies with Hazelnuts

Prep time: 20 minutes | Cook time: 10 minutes | Serves 6

1 cup almond flour	1 cup Swerve
½ cup coconut flour	2 teaspoons vanilla
1 teaspoon baking soda	2 eggs, at room temperature
1 teaspoon fine sea salt	1 cup hazelnuts, coarsely chopped
1 stick butter	

1. Preheat the air fryer to 350ºF (177ºC). 2. Mix the flour with the baking soda, and sea salt. 3. In the bowl of an electric mixer, beat the butter, Swerve, and vanilla until creamy. Fold in the eggs, one at a time, and mix until well combined. 4. Slowly and gradually, stir in the flour mixture. Finally, fold in the coarsely chopped hazelnuts. 5. Divide the dough into small balls using a large cookie scoop; drop onto the prepared cookie sheets. Bake for 10 minutes or until golden brown, rotating the pan once or twice through the cooking time. 6. Work in batches and cool for a couple of minutes before removing to wire racks. Enjoy!

Cherry Pie

Prep time: 15 minutes | Cook time: 35 minutes | Serves 6

All-purpose flour, for dusting	cherry pie filling
2 refrigerated piecrusts, at room temperature	1 egg
1 (12.5-ounce / 354-g) can	1 tablespoon water
	1 tablespoon sugar

1. Dust a work surface with flour and place the piecrust on it. Roll out the piecrust. Invert a shallow air fryer baking pan, or your own pie pan that fits inside the air fryer basket, on top of the dough. Trim the dough around the pan, making your cut ½ inch wider than the pan itself. 2. Repeat with the second piecrust but make the cut the same size as or slightly smaller than the pan. 3. Put the larger crust in the bottom of the baking pan. Don't stretch the dough. Gently press it into the pan. 4. Spoon in enough cherry pie filling to fill the crust. Do not overfill. 5. Using a knife or pizza cutter, cut the second piecrust into 1-inch-wide strips. Weave the strips in a lattice pattern over the top of the cherry pie filling. 6. Insert the crisper plate into the basket and the basket into the unit. Preheat the unit by selecting BAKE, setting the temperature to 325ºF (163ºC), and setting the time to 3 minutes. Select START/STOP to begin. 7. In a small bowl, whisk the egg and water. Gently brush the egg wash over the top of the pie. Sprinkle with the sugar and cover the pie with aluminum foil. 8. Once the unit is preheated, place the pie into the basket. 9. Select BAKE, set the temperature to 325ºF (163ºC), and set the time to 35 minutes. Select START/STOP to begin. 10. After 30 minutes, remove the foil and resume cooking for 3 to 5 minutes more. The finished pie should have a flaky golden brown crust and bubbling pie filling. 11. When the cooking is complete, serve warm. Refrigerate leftovers for a few days.

Strawberry Shortcake

Prep time: 10 minutes | Cook time: 25 minutes | Serves 6

2 tablespoons coconut oil	1 teaspoon vanilla extract
1 cup blanched finely ground almond flour	2 cups sugar-free whipped cream
2 large eggs, whisked	6 medium fresh strawberries, hulled and sliced
½ cup granular erythritol	
1 teaspoon baking powder	

1. In a large bowl, combine coconut oil, flour, eggs, erythritol, baking powder, and vanilla. Pour batter into an ungreased round nonstick baking dish. 2. Place dish into air fryer basket. Adjust the temperature to 300ºF (149ºC) and bake for 25 minutes. When done, shortcake should be golden and a toothpick inserted in the middle will come out clean. 3. Remove dish from fryer and let cool 1 hour. 4. Once cooled, top cake with whipped cream and strawberries to serve.

Vanilla Pound Cake

Prep time: 10 minutes | Cook time: 25 minutes | Serves 6

1 cup blanched finely ground almond flour	1 teaspoon baking powder
¼ cup salted butter, melted	½ cup full-fat sour cream
½ cup granular erythritol	1 ounce (28 g) full-fat cream cheese, softened
1 teaspoon vanilla extract	2 large eggs

1. In a large bowl, mix almond flour, butter, and erythritol. 2. Add in vanilla, baking powder, sour cream, and cream cheese and mix until well combined. Add eggs and mix. 3. Pour batter into a round baking pan. Place pan into the air fryer basket. 4. Adjust the temperature to 300ºF (149ºC) and bake for 25 minutes. 5. When the cake is done, a toothpick inserted in center will come out clean. The center should not feel wet. Allow it to cool completely, or the cake will crumble when moved.

Mini Peanut Butter Tarts

Prep time: 25 minutes | Cook time: 12 to 15 minutes | Serves 8

1 cup pecans	cheese
1 cup finely ground blanched almond flour	½ cup sugar-free peanut butter
2 tablespoons unsalted butter, at room temperature	1 teaspoon pure vanilla extract
½ cup plus 2 tablespoons Swerve, divided	⅛ teaspoon sea salt
½ cup heavy (whipping) cream	½ cup stevia-sweetened chocolate chips
2 tablespoons mascarpone cheese	1 tablespoon coconut oil
4 ounces (113 g) cream	¼ cup chopped peanuts or pecans

1. Place the pecans in the bowl of a food processor; process until they are finely ground. 2. Transfer the ground pecans to a medium bowl and stir in the almond flour. Add the butter and 2 tablespoons of Swerve, and stir until the mixture becomes wet and crumbly. 3. Divide the mixture among 8 silicone muffin cups, pressing the crust firmly with your fingers into the bottom and part way up the sides of each cup. 4. Arrange the muffin cups in the air fryer basket, working in batches if necessary. Set the air fryer to 300ºF (149ºC) and bake for 12 to 15 minutes, until the crusts begin to brown. Remove the cups from the air fryer and set them aside to cool. 5. In the bowl of a stand mixer, combine the heavy cream and mascarpone cheese. Beat until peaks form. Transfer to a large bowl. 6. In the same stand mixer bowl, combine the cream cheese, peanut butter, remaining ½ cup of Swerve, vanilla, and salt. Beat at medium-high speed until smooth. 7. Reduce the speed to low and add the heavy cream mixture back a spoonful at a time, beating after each addition. 8. Spoon the peanut butter mixture over the crusts, and freeze the tarts for 30 minutes. 9. Place the chocolate chips and coconut oil in the top of a double boiler over high heat. Stir until melted, then remove from the heat. 10. Drizzle the melted chocolate over the peanut butter tarts. Top with the chopped nuts and freeze the tarts for another 15 minutes, until set. 11. Store the peanut butter tarts in an airtight container in the refrigerator for up to 1 week or in the freezer for up to 1 month.

Graham Cracker Cheesecake

Prep time: 10 minutes | Cook time: 20 minutes | Serves 8

1 cup graham cracker crumbs	⅓ cup sugar
3 tablespoons butter, at room temperature	2 eggs, beaten
1½ (8-ounce / 227-g) packages cream cheese, at room temperature	1 tablespoon all-purpose flour
	1 teaspoon vanilla extract
	¼ cup chocolate syrup

1. In a small bowl, stir together the graham cracker crumbs and butter. Press the crust into the bottom of a 6-by-2-inch round baking pan and freeze to set while you prepare the filling. 2. In a medium bowl, stir together the cream cheese and sugar until mixed well. 3. One at a time, beat in the eggs. Add the flour and vanilla and stir to combine. 4. Transfer ⅔ cup of filling to a small

bowl and stir in the chocolate syrup until combined. 5. Insert the crisper plate into the basket and the basket into the unit. Preheat the unit by selecting BAKE, setting the temperature to 325ºF (163ºC), and setting the time to 3 minutes. Select START/STOP to begin. 6. Pour the vanilla filling into the pan with the crust. Drop the chocolate filling over the vanilla filling by the spoonful. With a clean butter knife stir the fillings in a zigzag pattern to marbleize them. Do not let the knife touch the crust. 7. Once the unit is preheated, place the pan into the basket. 8. Select BAKE, set the temperature to 325ºF (163ºC), and set the time to 20 minutes. Select START/STOP to begin. 9. When the cooking is done, the cheesecake should be just set. Cool on a wire rack for 1 hour. Refrigerate the cheesecake until firm before slicing.

Mini Cheesecake

Prep time: 10 minutes | Cook time: 15 minutes | Serves 2

½ cup walnuts	cream cheese, softened
2 tablespoons salted butter	1 large egg
2 tablespoons granular erythritol	½ teaspoon vanilla extract
4 ounces (113 g) full-fat	⅛ cup powdered erythritol

1. Place walnuts, butter, and granular erythritol in a food processor. Pulse until ingredients stick together and a dough forms. 2. Press dough into a springform pan then place the pan into the air fryer basket. 3. Adjust the temperature to 400ºF (204ºC) and bake for 5 minutes. 4. When done, remove the crust and let cool. 5. In a medium bowl, mix cream cheese with egg, vanilla extract, and powdered erythritol until smooth. 6. Spoon mixture on top of baked walnut crust and place into the air fryer basket. 7. Adjust the temperature to 300ºF (149ºC) and bake for 10 minutes. 8. Once done, chill for 2 hours before serving.

Indian Toast and Milk

Prep time: 10 minutes | Cook time: 20 minutes | Serves 4

1 cup sweetened condensed milk	1 pinch saffron threads
1 cup evaporated milk	4 slices white bread
1 cup half-and-half	2 to 3 tablespoons ghee or butter, softened
1 teaspoon ground cardamom, plus additional for garnish	2 tablespoons crushed pistachios, for garnish (optional)

1. In a baking pan, combine the condensed milk, evaporated milk, half-and-half, cardamom, and saffron. Stir until well combined. 2. Place the pan in the air fryer basket. Set the air fryer to 350ºF (177ºC) for 15 minutes, stirring halfway through the cooking time. Remove the sweetened milk from the air fryer and set aside. 3. Cut each slice of bread into two triangles. Brush each side with ghee. Place the bread in the air fryer basket. Set the air fryer to 350ºF (177ºC) for 5 minutes or until golden brown and toasty. 4. Remove the bread from the air fryer. Arrange two triangles in each of four wide, shallow bowls. Pour the hot milk mixture on top of the bread and let soak for 30 minutes. 5. Garnish with pistachios if using, and sprinkle with additional cardamom.

Coconut-Custard Pie

Prep time: 10 minutes | Cook time: 20 to 23 minutes | Serves 4

1 cup milk ¼ cup plus 2 tablespoons sugar ¼ cup biscuit baking mix 1 teaspoon vanilla	2 eggs 2 tablespoons melted butter Cooking spray ½ cup shredded, sweetened coconut

1. Place all ingredients except coconut in a medium bowl. 2. Using a hand mixer, beat on high speed for 3 minutes. 3. Let sit for 5 minutes. 4. Preheat the air fryer to 330ºF (166ºC). 5. Spray a baking pan with cooking spray and place pan in air fryer basket. 6. Pour filling into pan and sprinkle coconut over top. 7. Cook pie at 330ºF (166ºC) for 20 to 23 minutes or until center sets.

Chocolate Chip Cookie Cake

Prep time: 5 minutes | Cook time: 15 minutes | Serves 8

4 tablespoons salted butter, melted ⅓ cup granular brown erythritol 1 large egg ½ teaspoon vanilla extract	1 cup blanched finely ground almond flour ½ teaspoon baking powder ¼ cup low-carb chocolate chips

1. In a large bowl, whisk together butter, erythritol, egg, and vanilla. Add flour and baking powder, and stir until combined. 2. Fold in chocolate chips, then spoon batter into an ungreased round nonstick baking dish. 3. Place dish into air fryer basket. Adjust the temperature to 300ºF (149ºC) and set the timer for 15 minutes. When edges are browned, cookie cake will be done. 4. Slice and serve warm.

Boston Cream Donut Holes

Prep time: 30 minutes | Cook time: 4 minutes per batch | Makes 24 donut holes

1½ cups bread flour 1 teaspoon active dry yeast 1 tablespoon sugar ¼ teaspoon salt ½ cup warm milk ½ teaspoon pure vanilla extract 2 egg yolks 2 tablespoons butter, melted Vegetable oil	Custard Filling: 1 (3.4-ounce / 96-g) box French vanilla instant pudding mix ¾ cup whole milk ¼ cup heavy cream Chocolate Glaze: 1 cup chocolate chips ⅓ cup heavy cream

1. Combine the flour, yeast, sugar and salt in the bowl of a stand mixer. Add the milk, vanilla, egg yolks and butter. Mix until the dough starts to come together in a ball. Transfer the dough to a floured surface and knead the dough by hand for 2 minutes. Shape the dough into a ball, place it in a large oiled bowl, cover the bowl with a clean kitchen towel and let the dough rise for 1 to 1½ hours or until the dough has doubled in size. 2. When the dough has risen, punch it down and roll it into a 24-inch log. Cut the dough into 24 pieces and roll each piece into a ball. Place the dough balls on a baking sheet and let them rise for another 30 minutes. 3. Preheat the air fryer to 400ºF (204ºC). 4. Spray or brush the dough balls lightly with vegetable oil and air fry eight at a time for 4 minutes, turning them over halfway through the cooking time. 5. While donut holes are cooking, make the filling and chocolate glaze. Make the filling: Use an electric hand mixer to beat the French vanilla pudding, milk and ¼ cup of heavy cream together for 2 minutes. 6. Make the chocolate glaze: Place the chocolate chips in a medium-sized bowl. Bring the heavy cream to a boil on the stovetop and pour it over the chocolate chips. Stir until the chips are melted and the glaze is smooth. 7. To fill the donut holes, place the custard filling in a pastry bag with a long tip. Poke a hole into the side of the donut hole with a small knife. Wiggle the knife around to make room for the filling. Place the pastry bag tip into the hole and slowly squeeze the custard into the center of the donut. Dip the top half of the donut into the chocolate glaze, letting any excess glaze drip back into the bowl. Let the glazed donut holes sit for a few minutes before serving.

Lush Chocolate Chip Cookies

Prep time: 7 minutes | Cook time: 9 minutes | Serves 4

3 tablespoons butter, at room temperature ⅓ cup plus 1 tablespoon light brown sugar 1 egg yolk ½ cup all-purpose flour 2 tablespoons ground white	chocolate ¼ teaspoon baking soda ½ teaspoon vanilla extract ¾ cup semisweet chocolate chips Nonstick flour-infused baking spray

1. In medium bowl, beat together the butter and brown sugar until fluffy. Stir in the egg yolk. 2. Add the flour, white chocolate, baking soda, and vanilla and mix well. Stir in the chocolate chips. 3. Line a 6-by-2-inch round baking pan with parchment paper. Spray the parchment paper with flour-infused baking spray. 4. Insert the crisper plate into the basket and the basket into the unit. Preheat the unit by selecting BAKE, setting the temperature to 300ºF (149ºC), and setting the time to 3 minutes. Select START/STOP to begin. 5. Spread the batter into the prepared pan, leaving a ½-inch border on all sides. 6. Once the unit is preheated, place the pan into the basket. 7. Select BAKE, set the temperature to 300ºF (149ºC), and set the time to 9 minutes. Select START/STOP to begin. 8. When the cooking is complete, the cookie should be light brown and just barely set. Remove the pan from the basket and let cool for 10 minutes. Remove the cookie from the pan, remove the parchment paper, and let cool completely on a wire rack.

Appendix 1: Air Fryer Cooking Chart

Air Fryer Cooking Chart

Vegetables					
INGREDIENT	AMOUNT	PREPARATION	OIL	TEMP	COOK TIME
Asparagus	2 bunches	Cut in half, trim stems	2 Tbsp	420°F	12-15 mins
Beets	1½ lbs	Peel, cut in ½-inch cubes	1Tbsp	390°F	28-30 mins
Bell peppers (for roasting)	4 peppers	Cut in quarters, remove seeds	1Tbsp	400°F	15-20 mins
Broccoli	1 large head	Cut in 1-2-inch florets	1Tbsp	400°F	15-20 mins
Brussels sprouts	1lb	Cut in half, remove stems	1Tbsp	425°F	15-20 mins
Carrots	1lb	Peel, cut in ¼-inch rounds	1 Tbsp	425°F	10-15 mins
Cauliflower	1 head	Cut in 1-2-inch florets	2 Tbsp	400°F	20-22 mins
Corn on the cob	7 ears	Whole ears, remove husks	1 Tbps	400°F	14-17 mins
Green beans	1 bag (12 oz)	Trim	1 Tbps	420°F	18-20 mins
Kale (for chips)	4 oz	Tear into pieces,remove stems	None	325°F	5-8 mins
Mushrooms	16 oz	Rinse, slice thinly	1 Tbps	390°F	25-30 mins
Potatoes, russet	1½ lbs	Cut in 1-inch wedges	1 Tbps	390°F	25-30 mins
Potatoes, russet	1lb	Hand-cut fries, soak 30 mins in cold water, then pat dry	½ -3 Tbps	400°F	25-28 mins
Potatoes, sweet	1lb	Hand-cut fries, soak 30 mins in cold water, then pat dry	1 Tbps	400°F	25-28 mins
Zucchini	1lb	Cut in eighths lengthwise, then cut in half	1 Tbps	400°F	15-20 mins

Air Fryer Cooking Chart

Beef

Item	Temp (°F)	Time (mins)	Item	Temp (°F)	Time (mins)
Beef Eye Round Roast (4 lbs.)	400 °F	45 to 55	Meatballs (1-inch)	370 °F	7
Burger Patty (4 oz.)	370 °F	16 to 20	Meatballs (3-inch)	380 °F	10
Filet Mignon (8 oz.)	400 °F	18	Ribeye, bone-in (1-inch, 8 oz)	400 °F	10 to 15
Flank Steak (1.5 lbs.)	400 °F	12	Sirloin steaks (1-inch, 12 oz)	400 °F	9 to 14
Flank Steak (2 lbs.)	400 °F	20 to 28			

Chicken

Item	Temp (°F)	Time (mins)	Item	Temp (°F)	Time (mins)
Breasts, bone in (1 ¼ lb.)	370 °F	25	Legs, bone-in (1 ¾ lb.)	380 °F	30
Breasts, boneless (4 oz)	380 °F	12	Thighs, boneless (1 ½ lb.)	380 °F	18 to 20
Drumsticks (2 ½ lb.)	370 °F	20	Wings (2 lb.)	400 °F	12
Game Hen (halved 2 lb.)	390 °F	20	Whole Chicken	360 °F	75
Thighs, bone-in (2 lb.)	380 °F	22	Tenders	360 °F	8 to 10

Pork & Lamb

Item	Temp (°F)	Time (mins)	Item	Temp (°F)	Time (mins)
Bacon (regular)	400 °F	5 to 7	Pork Tenderloin	370 °F	15
Bacon (thick cut)	400 °F	6 to 10	Sausages	380 °F	15
Pork Loin (2 lb.)	360 °F	55	Lamb Loin Chops (1-inch thick)	400 °F	8 to 12
Pork Chops, bone in (1-inch, 6.5 oz)	400 °F	12	Rack of Lamb (1.5 – 2 lb.)	380 °F	22

Fish & Seafood

Item	Temp (°F)	Time (mins)	Item	Temp (°F)	Time (mins)
Calamari (8 oz)	400 °F	4	Tuna Steak	400 °F	7 to 10
Fish Fillet (1-inch, 8 oz)	400 °F	10	Scallops	400 °F	5 to 7
Salmon, fillet (6 oz)	380 °F	12	Shrimp	400 °F	5
Swordfish steak	400 °F	10			

Appendix 2: Recipe Index

T

V

W

Z

Made in the USA
Las Vegas, NV
01 December 2023

81892456R10059